Sharing the Table

A Northwest Chef Instructor's Quest to Recreate Memorable Meals

To Kaaren,
May you always
find Joy sharing your
table
Linda Hierholzer

L I N D A   H I E R H O L Z E R

Forward by Sheri Flies

To my family, friends and acquaintances,
with whom I have had the great honor of sharing the table.

Table of Contents

SALADS

BRUNCH

ENTRÉES

PASTAS

VEGETABLE MAINS

GRATITUDE

Grace Personified

After years of starting and stopping, changing directions and dabbling with a multitude of intentions, I find humble gratitude for so many individuals who nudged me on this life path towards the completion of this book.

I am grateful to Molly Johnston who spent hours and days with me contemplating the likes and dislikes of the numerous cookbooks that we each had read, helping me develop a vision for what this book would look like and how it would best be used by readers. Her ideas helped me shape the way in which I structured recipes. Her friendship, knowledge, humor and encouragement has been a constant on this journey.

I am thankful for Sarah Finley's dedicated commitment to grammar directives which has kept my writing on the straight and narrow. I am truly blessed that she is also my niece and goddaughter.

Infinitely patient, Roxann Jensen guided my writing style and sentence structure for which I am deeply grateful. We share a rich past from grade school days to the present where we each shared our talents with one another freely.

My gratitude to Paul Mills is twofold. Foremost, he recognized in the rough draft that I was not only writing a cookbook but also a memoir which ultimately inspired the book title and subsequent writings. Eloquently, as my musical sommelier and dear friend, he developed the music advice for Sharing the Table chapter.

I am appreciative for the chance meeting of my first Seattle student and dear friend, Sheri Flies. Through many years, we have shared the table and the kitchen with laughter and tears. Her curiosity and conversations fueled my creative side. Her friendship is one of my most precious relationships as are her daughters who are two of my godchildren.

Liz Abelsen has been graciously forthright in attention to details in testing recipes. Her knowledge and friendship have helped me to correct and develop difficult recipes. Also, her chickens and rescued farm animals like my excess homegrown produce and I enjoy those awesome eggs!

Special thanks to: The writings of Mother Teresa of Calcutta© by Mother Teresa Center, exclusive licensee throughout the world of the Missionaries of Charity for the works of Mother Teresa. Used with permission.

My heart is gladdened with joy that my parents bestowed upon me in the years of my youth the fundamental lessons of entertaining and the importance of being a gracious hostess. They also taught me to be a world traveler, to reach out and explore new places and customs. These lessons are fundamental to the development of this book.

I am joyfully grateful for my culinary students through the years at Seattle Culinary Academy at Seattle Central Community College, Culinary Arts at Spokane Community College and Seattle Center for Hotel & Restaurant Administration, Washington State University. I am in awe of how they have developed their careers and gone on to become cookbook authors, culinary instructors, chefs, restauranteurs and even James Beard award winners! The diverse background of each student taught me about their unique cultural cuisine. I am especially grateful to Becky Selengut who forged a path into the cookbook world and helped guide me as I have gone through this process. When students posed questions for which I did not immediately have an answer, I would begin researching. Quite often I would turn to Cynthia Wilson, dietitian and fellow instructor. I am grateful for her research assistance and lengthy discussions on a wide variety of food related topics which enhanced my teaching abilities.

When the call went out that my recipes were ready to be tested, friends and friends of friends answered with astounding encouragement and genuine feedback that have assisted in the final crafting of each recipe. I am deeply grateful to each and every one: Liz Abelsen, Ashley Harrison, Ben Lefor, Suzanne Harrison, Nancy Hughes, Roxann Jensen, Susan Olsen, Amy Peterson, Lindsay Lambert, Molly Johnston, Sharalynne Middleton, Lauren Ford, Mary Lee, Sheri Flies, John Lee, Jane Seyes, Linda Dulken, Jane Castro, Amy Tierra, Elizabeth Coffey, Melissa Grimaldi, Lori Horton, Jona Bolin, Craig Beymer, Paula Harper-Christensen, Beth Box, Annette Hutson Blake, Katie Marvin, Nick Musser, Ana Sainz, Ingrid Williams, Vivian Pantelich, Donna Schultz, Tara Johnston, Jodi McWhirter, Kris Dudak, Juli Guinasso, Dave Totton, and Annette Totton. They in return wish to acknowledge their recipe tasters.

And to my consummate food taster and gourmand, my husband John, I am grateful for your honest and perceptive flavor insights. It can be said that you have taste tested each dish in this book, often many times. And though that one time in New York City while sitting next to the New York Times food critic you proclaimed "no, not again!" when presented with a plate of my award-winning recipe you have persevered. For your belief and support in my creations I shall always be grateful.

FORWARD

When I asked Linda why she asked me to write her forward, she simply said, "we have shared so many meals over the years and this book is about sharing the table." For Linda, sharing the table means sharing her heart.

Over 25 years ago, I came to Linda as a student with a broken heart. For about a year, I visited her home weekly for private lessons; to learn the "how-to" of classical cooking from the basics to complex sauces to chocolate ganache filled chocolate truffles -- which bloomed, I might add, because I didn't conch the chocolate properly. Through cooking with Linda, my heart began to heal and our friendship grew. Today she is a dear friend and the godmother of my adult daughters. Linda has taught them to appreciate excellent food and to cook at "Godmother Cooking School" when they were children.

Linda and her husband John (who is an avid gardener) grow a good portion of their food these days and what they don't grow, she sources locally. As the world evolves and we all learn how interconnected we are to each other, so has Linda and it shows in her attention to detail. She is a big proponent of knowing where food comes from and how the people or animals that provide the food are cared for.

This exquisite book shares a big portion of Linda's life as a professional chef, teacher, mentor, life-long learner, world traveler and spiritual seeker. As I peruse this book, so many memories come to mind of good food, conversations and adventures together. My family was the fortunate Thanksgiving family referenced in the opening and the Amaretto Yams are now a "must have" tradition for us. There is a story behind every one of these recipes that complements the good taste, clean ingredients and beautiful presentation. This book gives you the opportunity to experience your own private lessons with Linda by learning the basics of equipment, tools, and knife skills, to individual artistic presentation and expression, to the integration of the senses into delicious and healthy food. You will not be disappointed.

May you now begin to more fully share yourself at your table with those you love.

Sheri L. Flies

2011 James Beard Foundation Leadership Award Recipient

ODYSSEY OF DISCOVERY

"Joy is a net of love by which you can catch souls."

-Mother Teresa

I once sat at a Thanksgiving table covered with an orange and brown plaid tablecloth. My companions were three friends, two godchildren and three circling, hungry Siberian huskies. We were surrounded by white cedar walls and warmed by a crackling fire in a river-stone fireplace. Outside the wood wrapped windows the sun was slowly disappearing from the ermine-white draped evergreens in this Cascade Mountain retreat. Big Bertha, the antique wood burning stove, surrendered lingering aromas of wood-roasted turkey which perfumed the air. Flickering candles lit the bountiful spread of dishes covering the table. Port-flavored gravy flowed like grace over mounds of fluffy mashed potatoes and dressing while Amaretto yams and sweetly-tart cranberries accentuated the succulent turkey. A crescendo of delightful dialogue and hearty laughter rose above the background ripple of a running river and Christmas music. *Joy was in the air.*

This book simply attempts to trace a journey that I have taken through the years of sharing many tables. My culinary journey began at a very early age and has continued up to this moment in time, when I have begun to reminisce on all the marvelous opportunities that have broadened and enhanced my experience of sharing the table. Much like the story in the book or movie of *Babette's Feast* this journey has taken its twists and turns.

In the small Idaho town of my birth, I was spoiled with cookies by my grandmother who lived upstairs but mostly enjoyed "real, whole foods" from our family's garden and my grandparents' farm. It was a charmed time with big family gatherings around the table cultivating a personal passion for that bounty of food that created and sustained community.

My first childhood memory was of pulling up a carrot from our family garden (organic, as that was all we knew then), washing it off with the garden hose and chomping down on pure orange delight! *This was the beginning of my lifelong quest to recreate that purely magical moment.*

Enchanted memories continued in my early childhood when I spent time on my grandparents' farm in a place named Treasure Valley. During the day, I would watch my grandmother prepare food from her garden and orchard for the men in the row-crop fields. I have fond memories of her cooking on a wood-burning stove all wonders of delightful dishes. In the fall, she would prepare duck, geese and quail shot in the early morning by the men. I knew and was taught to revere "Boss" the steer that would be our winter's mainstay. Grandma's garden was quite large as was her most delicious Beefsteak ripe red tomatoes. She would only adorn these with salt and black pepper as their flavor was so bold and endearing. For years, I have grown tomatoes in my own garden but never have any of those tomatoes tasted as good. Next to Grandma's garden was the chicken coup that was enclosed in a large fenced area where the chickens would run freely. One time in the summer I remember visiting my Great Uncle's orchard. He lifted me up and encouraged me to pluck a pink and golden yellow orb which I thrust into my little mouth, fuzz and all, juices running out the sides and down my cheeks. This would become known as a peach, one of my favorite foods to this very day. Often Grandma would let me assist her by rolling out the yeasty dough which would become cinnamon rolls that we would take to the field-hands mid-morning along with a black enamel pot of steaming hot and aromatic coffee. By lunch time Grandma would have multiple dishes of meats, vegetables, salads, potatoes (I grew up in Idaho, what you would expect?) and dessert prepared as the hungry men would file in. I did not understand how some of them could pile all the food on top of each other and then crown it entirely with ketchup! I would want to savor each morsel separately. Grandma was a great cook and gardener. *She was most lovingly my first cooking inspiration.*

I was in the first generation of children with out-of-the-home working moms. Our family had moved to a larger nearby town for the job opportunities of both my parents. So, from the age of eight I would come home from school, call Mom at work and get instructions on how to prepare dinner for our family of five. Often unsure of my task, I would run for advice to Katie, who rented our basement apartment. Katie was my own personal "Mary Poppins." She was a tall, thin retired woman with a gentle, kind demeanor. She was also an awesome cook who would once a week cook an entire meal for our family. She became family and my guardian angel. Patiently, she would instruct and help me prepare each dish that I was to make. One of the greatest lessons I would learn from her was to measure small amounts of ingredients in my hand rather than with measuring spoons. This would be followed by tasting and altering the amounts. To this day, I will often pour a spice or salt into my hand then check to make sure I can still accurately "eye" the proper amount. *The proof is in the tasting.*

Katie's sister-in-law was Mabel, a marvelous baker. Her chocolate cake was made with sour milk and was the best chocolate cake I have ever tasted in my entire life! To impress a boyfriend, I once asked her to teach me to make lemon meringue pie, his favorite. I still have that recipe that produces a flaky crust, tart lemon filling and mile-high meringue but the boyfriend who was most enamored with my baking abilities, has long since disappeared. *Sweets became a gift that I share with my loved ones.*

On weekends my mother's extended family of two sisters, a brother, their spouses, all their children and our family would land at my grandparents' farm. Depending on the season, harvesting and preserving the currently ripe crop would become an entire family adventure. Everyone would have a job that would contribute to the whole so that each family could take home canned and/or frozen food for the winter. Recently, at a cousins' party we all decided that the "frozen corn weekend" was a favorite. The men and older boys would go to the field in the early morning to pick gunny sacks full of corn. Then all adults and children would gather around an upside-down round cattle tank to remove husks and silk from the corn. The corn was then shuttled to the kitchen where my eldest aunt would blanch the corn in boiling pots of water. From there the corn was carried to the utility barn to be submerged in large sinks filled with water and large blocks of ice to be quickly chilled. The women would then slice the corn kernels from the cobs and place into freezer containers marked with the date. After that long day, we would all sit down at the kitchen table to enjoy one of Grandma's plentiful meals. *To this day, I devotedly grow and preserve all sorts of foods, some of which become gifts.*

My Father was a great fisher and outdoors man. He taught me to fly fish in the beautiful streams of Idaho. In those days, we would observe thousands of spawning salmon near the headwaters of the Salmon River. But mostly Dad would catch rainbow trout. Since he usually caught the limit we would freeze a few then with the rest, throw a big party for family and friends. My mother, who never really liked to cook but did love to entertain would, with the help of the entire family, lay out a buffet style feast. At these frequent parties, there would be so many people that the whole house became the table with extra folding chairs and tables to accommodate the masses. *This is where my love for entertaining took root.*

In my early twenties, preparing dinner parties for friends who had little cooking skills, began to give me confidence in my entertaining abilities. One day a friend called and

> One day a friend called and asked me if I would fill in for her as a cook for a college fraternity until they could find her replacement. I became that replacement.

asked me if I would fill in for her as a cook for a college fraternity until they could find her replacement. I became that replacement. I enjoyed making lunch and dinner five days a week from scratch for those guys. Interestingly, it was the next-door fraternity in Eugene, Oregon where scenes from the movie "Animal House" were filmed. *Thus, came the idea that I could make a vocation of my all so passionate avocation.*

After a time, I moved to up-state New York and answered an advertisement for a short order cook at a restaurant. The chef turned me down because he "only hired men on the cooking line" but offered me a job making salads and sandwiches in the morning then washing dishes in the afternoon. Little did I know at that time that this was a four-star restaurant of much acclaim called The Springhouse. I would hurry to prep my salads and sandwiches and then ask the baker or sous chef how I could help them, thus expanding my cooking abilities. During two years, they taught me many skills. One valuable lesson was left on my cutting board one morning. It was the garbage from the day-before trash can. Annoyed I returned it to the trash can and cleaned my station. A few minutes later the restaurant owner asked me if I got his message. Befuddled, he proceeded to tell me how each scrap that I had thrown away could have been utilized rather than discarded. *This became a lesson on food frugality and sustainability.*

In the seventies, women in this country could, for the most part, only find work in restaurant salad and sandwich pantries or in dishwashing. My next job in a West Coast hotel pantry would introduce me to my chef-mentor, Chef Don. He must have observed my eager passion for food and decided to promote me through a variety of jobs in the hotel including pantry manager of seven, baker, breakfast short order cook then sauté cook for the fine dining restaurant. Often, he would encourage me to create dinner specials which expanded my culinary abilities. I would then turn to Julia Child's book *Mastering The Art Of French Cooking* for inspiration. At one point the cast and crew of the movie *Animal House* stayed at that hotel. I became friends with

the set chef and he invited me out to the set to help him in his trailer, feeding the cast and crew. It was a fun time! Who would have thought then that it would become an iconic movie? After a year, as saucier, Chef Don called me into his office and said that he was going to fire me in one year. *What?* And he then told me that I was to apply to the Culinary Institute of America and prepare myself for culinary school, moving from the West Coast to the East Coast, as he thought it was time for women such as me to become chefs in our own right. *Encouraged and supported by my parents, I followed that dream.*

Culinary school was everything and more than I could have ever wanted. I think I drove my instructors' crazy with all my questions. In the five years of working in the hospitality field I had learned *how* to prepare many classical dishes but what I wanted to know was the *whys.* My curiosity led me to do independent research on week nights and weekends. Daily after classes I returned to my dorm room where my roommate and I would indiscriminately open *The New Larousse Gastronomic* to any page and read a passage to augment our daily lessons. I have never wanted to stop learning. After culinary school and a few jobs as a chef, I was called to fill in for an injured high school skill-center chef instructor for several months. Ah ha! *The highest form of learning is to become a teacher. I had now found that my new vocation as an instructor would keep me enthralled with my evermore passionate avocation of the table.*

For nineteen glorious, yet challenging, years I taught culinary arts at Spokane Community College then at Seattle Culinary Academy at Seattle Central Community College, the oldest culinary school west of the Mississippi. When I arrived at Seattle Culinary Academy it had just been reopened after having been shut down for a year's complete renovation. All our culinary instructor team members had taught in the field before and had the opportunity to recreate the entire curriculum and eventually expand and hire more instructors. The most profound change that we made was to base our curriculum on international cuisine

> Culinary school was everything and more than I could have ever wanted.

rather than exclusively French cuisine, which was a departure from most culinary schools at the time. Each of the instructors chose a part of the world in which to specialize. I was intrigued with Mediterranean and Latino cuisines. We would each travel to various countries to sample firsthand what we had been researching. *My travels opened my mind again to the importance of quality ingredients but also to new cooking styles and techniques.*

My first culinary trip was to Switzerland and France in 1994. This was a Culinary Institute of America tour which assured that we were treated to the best of cooking and restaurant experiences. One of my favorite restaurant experiences was at Restaurant Girardet. Freddy Girardet was considered one of the Chefs of the Century. As we worked our way through eleven courses I questioned the maître d', Jean Louis, about each dish, taking pictures to commemorate. Jean Louis was kind enough to steam off the wine labels for me for souvenirs and present me with a small house plate designed for Freddie Girardet exclusively by Paloma Picasso. My roommate Anne and I were also given a kitchen tour to meet the chef and kitchen brigade. Later in the trip we were treated to an outstanding meal at Bocuse outside of Lyon, France. Paul Bocuse was considered another of the three Chefs of the Century. This time I presented Chef Bocuse with a business card from one of his previous apprentices that I knew. When it was interpreted that I was also a Culinary Institute of America grad he insisted that I come see his kitchen and meet the brigade. With Anne and camera in tow we had a picture of the Chef, Sous Chef, Anne and me to memorialize the occasion. *The dishes presented to our table at these and other restaurants on this trip are some of my fondest food memories.*

Anne and I decided to attend a follow-up Culinary Institute of America tour of North and Central Italy two years later. As we flew from Zurich to Milan I noticed that after the breathtaking Alps there were flat rice paddies. We were about to land in risotto country! So many things about Italy were endearing, but I must say that touring the infamous

Emilia-Romagna region opened my eyes to pristine and quintessential foods. First there was the tour of a Parmigiano-Reggiano consortium to discover the entire process of making this incredible cheese which dates back eight hundred years. Our education included everything from the cow's diet to the brining and aging method. Then, just a few miles away, we learned that the pigs were fed the cream by-product of Parmigiano-Reggiano, thus creating the lactose sweet and lusciously fatty Parma Prosciutto that is massaged and cured in sea salt. In Modena, we were treated to a tour of an award-winning balsamic vinegar estate to study its simple yet complex progression and sipped glasses of vinegar much as one would sip a fine Port. And, of course, no central Italian tour is complete without a visit to a Chianti winery. *This trip afforded me with wonderful cooking schools and restaurant experiences. However, as I rested back at home having just cooked with Parmigiano-Reggiano, the lingering smell took me back to the realization that good dishes start only with the highest quality ingredients.*

On weekends, I would go on my own Napa Valley tasting tour. It was a glorious month of exploration!

When the instructor who specialized in Asian cuisine took a sabbatical to travel to numerous Far East countries, I volunteered to cover his classes and did a quick study of various Asian cuisines but was happy to return to my beloved Mediterranean and Latino specialties. I also took a sabbatical when I was chosen as a scholarship recipient of *Madeleine Kamman's School for American Chefs* at Beringer Winery. It was here that I learned two very important lessons. At the first class, Madeleine asked each of us nine chefs to describe how they would roast a chicken. Much to all our amazement, we each had a very different method. I had observed a similar outcome at a homeless shelter at a church where several members would bring a breakfast casserole (strata). Each used the same recipe but every time the dishes were all very different in taste, texture and appearance. Secondly, Beringer winery gave us classes about viticulture in the field on terroir importance (soil, site and climate) and food with wine pairings. We were also shown how the grapes were pruned. We were taken to vineyards where obsidian rock painted a black mosaic on the ground beneath the vines which contributed to the flavor of the grapes. They gave us wine tastings at private and exclusive vineyards. On weekends, I would go on my own Napa Valley tasting tour. It was a glorious month of exploration! *Ingredients, their terroir and techniques matter equally in the outcome of a recipe!*

While in Napa I also attended classes and a Mediterranean conference at the Culinary Institute of America at Greystone. What an outstanding education! When I returned home I had to complete a paper as stipulated for my sabbatical. I had chosen food history as I had been discouraged that most culinary textbooks began with history of French cuisine in seventeen hundred and discussed nothing prior to that. *I knew there had to be a rich history prior to that time which would uncover mysteries of the origin of indigenous foods, dishes and interesting trivia of the entire world's cuisines.*

The following year my husband and I traveled to Spain during spring break to explore Costa del Sol. We began in Madrid where we enjoyed the Prado Museum followed by afternoon tapas and late in the evening the finest lamb chops and olive oil fried potatoes we have ever eaten anywhere in the world. On the train trip to Málaga we saw olive and lemon groves the whole way. From a condo in Costa Mista we took day trips. In Jerez, we observed the solera process of Sherry production. In Seville, we munched on

the seafood menu in the restaurant called Faro Playa. We would watch the sunset over the North African mountains and Mediterranean while devouring the freshest of seafood prepared quite simply. *It was here that I embraced the notion that good whole food is best prepared simply. I was also impressed with how the history of the region influenced and changed countries depending on who occupied another's country.*

In 2002 I quickly signed up for a Women's Chefs and Restaurateur's culinary tour of Oaxaca, Mexico. The then-current president of WCR, Deann Groen Bayless and her husband Rick Bayless were the leaders and teachers. Having read that Oaxaca cuisine is considered the finest cuisine in Mexico and very different from our limited idea of Tex-Mex cooking I was not disappointed. As I read back through my travel diary I can literally smell the food that I am describing as it is profoundly distinct. After a couple of lectures on the culture and foods of the region we were split up in groups of four and given a grocery list written in Spanish. We were then taken to a local market to find, barter and buy the ingredients which we would use to learn how to cook the dishes. It was a lesson of complete immersion into the Oaxaca culture. *In this hot arid country, I learned to love many new foods such as chocolate flower blossoms, many varieties of chilies, squash blossoms, chayote, banana leaves, mescal, chocolate atole, different colored moles, turkey eggs, corn, fungus, epazote and even spicy crisp grasshoppers!*

While in Napa I also attended classes and a Mediterranean conference at the Culinary Institute of America at Greystone. What an outstanding education!

outstanding carrot tapas while watching flamenco dancers. One day we traveled through Gibraltar aboard a ferry bound for Tangiers, Morocco. Our exotic Moroccan lunch of lamb kefta, harira soup, chicken tagine, couscous, honey cakes and mint tea did not disappoint my expectations. Each evening we would return to our condo, walk under the coastal highway viaduct and work our way through

The more I taught, the more I learned, especially from an ethnically diverse student body. The more I traveled, the more educated I became, appreciating the authenticity of a country's cuisine, history, customs, colors, aromas and essence. The more I studied the more enlightened I became to the concept of *flavor transformation and table viability. In my surmounting quest to understand the fundamentals of "dish" and "table" I began to develop a "food philosophy," the premise of which flavor and culture preservation and development takes a paramount importance to all the other elements.*

I was about to travel to the Greek Isles when I was forced to retired early due to health issues. As soon as I was well again I remodeled my retirement home kitchen and began a cooking school called Leisurely Pursuit Cooking School. I missed teaching and had a wealth of information to share. It was here that I could devote focused attention to each cooking technique and to test recipes. Some of the information that I accumulated for these classes is in this book. More than just the research, the classes brought me back to sharing the table. The nine of us in the class would gather around the kitchen island that my husband has lovingly dubbed "the granite aircraft carrier," to consume the day's bounty which would encourage lively discussions about foods and flavor. We shared thoughts, memories, and more. Unfortunately, in the busy world we live in, the art of the table has become somewhat rushed. *Ultimately, "breaking bread together" is the catalyst of much delightful pleasure, joy, laughter, and discussions that creates rich connections among a group of people. It is worth pursuing, leisurely.*

In the past few years I have been able to travel to Germany, Switzerland, Austria, Scotland, Italy, Croatia, Spain and my husband's ancestral home in the Black Forest. Here again, I found a very clear and profoundly unique cuisine. *Distant relatives invited us into their homes and at their tables we delighted in rapport resulting from the universal appeal of food well-prepared.*

My table philosophy is rooted in the twists and turns from Formica tables to white linen draped tables. No matter the atmosphere, simple tried and true guidelines remain the same. Whenever possible, grown and procured food ought to be in season, local, organic, free-range, sustainable and fair-traded. The condition of that food ought to be at the peak of freshness or desirability when used. Cooking methods ought to be studied before execution of the recipe to have the optimum outcome. The dishes whether plain or complex, should serve to light up the moment with its flavors, aromas, textures, sights and sometimes sounds. The plated food should be set forth in an attractive manner as to heighten the visual appeal. The ambiance of the table sets the manner of hospitality which is the relationship between the host and guests and one another. *Passion for inviting guests, organizing, procuring, preparing, cooking, plating the food and readying the table will ultimately define the triumphant effect desired.*

The following chapters and recipes will explore ways to combine basic ingredients to highlight their greatest potential to be shared at the table with kindred spirits. First and foremost, the ingredients must be of highest quality, preferably organic and locally grown. If the ingredient is to be stored before preparation careful steps must be taken to preserve texture, flavor and nutritional quality. Often a food needs only be pared or cut a particular way to make it more toothsome and enjoyable. Then, how food is mixed with other ingredients and prepared by specific methods will alter their original essence, thereby creating a new flavor profile. Why certain techniques are used with specific ingredients will enable a greater perception of desired taste outcomes. How one flavor will balance or highlight another flavor will be examined. The collection of recipes illustrated in this book is based primarily on authentic Mediterranean and Latino cuisines, some adapted to the western kitchen. Additional recipes lovingly come from my family, friends and other travels on this odyssey of discovery. *My wish is for you to explore a world of delightful pleasures and how to recreate purely magical moments while sharing the table.*

MEMORABLE MEALS

During this lifetime adventure I have had the great pleasure of sitting at many tables and sharing meals with a wide range of family, friends, brief acquaintances, students, colleagues, chefs, cookbook authors, and traveling companions. I am profoundly grateful for having had the great fortune to do so.

Through the years, I have acquired hundreds of menus from restaurants, hotels, association events, and culinary tours. Fortunately, I had the presence of mind to carry small blank books to scribble in on my travel adventures. While writing this book, I was thankful for the opportunity to refer to them many times over. It has been most pleasurable to relive each occasion.

A few years back, I began to print menus for meals that I would prepare for my friends and family and to keep them in a notebook. This has enabled me to remember what I have and haven't served and to whom. I also made notes to myself about guest's likes, dislikes and allergies. As you enter my kitchen, you will first notice a chalk board with the latest party's menu printed upon it. Frequent visitors will gravitate immediately to the board to discover what they will be served that day. They have also enjoyed being able to take a printed menu home with them.

AIWF Northwest Chapter Luncheon with Julia Child
February 28, 1995

Sponsored by the Sorrento Hotel and Columbia Winery

Smoked Salmon Mousse on Puff Pastry

Spring Asparagus Wrapped Prosciutto

Crab Salad in Belgium Endive

Columbia "Woodburne Cuvee" Chardonnay, 1993

Lopez Island Saffron Mussel Bisque

Columbia "Chevrier" Semillion-Chardonnay, 1993

Roasted Filet of Canadian King Salmon

Fondue of Artichokes, Sunchokes and Fennel, Merlot Beef Essence

Columbia Valley Merlot, 1992

Bosc Pear and Almond Tart with Vanilla Ice Cream

Buttered Rum Caramel, Toasted Almonds

Columbia "Cellarmaster's Reserve" Johannesburg Riesling, 1992

JULIA

As I walked into the room, the sun was beaming brightly through the floor-to-ceiling windows, obstructing my view for a few moments. Searching carefully, my eyes slowly came to rest on a seated, slightly bent over, older woman illuminated by streams of light and seated alone in all her glory. This was my Julia, our Julia that I had patiently waited all those years to encounter in person. I sat across the room, contemplating the hours spent studying, word for word, her intriguing instructions, her voice rising from the pages and challenging me to take to the stove. Then in a moment of amusement, her chicken escapades came dancing to mind and I rose from my seat, fraying book in hand and moved toward the light. She reached her hand to greet me as I knelt on one knee to come face to face with this kind and gentle soul. After proper introduction, she asked what my profession was. I replied chef-instructor. A broad smile came across her face as her eyes lit up and she replied that she too was a teacher, a profession that she held with high regard. Handing her my 1960's *Mastering the Art of French Cooking* book to sign, I explained that her creation had been my companion through the years as I worked multiple positions within the kitchen brigade from restaurant to restaurant. She was notably pleased and encouraged me to carry on the work of inspiring a new generation of women chefs, a role that I eagerly embraced. The meal at the Sorrento Hotel was lovingly prepared by Chef, and friend, Eric Lenard. Adoration filled the room.

ALICE

Passing through the iconic trellis and up the pathway to the open door, I was about to embark upon a profound shift in the way I regard the *table*. I had planned our pilgrimage to the Bay area around reservations made at Chez Panisse restaurant several months in advance. California Cuisine was all the rage and it was based primarily around one woman, Alice Waters. From the time I entered the Culinary Institute of America to the time that I graduated in 1980, few women were in attendance. My only female kitchen instructor taught pantry and had a home-economics background. Trail blazer that I was, as a chef-instructor at Spokane Community College, I longed to find a woman mentor, someone to whom I could follow as a model. "You're Alice Waters" I blurted out like a star-struck groupie, amazed that she would be the one greeting and seating us. After composing myself, we chatted like reacquainted friends. Noting that I was a chef-instructor she insisted on introducing me to the chef and staff, gave my husband and me a tour of the small kitchen, wine cellar and office, then seated us. Each plate elaborated colorful schemes which enhanced the visual integrity. Each food spoke clarity of its unique characteristics. Our palettes tingled with bursts of flavor and texture. We reveled in the entire experience.

The menu was printed in exquisite calligraphy:
Menu August 20. 1985

Deep fried squid with tomato salad

Eggplant and pepper soups

Grilled free range chicken breasts with sauce béarnaise

Garden salad

Fraises des bois cream puffs

Scribbled notes:

First course: *Flour-dusted crisp fried squid tentacles and tubes surrounded by baby cherry tomatoes, fresh basil, minced red onions and vinegar with lemon wedge*

Second course: *Roasted, puréed eggplant and red pepper soups swirled together and topped with an extra-virgin olive oil crouton with fresh parsley leaves*

Third course: *Mesquite grilled free-range chicken breast with sauce béarnaise and fresh tarragon on a bed of wilted spinach and shallots. Sautéed baby yellow summer squash and green beans*

Fourth course: *Garden salad of baby lettuces, dandelion greens, nasturtiums and violets*

Fifth course: *Miniature syrup-glazed cream puffs, filled with whipped cream and adorned with wild baby strawberries in a pool of strawberry purée*

MUSTARD'S MENU

Appetizers, Soups and Salads

Cornmeal Pancake with homemade sour cream and Caviar

Warm Goat Cheese, almond coated with sun dried tomatoes and chives

Limestone and Butter Lettuces with seasoned pecans and bleu cheese

From the Wood Burning Oven

Half slab Barbequed Baby Back Ribs

Smoked Pork Loin with many mustards

Grilled Quail with Pasilla pepper vinaigrette

From the Grill

Fresh Fish (see chalkboard)

Sonoma Rabbit with red tomato salsa and black beans

Pounded Veal Chop with pan fried tomatoes, basil and garlic

Sandwiches

Smoked Pork Loin, molasses and orange marinade, with watercress

Barbequed Brisket of Beef

Smoked Ham and Jarlsberg Cheese, grilled, with tomato chutney

Sides and Condiments

Grilled Eggplant and red onion with ginger butter

Polenta

Homemade Ketchup

Turmeric Pickles

Desserts

Chocolate Pecan Cake, chocolate sauce

Tapioca Pudding, bourbon cream

Caramel Custard with pistachios and cream

Heading north on the St Helena Highway to a sunny day of winery exploration, my husband and I began looking for a restaurant so we could catch a quick bite. It was in August of 1985, which was slightly before the time when Napa Valley would become the destination hub of wine-tasting that it is today. Ahead on the left we saw what looked like a restaurant with a parking lot full of cars and pickups, a sure sign of the local's favorite eatery. The large sign read MUSTARDS GRILL in a golden yellow color, much like the masses of mustard flowers that proliferate the vineyards during the springtime. We had arrived at Cindy Pawlcyn's now-iconic creation. As we were escorted to our table I reveled in the heavy scent of burning wood, the clinking of fine wine glasses and the jovial chatter of the patrons. Little did I know that this roadside diner would be the catalyst that would change my perception of the barbeque joint forever. As I scanned the menu I realized that this was not a mere baby back ribs and pulled pork pit. The white linen tablecloths had immediately dispelled that myth. Yes, of course one could get ribs, pulled pork, hamburgers, or barbequed brisket but also available was Sonoma rabbit, pounded veal chop, and black bean and ginger prawns. I marveled at the sides of homemade ketchup, tomato chutney, and turmeric pickles. Now we were in a quandary of what to order. What a wonderful situation! Of all the dishes we ordered that day, it's the dessert that remains most clearly etched in my memory! It was a silken caramel custard in a pool of heavy cream, sprinkled with powdered sugar and garnished with candied pistachios and fresh raspberries. The very thought of heavy cream being a sauce was an epiphany which worked extraordinarily well! We could have called it a day right then, but of course we headed on to the wineries.

SWITZERLAND AND FRANCE 1994

One of the most enjoyable learning adventures of my life was specializing in Mediterranean and Latino cuisines for our culinary arts department. It meant perusing through hundreds of cookbooks and travel books in search of authentic and culturally diverse studies. Twists and turns down unusual alleyways, colorful sights, fragrant aromas and exotic flavors were my nightly companions as I explored page by page. One day a continuing education flyer arrived from The Culinary Institute of America featuring a fascinating tour of Switzerland and France. Intriguingly, it involved several once-in-a-lifetime dining experiences. Pinch myself, it included eating at two "Chef of the Century" restaurants. I was in, whole-heartedly!

Curiosity with a twinge of excitement resonated as I dared a solo flight from Seattle to my dream trip abroad. During a flight layover in New York's JFK airport I noticed a woman about my age and an elderly couple who just happened to be talking about the culinary trip that I was about to embark upon. I managed to approach them and introduce myself. In turn I learned that the woman, Anne was a dietitian from Kingston, New York. Harvey and Judy were a retired couple who lived near Rhinebeck in upstate New York. At that moment, we became instant friends bound by the love of travel and good food with whom I would sojourn for many years to come. So off we were on what was my first-ever European trip, the memories of which are profoundly etched on my heart.

Lausanne, our first stop, was nestled on three hills that borders Lake Geneva, Western Europe's largest lake. With emerging Swiss Alps as a backdrop, it boasted a charming old city center, Olympic museum, and the gateway to two outstanding table-sharing experiences.

After catching a good night's sleep, we began at Ecole Hoteliere de Geneve's hotel management school where we took a cooking class in their demonstration kitchen, the style of which I would recreate at Seattle Culinary Academy nine years later. This was followed by a tour of Nestle World Headquarters and Alimentarium Food Museum in Vevey where we were challenged to a scratch-and-sniff food game. Anne and I then strolled down a few blocks to the water's edge where we whimsically posed with a bronze statue of Charlie Chaplin's "The Tramp."

These charming and humorous moments were to be eclipsed by the evening meal at Auberge du Raisin, a two-star restaurant. Our group sat at a round white linen draped table near a charming fireplace where we were served an outstanding prix fix meal prepared by Chef Adolf Blokbergen. This was our first opportunity for the tour participants to get to know one another better. As often is the case, the food became a catalyst to lively conversation, laughter and pure multi-sensory joy.

AUBEREGE DU RAISIN
Menu by Chef Adolf Blokbergen, October 5ᵀᴴ, 1994

APERITIF
Croustillant de Ris de Vea en amuse-bouche

Champagne Pommery, en Magnum

MENU
Terrine de Pigeon et Foie gras, Pain brioche

Pinot-Gris, J.P Chaudet, 1991

Suprême de Loup de Mer à l'Exotique

Chardonnay, Clos des Ruvines, Ch. Cuénoud, 1992

Risotto de Crustacés à l'Aneth

Crème de Maïs

Filet de Chevreuil de la Nouvelle Chasse

Et sa Garniture

Plant Robert, Magnum, 1990

Choix de Fromages affinés

Cabernet Chamoson, V. Favre, 1992

Composition de Framboise

Petite Arvine Sous l'Escalier, Domaine Mont d'Or, 1992

After the meal, Chef Blokbergen graciously came to our table, answered our numerous questions then gave us a tour of the kitchen.

The following is a copy of the menu, proudly signed by the chef of that evening's odyssey, which is displayed with other cached memorabilia menus on my living room wall:

The following day we were to experience one of the preeminent, if not "the," finest dining restaurants of that era. Restaurant Girardet in the small village of Crissier, was the only three-star restaurant in Switzerland, and the hottest reservation in Europe. Monsieur Girardet dubbed his style of nouvelle cuisine, "spontaneous cuisine," explaining that perfecting a recipe and repeating it endlessly was not possible for him as ingredients vary considerably from day to day. He likened his work to an artist setting out the colors on a palette before starting to paint a picture, bringing constantly changing harmonies of nature to a life of their own. He most certainly was ahead of the trend to grow and source foods locally.

Before settling into our graciously appointed private dining room, Chef Girardet posed with our tour group on the front steps of his restaurant for a group photo. That picture has graced my office wall all these years since.

GIRARDET

Once seated and as the courses were presented, I began to quiz matre d' Jean Louis as to what ingredients were in every dish and how they were prepared. "One moment please" he would reply before disappearing into the kitchen and returning with the precise answer. After the third course, he would approach me with the next course and proceed to give a precise dissertation of the presented dish. With camera at hand I captured a visual memento of each masterpiece. He also presented me with each wine label that had been carefully steamed off the bottle to be preserved in my travel diary. Having noticed the unusual design on the beautiful china plates, I asked Jean Louis if it would be possible to purchase a small plate as a keepsake. He returned with a small slightly chipped plate that he said I could have for free. I discovered that the china was designed by Paloma Picasso exclusively by Limoges for Fredy Girardet. What a treasure!

Soon after the last course was presented, Chef Giradet appeared in the dining room to a spirited applause. He proceeded to pose for a picture at each table. As a final act of hospitality, he invited Anne and me to tour the kitchen and meet the brigade. I marveled at the immaculate kitchen and a new piece of equipment called an induction stove, which took many years to finally appear for use in American kitchens.

To this day, I have never eaten so many course at one setting, nor had each course be so amazingly perfect in sight, color, aroma and flavor. He was truly a "Chef of the Century."

HOTEL DE VILLE GIRARDET

Menu by Frédy Girardet, Chef of the Century, October 6TH, 1994

Domaine Blanchard

Tartegnin "Le Portillon" 1990 Cru d'Origine

FIRST COURSE

Consommé de truite

Consommé of Lake Trout

Cold consommé of lake trout: Aspic was potted with layers of dill and saffron custard, tomato aspic, custard again, and lake trout at the bottom of the cup. Garnished with sprigs of dill and chervil

SECOND COURSE

Râble de lapereau fondant en dodine au ris de veau, grecque de primeurs à la coriandre

Saddle of Rabbit, Sautéed Rabbit Leg, Vegetable Salad

Saddle of rabbit and sweetbreads galantine wrapped in savoy cabbage with aspic. It was garnished with three mustard seeds, sautéed rabbit leg in mustard mayonnaise alongside a salad of blanched broccoli, spinach, cauliflower, radish, artichoke heart and chervil in a balsamic vinaigrette

THIRD COURSE

Crème légère de bouchots et de coques aux herbes frites

Baby Mussels and Cockles in Fumet Cream

Baby mussels and cockles in a fish fumet cream were garnished with a mixture of tarragon, brunoise of tomato concassée and fine herbs (chives, parsley, chervil, tarragon). Topped with a sprig of deep fried tarragon

Les Deux Crêtes

Pinot Gris Malvoisie 1986 G. Galvien

FOURTH COURSE

Suprême de loup de mer aux aubergines, tomatoes confites et huile vierge

Sautéed Sea Bass in a Lemon Vinaigrette

Crackling skin side up sea bass was accompanied by frizzled shallots, peeled cherry tomato, deep fried eggplant croutons and a disc, with an emulsified extra-virgin olive oil and lemon vinaigrette, julienne basil, and brunoise of tomato concassée

FIFTH COURSE

Petit gateau de homard Breton au chou vert

Lobster Tart and Lobster in Shell with Sauce Américane

Lobster and savoy cabbage tart served with a shelled lobster claw in a crustacean demi-fumet with lobster head shell on curly parsley with Sauce American

Chaâteau Rochefort Allaman

Grand Cru Appellation D'Origine 1988

Choisi au Fût Par Fredy Girardet

SIXTH COURSE

Épigramme de pigeonneau en parures de truffles

Breast of Pigeon in a Black Truffle Demi Sauce with Chanterelles and Cépes

Sautéed épigrammes of pigeon breast sprinkled with parsley in a demi-glace with brunoise truffles, sautéed spinach, and timbale of purred carrots topped with a carrot disk and carrot strips on sides and five peas; sautéed chanterelles and cépes

SEVENTH COURSE

Fromages frais et affiné

Cheese Tray

Tableside presentation of an assortment of Roquefort, Gruyere, French Brie and Tom de Rougemout

Espresso or Cappuccino

EIGHTH COURSE

Dacquois d'ananas

Pineapple Tart in Passion Fruit Sauce with Jamaican Rum Raisin Glace

Warm pineapple tart with meringue in a passion fruit sauce with Jamaican rum raisin ice cream garnished with pistachios

NINETH COURSE

Sorbets du jour

Trio of Sorbets

Raspberry, pink grapefruit and banana sorbets

TENTH COURSE

Glace du jour

Trio of Glaces

Vanilla, coffee and chocolate ice cream

ELEVENTH COURSE

Friandises

Assorted Petit Four

Candies, small cakes, chocolates and truffles

Each successive day of the trip was unique and enlightening. Many other dining experiences were to follow such as the one in the Beaujolais wine region where we were to dine in the small village of Juliénas at Restaurant Le Coq au Vin. There we enjoyed a country meal of mixed greens with country-style pâté and grain mustard, red wine braised chicken with mushrooms and bacon, whipped fresh sheep's cream, and chocolate mousse.

BOCUSE

Finally, the evening for which most of us had been anticipating, arrived. We traveled from Lyon into the countryside. As we approached the restaurant we could see a well-lit sign with enormous letters spelling out PAUL BOCUSE! From the doorman's red hat, to the menu, china, glassware, silverware, napkins, and the washroom towels, all bore his name or initials.

A local chef from Woodinville, Washington asked me to give the chef his business card as he had apprenticed under Chef Bocuse years before. Once the waiter gave the card to the chef, he approached me and with the help of an interpreter I explained my connection. When he asked about my background as a chef-instructor he was delighted to learn that I was a graduate from the Culinary Institute of America where his own son was currently attending. He put his arm around me and whisked me off to the kitchen to meet his sous chef. Anne, with camera in tow, was just a few steps behind to memorialize the moment forever.

Vendredi 7 Octobre 1994

Apéritif Maison

Côtes du Rhône 1993 – Etienne Guigal

Beaujolais 1993 - Georges Duboeuf

Café

MENU

Amuse-gueule de l'Auberge

‡‡‡

Rouget Barbet en écailles
de pommes de terre croustillantes

ou

Nage de saumon au beurre de cerfeuil

‡ ‡ ‡

Canette rôtie à la broche au feu de bois

ou

Carré d'agneau persillé à la fleur de thym

‡ ‡ ‡

Sélection de fromages frais
et affinés "Mère Richard"

‡ ‡ ‡

Crème brûlé à la cassonade Sirio

Délices et gourmandizes

Petits fours et chocolats

The following day we took the TGV (train à Grande Vitesse, or "high speed train") from Lyon to Paris where we spent our last two days sightseeing and eating in more wonderful restaurants. So many moments of this trip were filled with chatter, giggles, awes and belly-laughs with good friends, Anne, Harvey, and Judy, that we decided on the flight back to go on another culinary trip together to Italy in two years hence.

ITALY, 1996

As I rested in a reclining chair from the busy day's preparations, the kitchen filled the whole house with the aroma of ripe red tomatoes stewing slowly in their own juices. But it was the smell lingering on my fingers that brought reflective visions of that bright morning, not long before but countries away, spent sipping Prosecco and feeling the mineral crystal bursts and pronounced flavor of well-aged Parmigiano Reggiano in my mouth. Never again would I use just any Parmesan cheese. My style of cooking had been forever changed, as had my perception of Italian cuisine. In fact, there are twenty uniquely different styles and regions of Italian cooking, which begs to ponder, "how Italian" restaurants in the US define their style of cooking?"

As promised in Paris with travel friends, Anne, Harvey, and Judy, we journeyed to Italy with The Culinary Institute of America's continuing education travel program two years later. As we flew over the majestic Swiss Alps the landscape gave way to a very flat land just before our arrival in Milan. It occurred to me that those flat fields were rice paddies, in fact risotto-style rice paddies. Looking back, I realize that this Italian culinary tour was as much, if not more about the exceptional ingredients of Italy as the cooking techniques of the region. I had always enjoyed the shopping part of cooking as much as the actual cooking itself, but now my shopping would become quests to find more perfect ingredients.

After a tour and good night's rest in Milan we headed to a Parmigiano Reggiano consortium in the Parma region of north central Italy. As we entered the large unheated room, the smell of Parmigiano Reggiano cheese was prevalent. Here we saw the entire process of making this eight-hundred-year-old cheese. Milk that had been acquired the previous evening had separated. The cream was sent off to slop the pigs that would eventually become Parma prosciutto. The evening whey was combined with the morning whole milk and heated in inverted church-bell shaped vats with fermenting whey of the preceding batch and rennet to help solidify the mixture. After about half an hour the curds were taken up in linen to drain before being placed in wooden molds to rest overnight and be given a written birthdate. The following day the molded cheese is removed from the molds, placed in a sea salt brine, and turned twice daily for twenty-six days. Then each one-hundred-pound wheel of cheese is aged for one to three years and branded with the trademark. After the tour, we toasted with chunks of cheese and Prosecco. They sent us on our way with cryovac-wrapped wedges of cheese which I would eventually bring home. Whenever I smell Parmigiano Reggiano (which is always in my refrigerator) my mind drifts back to that very special tour. We also toured a Parma prosciutto consortium, an authentic balsamic vinegar estate, and a Chianti winery where we learned about their unique processes, but those stories must wait for another day.

The most memorable meal of the trip was at the hunting hill-top villa of Sra Jo Bettoja. The bus could not make the difficult grade uphill so we proceeded on foot to the top of the hill where we were greeted with red wine and pâté under a huge wisteria arbor. A hired hand gave us a demonstration on a nearby picnic table on how to bone-out a suckling pig which was to be stuffed with local wild fennel and roasted to become Porchetta for our dining pleasure. We then began our luncheon which was served by courses in the small villa and enjoyed in the courtyard near the chapel. After the Primo course, the roasted pig with apple in mouth and carrot in the posterior was paraded for all to admire.

Porchetta Bettoja

Antipasto

Chicken Liver Pâté

Assorted Breads

Primo

Rigatoni Anointed with Mint and Pistachio Pesto

Secondo

Porchetta

Fingerling Potatoes

Tossed Green Salad

Dolce

Ricotta Cheese Cake

Hazelnut Biscotti with Vin Santo

Fresh Ricotta Cheese with Sugar, Rum, Cocoa and Fresh Ripe Strawberries

An hour after this magnificent meal we were touring the Vatican. While Pentecost services were proceeding, we stopped to admire a glorious painting of the Assentation. I then realized that we had just experienced at the hill-top villa a culinary bit of heaven on earth.

OAXACA

The Legend of the Sacred Mountain retreat was nestled on the hillside southeast of Oaxaca. Our travel-weary group from Women Chef's and Restauranteurs were welcomed with margaritas and a lively Mariachi band. As we settled in for the evening a heron landed on the mountain peak behind, an omen of moments yet to come.

I had read about this culinary destination for several years and eagerly signed up for the culinary tour when I knew that the WCR president, Deann Groen Bayless, her husband and co-author Rick Bayless and cookbook author Marilyn Tausend would be guides.

The first mornings' breakfast was simple yet authentically satisfying. Huevos ranchero in black beans purée with salsa and hand-made tortillas was accompanied by sweet bread, baby red bananas, papayas, mangos and chamomile tea.

We proceeded to the chapel for an informative lecture on the history, culture and ingredients of the local cuisine. Perusing the hand-out list of unique foods, I began to imagine their smell, appearance and flavor. Soon we were split into groups of four, given a shopping list, pesos, and an oilcloth shopping bag. We were about to embark on a scavenger hunt at the local outdoor market.

This scavenger hunt was not like the ones of my youth where we drove to friends' homes to collect a diverse group of household items, then raced to be first to return. This hunt was in a foreign land whose people spoke Spanish, where we had to negotiate for lower prices in a currency we were yet to understand, and where we had to look for ingredients whose appearances with which we were not familiar. Luckily, one person in our group spoke some Spanish, another knew how to bargain for lower prices, and I had seen pictures in books of some of the ingredients. Off we were for a great adventure. This experience was the most fun I have ever had in any international cooking school I have attended! Not only was it entertaining, but we were experiencing the daily routine of shopping in an Oaxacan market.

We ate in a traditional bodega, several restaurants, a hotel and a cooking school where we made several styles of mole. My favorite meal eaten was at the Tlamanalli restaurant which was run by a local family.

Chepil and Squash Blossom Soup

with Chayote and Cheese Quesadilla

Mole de Castilla

with Chicken, Rice, Peas and Carrots

Quava, Zapote Negro and Rosewater Ice Creams

Chocolate Aguas Fresca

We had arrived and were now fully immersed in this magical Central American land of Oaxaca. Many more culinary adventures were to follow, even that of eating chili-fried grasshoppers!

COSTA DEL SOL, SPAIN, 2001

The most romantic table that I ever shared was after a chain of events that led my husband and me to a magnificent restaurant on the shores of the Mediterranean.

After an otherwise beautiful flight over the polar ice cap from Seattle to Copenhagen, my husband and I, suffering from sore throats, fever, plugged ears and coughing made what we called the "Hierholzer Copenhagen Accords." We determined that after planning this trip for over a year, no matter how badly we felt, we would continue our tour as planned, visiting the small villages and historic sites around our condo on the southern Spanish coast. It was one of those "I don't care that I am deathly ill, the French air controllers are on strike so we have to fly around France, our flight is delayed and we will arrive exhausted in Madrid several hours late" moments.

On track after a few short hours of sleep, we walked to the Prado museum and viewed outstanding art work and the etchings of Goya that depicted the gruesome struggles with the French. After numerous ghastly drawings, I said that I felt like those poor peasants being tortured. So, on to tapas and more sleep we trudged, but still on track. As I packed a large bottle of water into the day-pack on my husband's back, a local man pointed at him and said "el burro," a phrase that we humorously use to this very day. The late dinner of very small grilled lamb chops, extra virgin olive oil fried potatoes, flan, cinnamon rice pudding and excellent red wine did boost our spirits.

The next morning, we boarded the train to Malaga. We sat back and rested and enjoyed the view of olive and citrus groves and the beautiful Sierra Nevada mountain range. We managed to get our car rental and find our way out of town to our costal condo. The next day we learned just how fast Spanish motorists could drive as we navigated our way to the Alhambra. It was magnificent but finding parking and a place to eat seemed challenging. Back at the condo office while inquiring about a place to eat nearby we noticed that they offered daily bus tours to the very sites that we had planned to visit. We signed up for every one so that we could rest as they drove, parked and gave us guided tours. As for dinner, we only had to walk a short distance under the coastal highway to the sea and up some stairs to a wonderful seafood restaurant called Faro Playa. There we sat and watched the sunset on the distant mountains of northern Africa. The seafood was so fresh and simply prepared that we would return every night from our day tours and work our way through the

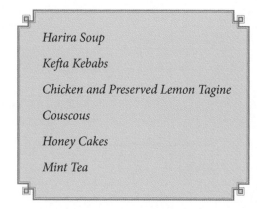

Harira Soup

Kefta Kebabs

Chicken and Preserved Lemon Tagine

Couscous

Honey Cakes

Mint Tea

entire menu with the dreamy Mediterranean as ambience. No other place before or after was as romantic as this. Sick or not we had a wonderful time.

On one of our days, we toured Seville's third largest cathedrals in Europe then on a river cruise. The next day we sipped Sherry in Jerez. Actually, we guzzled Sherry because the tour guide had just announced we had ten minutes to be back on the bus. Six different Sherries had just been poured and were sitting in front of us. By the time, we had boarded the bus and arrived at the restaurant for lunch, we were quite happy and famished. Luckily, carrot tapas that were astonishingly good were quickly served. We had several cazuelas full of these tasty bites while watching flamenco dancers twirl and entertain the audience to the brilliant rhythm of Spanish guitar. Then it was off to the majestic Andalucía horse show that lived up to all I had anticipated.

I had hoped to travel by ferry to Tangiers, Morocco and indeed there was a day tour which we were able to join. The trip from Gibraltar by catamaran was about one and a half hours then we were met by a tour bus. A tour guide steered us through the streets amidst poverty and filth and down into the underground marketplace. Here we saw huge piles of colorful spices, fresh fruits, vegetables, and chickens, quail and rabbits in full coats, heads and all. Then we enjoyed an exotic lunch that I had been anticipating and which did not disappoint.

We returned to our favorite seafood restaurant that evening for one last romantic meal. In my travel journal I wrote "Time will hopefully allow us to forget our illnesses and just remember how much we enjoyed our trip". Mission accomplished!

SHOPPING SAVVY

"Do we not see some in our own days that can distinguish by its superior flavour the thigh on which the partridge leans while sleeping? And have we not plenty of who are able to indicate the latitude under which a wine has ripened . . . That we should render to Caesar that which is Caesar's, proclaim man the great gourmand of nature, and not be surprised if the good doctor nods sometimes like Homer." *-Brillat-Savarin*

Many a great cookbook begins with the importance of choosing foods with the highest quality. Locally grown, organic and sustainable ingredients most often present the finest flavor and nutrition profile. What you, the cook, **do with these ingredients** is also of paramount importance to the flavor outcome of any recipe. The finest raw ingredient handled poorly will not produce desirable results.

In today's market, all manner of options present the shopper with the dilemma of which is the best product to buy that will produce the finest, healthiest, sustainable and flavorful dish. Current knowledge of ingredients can make the shopping trip part of the enjoyable experience of preparing a delicious, nutritious meal. Shoppers' confession: "I have been known to swoon over a perfect enormous head of bright white cauliflower, so much so that I took a picture for memories sake." Hopelessly in awe of nature's finest foods I strive to stay abreast of the latest information of produce, meats, poultry, seafood, grains, legumes and nuts. In doing so I have developed a criterion that helps me navigate the many markets available in my area.

1. Shop locally and in season whenever possible. Recently at a dinner party, I boasted that the salad greens were purchased the day before at a farm stand 2.2 miles from my home. Though my husband cringed, I truly was proud of that salad. Since that time my weekly visits to that farm are referred to as the "2.2-mile" farm day" and my husband is currently cultivating our own organic garden plot. I am also known to order my Thanksgiving organic heirloom turkey two months in advance and pick it up in the parking lot of a local food co-op. I find these adventures as exciting as the plans and preparation of the meal.

There are now many ways to find your closest farm fresh foods. There are several on-line sites that will direct you to these sources. Farmer's markets have also become a weekly source of fresh, locally grown foods and a fun way to connect with farmers. If time is of the essence, set up neighborhood groups that will take turns shopping and sharing the bounty. There are also Community Supported Agricultural (CSA) subscriptions that will deliver fresh produce to your door once a week. It is like opening a gift when the box of produce arrives and you can begin planning for the week's menus.

2. Buy organic, free-range, grass-fed, sustainable foods if possible. In the mid-eighties, I had the great opportunity of meeting Alice Waters and enjoying a unique and delicious meal at her restaurant, Chez Panisse. My husband, who at that time was not a gourmand, and I were so impressed we proceeded to go to our hotel room and write down all our observations. From then on I was on a path to learn all I could about the "organics movement." I now am a member of Slow Foods and read all I can about the latest information on how our food is grown, raised, processed and shipped. I also follow Organic Consumers Association which keeps abreast with the latest in ingredient authenticity.

   As a child, when I pulled up a carrot from our organic garden to munch on, the revelation was pure joy. I even sliced off the top of the carrot, stuck toothpicks in it, propped it in a glass of water and watched it slowly sprout new roots. Try that with a store-bought carrot today and you will watch until the carrot rots. The simple reason is that those carrots have been chemically treated to not sprout. Leave an organic carrot in the fridge too long and it will begin to sprout. Try a side by side comparison of an organic and chemical carrot to discover that sprouting is not the only difference. Flavor abounds in the organic carrot as does the nutritional value. Pesticides are meant to kill insects and other harmful substances that would destroy the carrot crop. Unfortunately, they also kill some of the nutrients and flavor. Pesticides used on large corporate farms also destroy all the living organisms in the soil, creating what is called "hard pan" soil that is literally dead. Without those living organisms, the "hard pan" easily erodes and takes precious top soil into the rivers and ultimately to the seas. This is just one example of the organic vs pesticide dilemma choice.

Organic foods are currently more expensive, but as they become more popular and more farmers see the value in going organic, the price is slowly coming down. I went through a prolonged period of chronic illness which left me with a lasting determination to do all I could to maintain good health. I have chosen to spend more money on organic foods in my budget. It has paid off with increased health and a more flavorful diet.

To become knowledgeable of other reasons that organic, free-range and grass-fed foods are vital to your family's health and the health of our planet as we have known it, I highly recommend viewing documentaries such as Robert Kenner's Food, Inc., Eric Schlosser's Fast Food Nation or Michael Pollan's Botany of Desire or read the books by these authors.

3. Spend time preparing weekly or daily menus to develop a grocery list, then be prepared to change the list when finding an outstanding specimen of a different product at an agreeable price. Even though I am retired and able to go shopping daily I prefer to spend some time in the evening planning menus for the week and do my shopping on Saturdays when most farmer's markets are open. Fresh foods from farmer's markets will keep longer than grocery store produce. I do my seafood shopping on Fridays because that is when most seafood is delivered to retail outlets and is at its freshest. Seafood only keeps for one or two days refrigerated.

   Plan the menu with season and variety in mind. It is best for good health to eat a wide variety of foods in small portions. Consider that on the plate you should have two thirds plant-based foods and one third animal products (if you are an omnivore). Four to six ounces of animal based protein is ample. That leaves eight to twelve ounces of plant foods including fresh produce (fruits and vegetables), legumes (beans and peas), nuts, seeds and whole grains.

4. Become familiar with what foods you find at which venues. Read the newspaper ads for specials or coupons. Through the years, I have become fond of four places where I have a mental list of "what to buy here." First is my local food co-op where I can find mostly organic and in season local whole foods. It also affords a large selection of bulk ingredients, especially organic spices which I buy in small quantities to ensure freshness. Second is Trader Joe's where I can buy organic dairy, egg, coffee, tea, produce, canned goods, extra virgin olive oil, special vinegars and nitrate-free cured meats. The appeal here is organics at a reasonable price. Third is Whole Foods (I know, you say Whole Paycheck but I am selective and cost-conscience) where I can find truly exotic and special ingredients. Their cheese selection is fresh and comprehensive. And if I find myself in the vicinity I can enjoy a nutritious and organic lunch. Fourth, but of equal importance to the previous three, I shop at Costco for large quantities of foods. In recent years, they have embraced a sourcing philosophy that searches the world for organic, sustainable, free-trade, grass-fed and free range ingredients at low cost to quantity prices.

    Find your closest outlets that stock foods which are fresh and cost-friendly. You probably have a Costco nearby but have you tried your local food co-op? And when you visit Whole Foods take a list that you can stick to and splurge on one new exotic ingredient. After all, shopping should be a fun activity.

5. Shop the perimeter aisles of your local grocery store for most your food. I do like my very close independent grocer; however, I rarely go down the center isles as these contain expensive, sugar-full, artificially flavored, GMO and pesticide-laden products that are costly to one's health and pocket book!

    Becoming aware of which foods and brands are damaging to your health and will save you in health-care costs. Remember that it must be a whole food with little or no additives to meet this objective.

6. Become familiar with the food you are about to purchase to ensure choosing the freshest, most nutritious specimen. I recommend The _Oxford Companion to Food_ by Alan Davidson as a comprehensive food guide for the serious cook. Googling the specific ingredient will give you a whole list of useful information, and you can use your smart phone at the market. We live in an age where knowledge is at our finger tips. How fortunate to be able to ask questions about that ingredient in front of you and then determine if it is fresh and flavorful. Remember that your sense of smell is also a great tool in determining food quality.

7. Read the ingredient and nutritional analysis lists on packaged foods. It is important to know that ingredients are listed in order of predominance. If corn syrup or hydrogenated shortening is the first ingredient you can be sure that I will set that food back on the shelf immediately! Become a label reader! Your health and flavor enjoyment depend upon it.

8. Pay attention to shelf life dates on packaged foods as they help you determine the freshness and storability of a packaged food, the sell-by date refers to the last day the grocer can display it for sale. It is usually still safe to eat for ten days after that date, if stored properly. The use-by date denotes the last day a food is palatable before it begins to deteriorate. The expiration Date signifies the date the product should be thrown out.

9. Travel with insulated bags or ice chests with ice packs to maintain proper food temperature. Unless you are going to the corner store within a mile of home and immediately returning, then you should assure that you can maintain the temperature of the food you purchase. Even in the dead of winter an insulated bag or chest will keep the food at the correct

temperature. You aren't really going to leave that gourmet ice cream in a hot car on the hottest day of the year, are you? So why would you leave milk in a bag in that same car for more than a few minutes?

10. Unpack your provisions carefully and store each food to sustain optimum nutrition and flavor. Did you know that the best way to store asparagus is by cutting off the tip of their ends, placing them upright in a bowl with a wet paper towel on the bottom and covering them loosely with a plastic bag in the refrigerator? You would have, had you paid attention to #6: Google it!

Once you get all those delicious, nutritious foods home learn how to store and use them quickly. Then it is time to put your feet up, enjoy your favorite drink and contemplate your next step.

"The materials you buy must always concord with the techniques you apply to them."
–James Beard

TOOL TALK

The most important tool you as a serious culinary adventurer can possess is the keen use of your own five senses. With basic culinary knowledge, the senses of sight, touch, smell, taste and hearing become the essential tools to guide you through the various steps in preparing any recipe. While navigating through a recipe, being mindful of these fortuitous gifts makes the journey to ultimate flavor become not only a simple task but also a delightful pleasure.

Sight allows you to choose the best possible ingredient at market then to cut, shape, prepare and fashion it into a lovely display. Observe and preserve the colors and shapes of individual foods for the best outcome.

Colors of food can denote freshness or spoilage of a raw ingredient, although organic and locally grown foods are not always the colors to which we have become familiar. They may have blemishes that are not found in their mainstream market counterparts. These blemishes may not always indicate spoilage. Color alone does not make them desirable or undesirable depending on the food. Each ingredient must be examined on its own merits. Colors of some foods change when exposed to oxygen by paring or cutting them. Apples, pears, avocados, bananas, potatoes, and meats are the most obvious. A simple dip in acidulated water can temporarily ward off unwanted colors of some foods. In the case of meats, the oxidation is not always detrimental to the dish once cooked. Colors of foods generally change when cooked and can signal a crucial state of doneness. Often the color will change from translucent to opaque or opaque to translucent when heated depending on the nutritional profile of the particular food. A sea scallop will change from translucent to opaque when cooked whereas an onion will turn from opaque to translucent. Color combinations of foods on an attractively-arranged plate can excite and encourage the dining pleasure.

Shapes also denote freshness or spoilage of a raw ingredient. Fruits and vegetables each have specific shapes that specify their freshness. Sometimes the shapes are firm and other times soft. Sometimes their shape will be smooth and others will be wrinkled. Again, each one must be judged on their specific merit. A wrinkled passion fruit will be at the height of ripeness whereas a wrinkled Bosc pear would be deteriorating. A firm carrot would be sought-after whereas a firm carrot with a vertical split in the skin means that the carrot has absorbed too much water before or after harvest and therefore not acceptable. A limp, soft carrot would indicate dehydration and not be preferred. The shape and texture of meat, poultry or fish can signal how they were handled during maturation, production or processing. Broken or deformed bones and mushy textures are not desirable. Grains and legumes should be well formed and whole, not broken or split. Often the shape of cooked ingredients is altered by cutting, forming or heating through various methods. These shapes add to the aesthetic appeal of the finished dish.

Procure raw ingredients by observing their color and shape. Researching the qualities of a main ingredient before shopping is advisable. While preparing the food, you can alter the shape of the food to cook evenly and add interest to the resulting dish.

Touching raw food will have a certain feel, while touching cooked food will be a much different experience. This is especially true of high protein foods such as meats, poultry, eggs and seafood, which will generally change from a soft raw form to a firm resilient form in its cooked state. Foods high in carbohydrates and fiber such as fruits, vegetables, grains and legumes generally will adjust from a raw firm structure to a soft texture when cooked with an occasional exception. Professional chefs will touch with their fingers to determine the state of doneness of a grilled steak or will pop a grain of rice into their mouth between their teeth to determine its degree of doneness. A pastry chef will use her or his hands to judge the proper consistency of a batter or dough. Observing these transformations will help you become more skillful in your approach to cooking. It will put you in contact with the true nature of that food. Also, food touching your tongue stimulates the nerve endings just under the taste buds, assisting your sense of smell to assimilate the impression of flavor. In addition to color and shape the cook should often procure individual foods by touching them to determine their freshness and suitability. The tactile experience of using one's fingers, hands, teeth and taste buds is not only necessary to cook well but makes it truly enjoyable.

"Smell and taste form a single sense, of which the mouth is the laboratory and the nose is the chimney; or to speak more exactly, of which one serves for the tasting of actual body, the other for the savoring of their gases." – Brillat-Savarin

Smelling raw food can detect ripeness or spoilage. This is especially true of fruits, which are best selected by their smell. Their raw smell will directly relate to their taste when eaten. This is true of vegetables to a much lesser extent depending on the vegetable. Smell denotes freshness of fresh or dried herbs and spices which give dishes very distinct flavors. Smell of meats, poultry, eggs, fish, shellfish and dairy products have very telling signs of freshness. As foods

cook, their flavor compounds vaporize to give off telltale signs of balance and the degree of doneness. It is the pleasurable experience of breathing in these vapors that truly combines with taste buds and saliva to form the perception of taste.

When you select an ingredient for a dish, evaluate its suitability using the sense of smell. When cooking that ingredient, you should be aware of the smell at each stage of flavor development to detect changes and, ultimately, doneness. Wave your hands from the cooking food towards your nose then inhale the vapors to savor its goodness.

Tasting raw and cooked foods gives you very dissimilar flavors depending on the nutritional profile of that ingredient. If the food is starchy when raw it will become increasingly sweet while cooking, as the starch will convert to a sugar. One only needs to taste a raw and cooked onion to appreciate this principle. Depending on the type (white, sweet, yellow, red, or green) and growing factors such as soil, climate and sunlight, onions will have a very starchy flavor and a sulfur compound that is perceived as pungent. As that onion is cooked it will begin to change in color from opaque to translucent, which is often called "softening" in recipes. It will also become sweeter and less pungent. If the onion is allowed to cook until it turns brown or "caramelizes", it will take on a pronounced depth of sweetness. An onion cooked beyond caramelization to "carbonization" (burnt) will turn the sweetness to bitterness, which is generally undesirable. Occasionally though, carbonized foods are used in small amounts in complex recipes to "layer" and punctuate other flavors. An "onion brûlé" is a French preparation in which a peeled onion is cut in half to expose the rings then placed flat on a very hot cast iron griddle and allowed to burn on the ringside while the top of the onion becomes soft and translucent, which indicates that the starches have been converted to sugars. This "onion brûlé" is then used in recipes like brown beef stock to add color, sweetness and a slight bitterness, which give a complex flavor profile to the stock.

The texture of raw and cooked foods is perceived on the taste buds as "mouth feel," adding a poignant interest to the food. A starchy or starch-coated food that is fried will

SHARING THE TABLE

become crispy and crunchy. If the food is high in protein when raw it will generally be soft and supple. When this protein rich food is cooked, it will begin to change in texture to become increasingly firm and resilient. Depending on the protein based food this firmness and the degree to which it is cooked may be enjoyable on the palate. Foods high in fat tend to coat the tongue trapping whatever flavor is present in the food for a longer time, which may or may not be an enjoyable quality depending on the other flavors. Oils and fats stored improperly, held in sunlight, exposed to oxygen or salt for too long will become rancid. Oils that are heated too long and/or at too high of a temperature will become bitter and putrid. Foods with high water content can become dehydrated which is sometimes desirable as in beef jerky or sun dried tomatoes. As these foods are cooked their water begins to evaporate, changing the nature of their texture and flavor.

Raw ingredients should be tasted to enlighten you as to their suitability for a specific dish. When a dish is cooking, you may begin to taste the flavors as they are developing. This will give you an insight as to how much longer the dish needs to cook, what other ingredients may be needed to alter the flavors and/or how the temperature may need to be adjusted. At the end of preparing or cooking a dish you should taste the food and adjust the flavor intensity by adding salt and/or an acid such as lemon juice.

Hearing the sounds of some raw ingredients can determine freshness. Consider the sound of the snap of a carrot when broken, which denotes a degree of crispness, or the crackle of commercial pasta, which means it is sufficiently dry and made of quality ingredients. More often you hear the sounds of food as it cooks. Listen for the sizzle of a small amount of flour added to a pan lightly coated with hot oil which will alert you to the readiness of adding a food coated with flour so that it will not stick to the pan. The rapidly bubbling sound of water will signal you to add pasta to be boiled. The sizzling sound of vegetables sautéing necessitates you to flip them occasionally to promote even doneness and prevent them from burning. Loud burping sounds from a pot of tomato sauce require you to reduce

the temperature to prevent the tomato sauce from coating the entire cook space!

Listening for telling sounds of raw and cooking foods is a tool used by the ever-vigilant cook. Hearing is especially important when you are multi-tasking in the kitchen because your eyes may be on one item and your ears may be hearing sounds of yet another, allowing for your prompt attention when necessary.

Consider just one ingredient: green asparagus.
Look for a spear of dark green asparagus with slightly purple tips, which alert you to a very fresh vegetable. Should that same asparagus spear be a dull grayish green with yellow tips, buyer beware! That same asparagus spear may either be pencil thin or thicker depending on the age and breed of the plant. Either size is acceptable but the thicker ones may need to be peeled before cooking. The stalk should be thicker at the base with a thin pointed tip. The heads should be tightly formed and compact. Asparagus is a fern whose tips will begin to bolt from the base and head if allowed to fully develop. This will make the shoot stringy and tough and may taste bitter when cooked. It should have a smooth skin, not wrinkled or wilted. Break one stalk to hear a crisp snap denoting freshness.

If the asparagus must be stored prior to cooking it is best to keep the spears together with rubber bands or string. Slice off a small portion of the ends and place in a small flat bowl with very wet paper towels. Place in the refrigerator and cover loosely with a plastic bag.

Break one spear at the point near the base where the green begins to turn white, which is the part grown underground that is tough and bitter. Line up the other spears by their tips and cut all that same length. Peel thick asparagus by placing each spear flat on a cutting board. Using a vegetable peeler carefully peel from the point where numerous tips begin to the base of the spear. A bunch of asparagus may be tied together with string to cook them standing up. The tender tips will be just barely above water to be steamed, while the thicker bases are boiled at a higher temperature.

Boiling water is detected by the appearance of large bubbles that break at the surface giving off a popping sound. When plunging the asparagus, tips up, into the boiling water, the green spear will turn a vibrant green, which indicates a degree of doneness. Conversely, if cooked too long the vibrant green will turn to a grayish green, which is generally undesirable. When cooked, the asparagus should keep its natural shape, not break apart. Testing one spear between your front teeth will determine doneness which generally should be al dente, an Italian term that means "to the bite" or just tender on the outside giving to a slight crunch on the interior.

A sprinkle of sea salt and a splash of lemon juice just before consuming will highlight the earthy, grassy natural taste of asparagus.

Organizing ingredients in a recipe is called "mise en place" in French. Quite literally it means "everything in its place." Thinking logically and in order comes naturally for some, for others it may take special effort, but in time it will become natural.

Read the list of ingredients in a recipe. Should an ingredient need to be washed, peeled, chopped or cut into a specific shape then this must be done before ever following the directions. Organize each prepared ingredient in a small cup or bowl on a sheet pan in the order that each is used in the recipe. Now that the mise en place is prepared it is time to mix, cook or bake. Once this becomes a habit, cooking or baking will become a pleasure and the outcome will assuredly be improved.

Likewise, organize an entire dinner party in much the same way. First organize the menu, then the recipes, then the shopping list, then the prep-sheet. Divide the prep-sheet into two or three days. Doing advanced preparations without loss of quality will make the day of the party much more enjoyable. Always plan to be ready at least one-half an hour before guests are due just in case unforeseen events happen.

Referencing one or more food encyclopedias or ingredient or technique-specific cookbooks will allow you to become better equipped to try a new recipe using your five senses. Prior to testing a new recipe, I often turn to *The Oxford Companion to Food* by Alan Davidson, *On Food and Cooking* by Harold McGee, *Chez Panisse Fruit* by Alice Waters, *Chez Panisse Vegetables* by Alice Waters, *The Herbfarm Cookbook* by Jerry Traunfeld, *good fish* by Becky Selengut and *Culinary Artistry* by Andrew Dornenburg and Karen Page to name just a few. My collection of books is ever as much an essential tool in my kitchen as is an oven, a saucepan, a chef's knife or a whip. The amount of time referencing an ingredient or technique will contribute to the successful outcome of your recipe and, will over time, establish your culinary prowess.

Equipping your kitchen with proficient implements depends on your knowledge of each tool, including their function, composition, shape and durability.

Mastering the use of each of these tools will enable you to skillfully perform tasks that will produce the ultimate flavorful dish. Consider the type and purpose of the tools required when first reading through a recipe. Each tool has a specific purpose and how it is used will determine a precise flavor and/or texture outcome. Using a gas stove top will be different than electric or induction tops. Pans will vary from aluminum to stainless steel and on it goes through each type of tool to be used. Let us now explore the differing effects of knives, hand tools, cookware and bakeware.

Knives

The chef's knife is also known as a French knife. One of the first requirements to becoming a cook is the knowledge of the proper use of a chef's knife. The second requirement is to acquire skill and speed with this knife. The blade is shaped and worked so that it can *peel, trim, slice, chop, mince, fillet fish, and fabricate meats and poultry*. A good quality chef's knife should be well balanced, with the weight of the blade equal to the weight of the handle.

The chef's knife is used on a cutting board secured with a rubber mat. A paring knife is used in the hand as well as for jobs off the cutting board.

A sharp knife allows for rapid and accurate work with a minimum of effort. A dull knife usually results in poor appearance of food product and poor uniformity and it poses a safety hazard because it may easily slip and cut fingers.

Preparation sizes

In this book use the following size recommendations for shapes:

Small dice = ¼ x ¼ x ¼ inch

Medium dice = ½ x ½ x ½ inch

Large dice = ¾ x ¾ x ¾ inch

Julienne = ⅛ x ⅛ x 1 ½ inches

Chiffonade = finely sliced (⅛ inch or smaller) herb, lettuce and greens

Please use a ruler until comfortable and accurate with each size to ensure the desired result of the recipe.

How to sharpen a knife

1. Secure the sharpening stone (found at professional restaurant shops) with a damp cloth to keep it from slipping.

2. Place a small amount of sharpening oil or water (but never both) on the stone.

3. Use the coarse side of the stone first then the smooth side.

4. Place the knife at a 20° angle to the stone and drag the knife with the holding hand across one side away from you then on the other side towards you with pressure from the guiding hand.

5. Sharpen the knife until the blade feels equally rough on both sides from the tip to the heel.

6. Wipe the knife clean with a paper towel.

Hone (realign) the knife with a sharpening steel to remove the small burrs. Hold the sharpening steel tip down on a cutting board dragging the knife gently at a 20° angle up and down each side of the steel.

Knife-handling:

1. Safely secure a cutting board by placing it on a damp towel or other non-slip material.

2. The predominant hand holds the knife with the thumb and index finger on either side of the blade and the other three fingers hold the handle of the knife.

3. The other hand is called the guiding hand. This hand should be held so that the fingertips are tucked slightly under to hold the food with the thumb held back behind the fingertips. The knife blade then rests against the knuckles, preventing the fingers from being cut.

Five basic knife movements:

1. Straight down motion for firm but not hard foods such as celery or onions.

2. Straight down and back motion for foods with a tough peel such as peppers or tomatoes.

3. Down and forward motion for most hard foods such as carrots or root vegetables. Often this cut is performed with the tip of the knife resting on the cutting board, however the cuts from this action become somewhat triangular shaped and not very uniform.

4. Rocking with the hands on the top of the knife and acting like a teeter-totter is used for mincing herbs or aromatic vegetables such as garlic or shallots.

5. A sawing motion is best for shredding delicate leaves from lettuces to herbs.

Hand Tools

When first setting up my home kitchen I had very few hand tools. As the years have gone by, I have acquired many new and some improved tools that may or may not make their principal jobs easier. Categorizing them as to their purpose may help to understand their necessity. Some hand tools have now become attachments to mixers or food processors, including slicers, shredders, graters, grinders, strainers, pasta rollers and sausage stuffers. The following list of tools is essential but not comprehensive, as many more tools are available but not always necessary.

Utensils that cut and change the shape of ingredients:

Zesters have to be one of the best inventions that have entered into every day preparation. They come in a wide variety of shapes and sizes and are sometimes called rasp graters. They are excellent for producing finely grated citrus zests, garlic, ginger, chocolate, nutmeg and select cheeses.

Box Graters usually have two to four sides. The fine and coarse grates are most useful for grating cheese, fruits and vegetables. For safety, hold the food flat against the grater with your thumb pushing the food through. Should you grip your hand around the food, you will most likely grate your knuckles - a most unfortunate move!

Peelers come in two varieties. A flat blade peeler is best used for peeling fruits and vegetables either toward you, or away from you onto a cutting board (as with a carrot). Delicate vegetables such as asparagus should be laid flat so as not to break the stalk while peeling. A serrated peeler is used to peel delicate fruits and vegetables such as peaches and tomatoes.

Mandolines are very useful for thinly and uniformly slicing fruits and vegetables. I have found the less expensive Japanese varieties have and keep the sharpest blades. For this very reason, I always put a food-grade glove on the hand that guides the food so I don't slice my hand, which of course, has happened on my culinary journey!

Poultry Shears are indispensable for easy dismemberment of raw or cooked poultry.

Herb Snippers are especially useful should you grow your own herbs in the garden or on the deck.

A Set of Round Cutters comes in several sizes to be used to evenly cut different types of food or baked goods into rounds. In the early days, I used the top of a water glass, which was neither safe nor accurate but conveniently inexpensive.

Melon Ballers or Parisian Scoops are used not only to create perfectly round melon balls but also to core the pits of fruit such as apples or pears. Look for sturdy ones with a solid solder where the scoop is attached to the handle. These will not break when used on hard vegetables such as carrots.

Utensils that scoop, stir and move ingredients:

Spoons are used to stir and lift ingredients. Slotted spoons allow for drainage when lifting solid ingredients from liquids or fats.

Wooden Spoons are inexpensive and indispensable for stirring hot pots of food. They do not scrape any of the metal from the pan into the food. They are especially important in the jam and jelly making process.

Ladles are useful to move liquids from one vessel to another. Good ones will have the measurement size on the handle (i.e. 4 ounces or ½ cup), which may be very helpful.

Scoops come in various sizes. They are not only helpful with ice cream but measuring and moving cookie or cupcake batter, etc.

Spatulas come in two varieties. Those that are used to scrape down a bowl and mix and those that are used to lift and flip foods. I have several sizes and shapes of flat spatulas, each geared to a specific task.

Bench Scrapers are helpful in the baking process or in making fresh pasta by doing just what they say, scraping the bench. They can also cut and portion various kinds of doughs.

Brushes come in two varieties. The first is a bristle hair pastry brush used to brush flour from doughs. The second is a high-heat silicone brush used to brush melted butter, oil, marinade or egg wash onto foods.

Tongs become the extension of one's fingers or hand to move and turn hot food.

Utensils that incorporate other ingredients and create air bubbles in foods:

Whips are found in many shapes, sizes and forms. Two are all that are necessary. They are also sometimes called whisks. A sturdy whip will have thick tines (wires) that enable the mixing of thick batters or sauces. A fine-tine whip will move freely when bounced from the side of a pan or bowl. Its purpose is to whip air bubbles into foods such as egg foams (Hollandaise sauce, meringues, etc.) and heavy cream (whipped cream)

Utensils that change the texture of ingredients:

Food Mill is the original food processor without electricity. It is a bowl with a perforated bottom and a hand-operated crank that moves the food through the holes, making a purée. It can separate skin or seeds from the food. I find that it still makes a better tomato purée than a food processor does. It also removes seeds from berries more easily than pressing them through a fine-mesh sieve.

Mortars and Pestles are excellent for grinding spices. Larger ones are good for mashing avocados into guacamole. I also keep a small electric coffee grinder to grind spices, well-marked so that it is never used to grind coffee beans.

Juicers come in several varieties. The one I turn to most often is a small two-piece Tupperware model if I only have one or two citrus fruits to juice. I also have an electric citrus juicer for larger quantities. Juicers for hard vegetables such as beets or carrots are expensive and tend to break quite easily.

Potato Mashers are used to make mashed potatoes and other cooked vegetable purées. I prefer the hand held manual type, which produces a better texture than an electric mixer.

Rolling Pins are usually made of wood and come in a variety of sizes and shapes. They are used to roll out dough into an equal thickness.

Utensils that measure liquids, solids, temperature and time:

Measuring Cups come in metal, glass and plastic varieties. I keep two sets of metal measuring cups, one for liquids and one for dry ingredients. They come in sets of four: one cup or eight fluid ounces, one-half cup or four fluid ounces, one-third cup or three fluid ounces and one-fourth cup or two fluid ounces. I also have plastic and heat-resistant glass measuring cups. These measurements are usually for pints, which are two fluid cups, quarts, which are four fluid cups, and gallons, which are sixteen fluid cups. Measuring cups are best for liquid ingredients but are also used here in the United States for dry ingredients.

Measuring Spoons come in metal or plastic varieties. Sets usually include one tablespoon, one teaspoon, one-half teaspoon, one-fourth teaspoon and one-eighth teaspoon. I keep at least two sets on hand, one for dry (herbs, spices, etc.) ingredients and one for liquid ingredients (milk, vanilla extract, lemon juice, etc.).

Digital Scales are very useful in weighing solid ingredients and for professional baking recipes. They should weigh a minimum of five pounds and up to ten pounds.

Thermometers are available in instant-read, meat, oven and deep-fry/candy varieties. All are necessary. Instant-read digital are necessary to measure the temperature of meats, fish and poultry and usually read up to 220°F. Oven thermometers help gauge your oven's true temperature which can change after much use. The deep-fry/candy thermometers are essential for those functions and should have a metal clasp that will attach to the pan for easy reading.

Timers come in handy, especially when multi-tasking, as a reminder to check the doneness of a dish.

Cookware

There are many types of cookware but first and foremost it is important to understand the different type of metals used to make the cookware as they determine how well the vessels will cook the food. The best conductors of heat are copper, cast iron and aluminum. Copper must not come in direct contact with the food because of its reactive nature (except for egg whites and high-sugar foods). Copper cookware must be lined with another metal. It is also very expensive. Cast iron heats more slowly but holds the heat for a longer time making it desirable for griddling or frying foods. It is porous so it absorbs the flavors and fat of the foods cooked in it. Enamel lined cast iron is very useful for braising foods that must remain at a constant low temperature for a long period of time. The unlined variety must be seasoned by heating with oil or fat several times to produce a non-stick surface. Aluminum is also a good conductor of heat but it is a reactive metal that is soft and easily scrapes off into the food, leaving an undesirable taste and color. It is most often lined with other metals or anodized (heat-treated to make the surface non-reactive). Stainless steel is a very poor conductor of heat; however, it is non-reactive and when combined with a sandwich of other metals, becomes an excellent cooking vessel. Most nonstick cookware has surfaces that, when scratched become unsafe for cooking and I do not recommend buying or using them. The new ceramic- lined nonstick pans are excellent for sautéing or frying but must be seasoned with oil or fat occasionally to keep their nonstick surface viable.

Listed below are a variety of common kitchen cookware. Select the right cookware for the desired effect on the food being cooked.

Pots versus Pans

There are many specialty pots and pans but only two basic ones are necessary in most kitchens. The main difference between a pot and a pan is that a pot has two short looped handles and a pan has one long handle. Both are used to boil, simmer, poach and braise foods. The second difference is the width and depth of the pot or pan. The wider the pot or pan the more readily liquids can evaporate, and the taller the pan the less the liquids will evaporate. A stockpot is tall with a minimum width for cooking stocks and broths for a long period of time, retaining maximum liquid. A sauce pan is shorter and sometimes wider to enable frequent stirring and less retention of liquid. A sauce pan is good for making sauces but also a good choice for cooking grains such as rice or simmering vegetables. A tight fitting lid is most helpful.

Sauté versus Sautoir Pans

A sauté pan has sloped, short sides with one long handle. It will wick off excess moisture, making it best for frying or sautéing small amounts of food. The sloped sides and long handle will also allow the pan to be kept in constant motion and assist in flipping foods over. (Practice the flipping motion by flipping a slice of bread. When good at bread, substitute an egg to fry on one side and flip to the other.) A sauté pan is good for frying and caramelizing ingredients. A sautoir pan (pronounced saw-twahr) is a short-sided pan with straight sides, which keeps moisture in the pan. A sautoir is good for sweating (releasing liquids) ingredients that are not meant to be browned but to be cooked without color.

Cast Iron Skillet and Griddle

Cast iron skillets are the perfect non-stick pan. Not only are they good for frying but are also good for baking. Because they are porous, they are not suited for liquid-based cooking. They must be seasoned by very lightly oiling and baking for one hour in a 350°F oven. Repeat this process until the pan becomes black. Clean the skillet by heating on the stove top and rubbing with kosher salt to remove debris. If this does not work, quickly wash in soapy water, rinse thoroughly and dry over a hot stovetop burner. While it is still hot, lightly oil it with a paper towel. I have several sizes of pans and a large rectangular griddle but my favorite is the one I inherited from my grandmother. Years of use makes cast iron cookware superior.

Braiser, Dutch Oven or Rondeau

These three pans are excellent for the two-step process of braising. The food is first browned in oil on the top of the stove, then deglazed with liquid, covered with a tight-fitting lid and slowly baked in the oven. The difference in pans is the metal, size and shape. All three should be lined with non-reactive metal such as stainless steel or enamel. Braisers are generally stainless steel lined, short-sided and round. A Dutch oven is usually enamel lined cast iron and round or oval in shape. Rondeau (pronounced ron-doe) means round in French. It is a straight-sided pot. Select the size and shape according to the food being braised. A round pot roast would do well in a Rondeau. A beef stew would do well in an oval pan. The tight-fitting lid is essential to the process of braising, as it does not allow liquid to escape but to caramelize and drip down onto the food below.

Roasting Pan

A roasting pan should be very sturdy and fitted with a rack so the food (usually meat or poultry) is surrounded by heat. Drippings in the bottom of the pan are generally used to make gravy or sauce.

Paella Pan

A paella pan is a shallow, sloped sided steel or enamel lined pan with two looped handles. They come in various sizes depending on the number of servings per dish. It is seasoned and re-seasoned like cast iron. Dimples are generally on the bottom of the pan to suck the liquid and rice to stick to the bottom of the pan creating a much-desired upside-down crust called "socarrat" in Spanish.

Wok

A wok is used to stir-fry, which is similar to sautéing, as items are tossed over very high heat. A wok may also be used to deep fry and steam foods. It has a deep bowl base with sloping sides and generally two looped handles. Carbon steel is recommended but non- stick varieties are available. The carbon steel variety will rust if not seasoned with a small amount of oil between uses.

Bakeware

Baking Pans and Molds: Loaf Pans, Pie Pans, Cake Pans, Bundt Pans, Cheesecake Pan, Muffin Tins, Tart and Tartlet Pans, Gratins, Casseroles Baking pans and molds usually come in tempered glass, heat-resistant porcelain, enamel-lined metal or metal (sometimes non-stick lined metal). They also come in a multitude of shapes and sizes. Each shape and size of pan is intended for a specific recipe. For uniform baking, custards are sometimes placed in an individual mold then placed in a hot water-bath in a large baking dish. A gratin is usually an oval-shaped, heat-resistant porcelain pan in which ingredients are baked and topped with either cheese or bread crumbs then browned. Casseroles can be round, square or rectangular tempered glass or heat-resistant porcelain in which recipes like lasagna are baked. Each recipe should specify the preferable type and size of baking medium. If other substitutions must be made, extra care must be applied for the best results.

Sheet Pan

In a home kitchen, rimmed half-sheet pans are generally used to bake items such as cookies and roasted vegetables. They are generally made of aluminum and must be lined with parchment paper or a high-heat silicone baking mat when baking acidic foods such as tomatoes or eggplant. Often a sheet pan is used to hold other pans whose contents may bubble over. They make a perfect tray for holding prepping cups or bowls with ingredients for a recipe or for holding cold plated salads or desserts that go in the refrigerator.

Wire Rack

A wire rack has two purposes. First, baked dishes or pans hot from the oven can be placed on them to allow air to circulate around the food while it cools. Second, with a sheet pan underneath the rack, foods such as bacon can be placed on them to catch drips and to keep them from stewing in their own juices.

Silicone Baking Mat

The high-heat silicone baking mat has become a wonderful, recyclable sheet pan liner. It is durable and can be washed and reused repeatedly. Parchment paper is a good substitute however it is expensive and non-recyclable. It is best to invest in a high-quality silicone baking mat.

Baking Stone and Peel

Baking stones come in round or rectangular shapes and are made of stone or terra cotta. They are necessary to create a crust on the bottom of bread, flatbread and pizza. A peel is a large wooden or metal flat spatula used to move the bread or pizza to and from the stone. For crusty breads the stone is put in a cold oven and heated to a high temperature. The bread is put on the stone with the peel then a baking pan of hot water is placed below in order to create steam in the oven.

The right tool for the right job will make a vast difference in the outcome of a recipe. Choose wisely.

FLAVORS FROM THE ARTIST'S PALETTE TO THE CULINARY PLATE

"A good cook who is born with an interest in gastronomy will naturally become, under favorable circumstances, a more accomplished artist than the individual to whom cooking is an unpleasant task." – *Escoffier*

Artists of all types rely on many tools and capabilities to express their talent. A musician has an instrument, a sense of timing, and exacting motor skills to name just a few. A painter chooses a medium with which to paint, a palette for mixing the colors, a special brush or technique, a unique focal point and finally a frame. A culinary artist also has a variety of tools and techniques that define efforts to produce a flavorful dish.

* * *

The artist's support is the foundation upon which they may express their images such as canvas, rice paper, parchment paper, cloth or ceramic.

The culinary artist's support is the base of the dish upon which they may express their recipe's inspiration. It is the starting point at which flavors and techniques may be applied to produce a unique dish. These bases are usually meat, poultry, fish, shellfish, eggs, fruits, vegetables, grains, legumes and dairy products. These basic foods will vary in flavor and texture depending on their terroir, harvesting, processing and storage prior to being used as the foundation of a recipe. As a platform, they will ultimately absorb and reflect the artist's vision in a variety of ways.

Meats and poultry have the "umami" or savory core that can carry a multitude of other flavors to great depths. Fish and shellfish have the salty, sea essence that pairs especially well with acidic, sour, and sweet flavors. Eggs are a unique foundation that depend directly on the techniques applied to them as to how they carry flavors. Raw egg yolks may be a thickening agent that carries flavors in dishes such as an aioli or hollandaise sauce. Boiled eggs may be "deviled" with many flavors or simply seasoned with salt. Whipped egg yolks and or whites create diverse structures for sauces, omelets, custards, soufflés, cakes, cookies, and pastries. Fruits and vegetables have earthy, garden patch, floral, grassy, woodsy, sweet and savory modes of flavor platforms. Grains in their whole form generally have a nutty, earthy, starchy base. Ground and processed grains known as meal or flour provide the framework of breads, fried breaded foods, cakes, cookies and pastries. Flours and meals also can expand and absorb liquids, thus becoming "thickeners." Whole legumes such as beans and peas have a vegetarian meatiness that is often seen as a base in many different country's' peasant foods. Fresh legumes tend to have a sweet base, while dried legumes have a starchy base. Soy bean curd or tofu has a neutral density that absorbs any flavoring or seasoning applied to it. Milk is transformed into numerous varieties of cheese which can carry almost any flavor or seasoning. Cream and milk can also be the stage for sauces and custards to entertain a gamut of flavors. These are the foundation ingredients that host a multitude of flavors to express culinary visions.

* * *

The artist's colors are the primary colors of red, yellow and blue. The mixing or layering of two or more of these colors and their progeny will produce a vast number of new colors.

The culinary artist's colors are the primary flavors of sweet, salty, sour, bitter, and umami, also known as savory. The blending or altering of any of these flavors will create new mingled or layered flavors. Flavors that are blended will have a certain aroma and taste. This blending of flavors is sometimes called "married" as it has a homogeneous taste even with separate ingredients. Flavors that are layered tend to approach the nose and palate in succession of one another. There are several excellent books that have lists of ingredients and their complimentary ingredients that pair well with each other.

* * *

The artist's paint is pigment bound in a substance such as oil, acrylic or watercolor that will adhere the color to the medium.

The culinary artist's paint binds colorful flavors to the foundation ingredient creating a sensation when eaten called "mouth feel." Fats and oils found in assorted foods are the primary binders as they attach to most ingredients. When the food is eaten, they coat the tongue thereby holding lingering flavors to be savored for a longer time. When fats and oils are absent in a recipe the perceived flavor disperses quickly in the mouth. Tannins found in foods such as red and purple plants (those with the anthocyanin pigment), immature fruits, some wines and the skin of nuts create the mouth sensation called "astringency." These foods will also linger on the tongue and create a tactile sensation. Pungent flavors from foods such as onions, garlic, radish, horseradish, ginger, mustard, black pepper, and chilies create a pain sensation that can have fleeting or lingering tactile sensation. Depending on the proportion of each used and how they are prepared they can merely highlight or conversely dominate a foundation flavor. The raw onion family including garlic has sulfur compounds that have a somewhat fleeting pain in the mouth. Cooking them will moderate their pungency. Horseradish, ginger, black pepper and all chilies tend to bind to any bodily cell and create lingering pain. Used sparingly they can push other dish-predominate flavors forward on the palate; whereas used in abundance they tend to dominate other flavors, and often burn long after the morsel is swallowed.

* * *

The artist's palette is a large curved half-moon board upon which the artist can mix various colors with other colors to develop a completely new color. The artist holds the palette in one hand while the other hand mixes colors and applies the paint to the medium.

The culinary artist's palette is the transfer of heat and/or coolness to the ingredients that alters one or more flavors of a recipe. Heat and coolness can be conducted by one item touching another item. For example, the gas flame conducts heat to the pan and the pan conducts heat to the steak in the pan thereby conducting heat. The surface of steak that touches the pan begins to transfer the heat to the interior of the steak along the meat fibers. In the case of coolness, a hot pan of custard sauce is cooled by placing the pan in an ice water bath which conducts the warmth of the custard to the ice water bath. The flavor of the steak and the custard takes on new nuances depending on how long they are heated or cooled. A raw steak has a silky, buttery flavor as in steak tartar or carpaccio, whereas a medium rare pan fried steak has a caramelized crusty flavor with a juicy center. Hot custard has a strong creamy egg and vanilla flavor, while cold custard has more subtle flavors. If the custard is frozen the flavor is understated, yet refreshing on the palate.

If movement is added to the heating or cooling process the transfer occurs faster. Stirring the hot custard while in an ice water bath will cool the custard much faster. If the cooled custard is put into an ice cream machine the churning paddle will develop a smooth texture, whereas, if that same custard is merely put in the freezer it will develop rough ice crystals. A piece of meat put into an oven with a fan (called a convection oven) will cook the meat much faster than an oven without a fan. When a pot of water is put over a heat source, hot gases rise to the surface of the water in the form of bubbles. As the temperature of water rises the bubbles become larger, breaking at the surface and the cool gases then sink to the bottom. This act of boiling produces a natural type of churning. If pasta is placed into this boiling water it will be naturally stirred and pieces will not stick to each other. Convection will change the flavor and texture of the foods being cooked or cooled but mostly affects the speed of the temperature transfer.

Radiation is heat that is transferred by waves of pure energy to the food source. On a hot day one can observe heat waves radiating from a hot asphalt street. Likewise, when broiler elements heat up, heat waves are transmitted to the food directly below. In the case of a grill they are transmitted to food directly above. Radiant heat is usually quite hot to be able to cook the food above or below. It is also used to brown or "gratinée" the top of a food. In microwaves radiation penetrates a food and the water in the food begins to move rapidly causing friction, which in turn causes heat. Because these microwaves are indiscriminately bouncing around in a microwave oven it does not always cook the food uniformly and needs foods that have sufficient water to vibrate.

New to the cooking scene is induction cooking, which is a form of electromagnetic radiation. A cooking vessel must be made of a magnetic material to be used on a ceramic cooking surface with a wire coil that creates a magnetic field between the two. This field induces heat in the pot or pan. It is a constant heat that reacts very quickly and produces excellent cooking results with minimal electricity and no noxious fumes.

Conduction, convection, radiation and induction are all methods in which ingredients can be altered to develop new flavors and/or textures. They are usually used in conjunction with a vessel or tool much as an artist uses a brush to mix and apply colors.

* * *

The artist's brushes are tools that allow the artist to mix color and apply it to a canvas or other medium. The type and style of brush will create varying outcomes.

The culinary artist's brushes are the tools or vessels that are usually used in concurrence with the active forms of heating and cooling. They serve as implements that slice, peel, mix, season, flavor, brush, grind, puree, mash, juice, measure, weigh, strain, scrape, scoop, ladle, whip, lift and hold. They are also used in the processes of boiling, steaming, poaching, blanching, roasting, baking, broiling, grilling, griddling, sautéing, pan frying, deep frying and braising. Specific tools that accomplish these methods are discussed in the chapter called Tool Talk.

* * *

The artist's focal point is the object which the artist sketches within the picture to draw the spectator's eyes into the entire picture.

The culinary artist's focal point is often a garnish that visually draws the eye into the whole plate. The visual expression of a garnish invites the diner's attention to the dish about to be consumed. That garnish can be a mere sprinkling of foods compatible to the dish such as nuts, cheese, croutons or chopped herbs. It also can be the shapes of the food, how the food is arranged or the colors of the foods on the plate. Garnishes should always be edible, well-matched to the other ingredients and inciting.

The focal point can also be a texture that brings contrast to the dish. Crunchy, crisp, granular, smooth, creamy, buttery, flaky and chewy are some of the textures that when put in the mouth, attracts attention to the whole tasting experience. These tactile expressions invite the tasters to explore all aspects of the food they are moving around in their mouths.

Bitter flavors such as Belgium endive, watercress, arugula, radicchio, escarole, celery root, Swiss chard, kale, mustard greens, chicory, dandelion, broccoli rabe, artichoke, horseradish, daikon, caraway, coriander, cumin, cinnamon, cranberries, kumquat, almonds, and burnt sugar can foil and bring immediate attention to the dish. Often these bitter components are combined with their opposing flavor of sweet and sometimes fatty ingredients which tend to balance them, but they generally always attract attention.

* * *

The artist's strokes (highlights) are the moving accents that bring to light the theme of the painting.

The culinary artist's strokes (highlights) are flavor accents that bring to light and emphasize the foundation ingredient. These are the spices, herbs, and aromatic vegetables and fruits. They also are the pungent flavors of cruciferous vegetables (cabbage family), horseradish, most of the onion family, pungent cheeses, truffles, mustards, fermented and pickled fruits and vegetables. Tangy and sour flavors from vinegars, citrus fruits, cheeses, sour cream, yogurt and wines as well as picante flavors from chilies and ginger round out the various ways to heighten and compliment the foundation ingredient in a dish.

* * *

The artist's frame is the way the finished painting is presented to further enhance the artist's vision. It may be gilded, elaborate, or austere. Whatever its nature, it effects the overall impression of the art work.

The culinary artist's frame is the presentation of the various elements of the dish that bring it all together. This of course would be the choice of plate upon which the food rests. However, it is also the basic parts of the dish such as the support, body, sauce or topping and garnish or accompaniment that augment the total image.

Plates come in numerous colors, shapes and designs. Personally, I am of the school that believes that the plate should not overwhelm the food. Therefore, I most often use white or ivory colored plates with little or no design. I do believe varying shapes of dishes can accentuate the dish nicely. Whatever you choose, consider making the plate the background upon which to best present the food.

The parts of the fare depend on the type of dish being presented, from appetizer to soup, salad, entrée or dessert. Not all parts are necessary or desirable. The support can be as simple as a leaf of lettuce to as complicated as a major complex recipe upon which the foundation food is presented. The body is the main dish. The sauce could be hot or cold, a dressing, or drizzle of a flavorful liquid such as vinegar, lemon juice or flavored oil or a swirl of sour cream, yogurt, or flavored butter (compound butter) which flavorfully moistens the body. A topping could be a crunchy nut or crouton, a sprinkling of chopped fresh herbs, citrus zest, or a tangle of micro-greens that give the dish a tactile interest. The garnish may be the topping or the sauce but it could just as well be a sprig of the dominant herb or a colorful slice of vegetable or fruit.

The choice is truly in the eye of the artiste!

ODE TO AN ONION AND THOSE AWESOME AROMATICS

Ode to an Onion
This orb of concentric delight
Be yellow, purple or white
Reveals a culinary core
A genesis of great taste . . . and more.

–John Hierholzer

Much like setting the table to enhance the outcome of the upcoming meal, aromatic vegetables, fats, oils, meats, herbs and spices are the cache of applicable flavors, the foundation to which the major ingredient of a dish is underscored and highlighted. Most of the countries represented in this book usually have specific combinations of aromatic vegetables, meats, herbs and spices that become the base to their respective dishes. For example, the French have mirepoix which is a combination of onions, carrots, and celery occasionally with the addition of thyme and bay leaves cooked in butter, olive oil or poultry fats. The Italians have soffritto, which may contain onions, garlic, fennel, prosciutto, pancetta, parsley, sage and bay leaves cooked in olive oil or butter. The Spanish have sofrito or sofregit which may have onions, garlic, tomatoes, jamón, bacon saffron, paprika, oregano, parsley, bay leaves and dried chilies cooked in olive oil or lard. And on it goes.

Setting a table with a cloth, plates and silverware sets the tone of the meal to come, likewise aromatic vegetables add to the distinct depth of a recipes' flavor. Take the humble onion for example: In its raw oblique form, it may render an edgy, starchy and crunchy profile. Sweat it in a fat or oil until translucent, soft and releasing juices, and it will give off a mellow, slightly sweet essence. Taken a step further by sautéing in a fat or oil until golden brown, it now takes the dish to a predominate sweetness. Sliced lengthwise from stem to root, with the cellulose grains, it will hold its shape when cooked, thus holding up to a long cooking time. When sliced across the hemisphere, between the stem and root, it will break down into smaller pieces whether eaten raw or cooked. This is also true for leeks, shallots, garlic and scallions, which are all in the allium family. Carrots, celery, fennel and tomatoes are other commonly used aromatic vegetables.

The different type of fat or oil used to cook the aromatics is usually based on availability in a specific country as well as flavor preference. Oils tend to have a higher smoke point than fats and are used for high heat cooking, except for nut oils. Fats tend to have a lower smoke point and are therefore better for low heat cooking.

Meats, whether raw or cured, may be rendered of fat with which to cook the aromatics. However, they also add a different flavor dimension such as umami, savory or salty, if used in the base.

Aromatic herbs and spices add a color and fragrant component to the dish, much as flowers do on the table. Consider saffron and turmeric adding a yellow color to the entire dish. Herbs added in the beginning of a recipe tend to marry with other flavors and colors, whereas green herbs used to finish a dish amplify a bright green and refreshing taste to the final preparation.

Much as the table is prepared and brightened, inviting guests to partake of the meal at hand, so to the basic aromatics separately or combined, enhance the colors, flavors, textures and aromas of a recipe. Deeply appreciated by all who participate. Awesome!

TASTE, THINK, TRANSFORM

"Cookery becomes an art when judgment, skill, creative ability and fine appreciation of flavors enter into it."

– Chester H. Smith, Pictorial Review Standard Cook Book, A Sure Guide for Every Bride, 1933

How often does the cook, in a rush to put food on the table, stop to sample the food, evaluate the flavor and modify with a few finishing touches? Unfortunately, this is not done often enough to affect the integrity of the dish. This last method of *"Tasting, Thinking and Transforming"* can be the most important of all the previous steps. It will, most importantly, determine how the dish is received by those waiting to indulge. As a chef-instructor, students would bring their finished dish to me for evaluation. We would both take a small sample and then I would ask them to tell me what they thought. More often than not the student would reply with "it seems bland" or something to that effect. (Although I must confess that sometimes they had hit the mark with a well-balanced dish. These were the students who I had observed tasting at various steps of their recipe and had already applied critical thinking.) My next question was: how would you change it? At this point the dialogue could go many directions. It was the perfect teachable moment.

Taste, Think, Transform is a phrase that is present in most of the recipes in this book. This is the point in the recipe where the cook is to decide if the dish's flavor needs to be altered or adjusted. Too often recipes are treated like they are perfect as written. In reality, we all perceive taste differently. Some people have a high tolerance for salt or hot chilies for example, while others have a low tolerance. If too much salt is present in a watery dish like soup, potato cubes can be cooked to absorb some of the salt and discarded. If too much chili heat is perceived, adding a small amount of sugar, dairy product or nut butter may tame it. Salt and acidic foods like citrus juice, vinegar or wine can counter-balance one another to create balance. It is advised to add small amounts of transforming ingredients at a time. It may take several alterations to get the desired results. So, take a moment to taste the food, think what is missing or too predominate, then go about transforming the final flavor.

TASTE

Tasting is the art of placing a portion of food in one's mouth, chewing, savoring and punctuating the flavor with air taken into the nose, and forced into the mouth. Each one of us has different abilities to taste determined by heredity, age, sense of smell, body needs, personal preference and psychological aversions. This most certainly poses a biased evaluation. Nonetheless, as a cook, one must to the best of one's inherent abilities appraise food and its balance or lack thereof. A set of questions may be helpful here:

- What flavor is appropriate here?
- Is that flavor pronounced or bland?
- Is the flavor shallow or deep?
- Does it need more salt or more acidity? (The two can create a flavor balance much like a teeter totter.)

- Does it need more aromatics?

- Is it too bitter?

- Is it too spicy or not spicy enough?

- Is it too sweet or not sweet enough?

- Is the texture pleasing?

- What is doneness?

- Would one change the flavor or mouth feel, and if so, how?

THINK

Aha! It has come to this. The recipe has not made a robot out of a cook! It is time to apply those past experiences and academic endeavors. Again, each and every one of us brings different skills and abilities to the recipe at hand. Consider if the food is balanced, flat, or overpowering. A second opinion often helps. Then begin to contemplate what changes need to be made, if any. What may be useful are some answers to the questions one has posed at the tasting:

What flavor is appropriate here?

Does the recipe have a single flavor, layered flavor or balanced flavor?

Roast chicken would be an example of a single flavor. So most likely a simple balancing of salt and lemon or vinegar will brighten, balance and bring forth the single umami (savory) flavor of chicken.

Pan roasted halibut with fennel, tomato and kalamata olive compote is an example of a layered flavor. To evaluate, each bite should include a bit of halibut, fennel, tomatoes and olives. The flavor of each ingredient must be pronounced and different creating an orchestra of notes in the mouth. Here the violin, now the piano, then the horn. Each ingredient flavor should be discernable.

Wine braised duck legs are an example of balanced flavor. Long slow braising can bring many flavors together and finally balance them so that no one flavor stands out but a new single flavor emerges. One might ask if the recipe has had time enough for the ingredients to meld together. This

is the reason that braised items like stews are better the day after they are made.

Is that flavor pronounced or bland?

If the desired flavor stands out, then the cook's work is done. Should the dish be bland, other questions must follow and be answered.

Is the flavor shallow or deep?

Does the dish just barely satisfy or is it profound? What intensity is suitable to ensure maximum enjoyment?

This is a question that conjures up images of pushing or pulling flavor notes to strengthen the dish. Much as one pushes a heavy door open or a horse pulls a cart, the cook can thrust or set in motion the essence of a dish by cooking methods.

Whether poaching, searing, caramelizing, roasting or frying an item, has the cook made the most of the method? Studying a recipe and its technique(s) *before* preparation is the best way to ensure depth. At the end of the cooking process the cook may need to determine what more can be done if the flavor falls short. Could a few more minutes in the pan, a splash of hot sauce or lemon juice restore the integrity of the dish?

Does it need more salt or more acidity? The two can create a flavor balance much like a teeter totter.

Salt of course is perceived differently by different people. It is still a question that must be answered.

If "bland" comes to mind, then it is time to try salting by adding a small amount at a time and testing again. If salted enough, does it still fall short? If it does, add a bit of lemon juice or an acid used in the recipe such as vinegar or other citrus fruits and tomatoes. One can teeter back and forth until a balance is achieved.

TRANSFORM

Time to change the character of the dish, taking small steps to not overreach the perceived goal.

Act in small increments. Also, consider additional cooking or baking time. If unsure what to do, consider what you perceive the final flavor should be and how that might be achieved. Need suggestions? Look for clues in the recipe and its ingredients. Also, look online at similar recipes or videos. It is amazing what help is available online.

By taking the time to *Taste, Think, and Transform,* the dish is enhanced and becomes the art of the cook to share with the guests. Time worth taking!

For more in depth discussion on this topic I highly recommend Becky Selengut's book: *How to Taste: the curious cook's handbook to seasoning and balance, from umami to acid and beyond.* It will be out in the spring of 2018.

SHARING THE TABLE ESSENTIALS

"Every science begins as philosophy and ends as art."
~Will Durant

Sitting at a friend's well adorned table three thousand miles from home, I felt the room radiate with conversation, laughter, joy, grace, fulfillment and genuine hospitality which brought about happy moments that linger in my mind to this day. The conversation led to a discussion about the art of the table and how some have lost this most precious experience. That day however reminded me of the sanctity of a well-set table.

Hospitality means generosity and friendliness. The Latin word "hospes" describes the relationship between the host and guest. That endearing relationship can be enhanced by the ambiance, the china or dishware, the crystal or glassware, the silverware or flatware, the candles, the flowers, the tablecloth and without doubt, the food and wine. In fact, each and every detail of the table creates the opportunity for hospitality to flourish. It is hospitality that truly sets the table.

The details of creating the possibility of hospitality begin with a game plan even for this crusty old chef. A meal for friends and/or family can be as simple or elaborate as one may choose. It also can be a **potluck** event where all invited bring one dish (written recipes can be exchanged). **Hors d' oeuvres** (the French word meaning "outside the meal") can be the gathering event before a formal sit-down dinner. In these modern times of traffic jams and busy schedules it is wise to have some type of hors d' oeuvre to buffer the hunger factor. As guests arrive each can begin nibbling while waiting for any guests that may be running late. **Buffet dinners** are a type of party that many enjoy because they can choose the amount and type of food with which they are comfortable ingesting. **Sit down dinners** are a way to put the guest at ease while the host serves each plate or serves on platters, family style. Following are a few guidelines that help in planning that special event.

VENUE

First, determine the type of dinner party. What setting is best for accommodating the event? If it is to be held at a rented hall, hotel, or restaurant, arrangements need to be made for the date, time and details. If it is to be in a home, considerations need to be made as to where in the home the hors d' oeuvres and dinner will be served.

Currently most people enjoy kitchen staged parties, especially if they are informal. The kitchen is the proverbial heart of the home. If it is a large gathering, have hors d' oeuvres placed at various tables in the room where the guests will gather. Inform the guests with small place cards next to the dish with the name of the hors d' oeuvre and ingredients for the curious or allergic guest. Another alternative is to have a person hand carry platters of hors d' oeuvres and beverages from guest to guest.

Will the guests be seated for the dinner? If so, much attention must be made to the seating arrangement. A small party generally is one where all the guests are seated at one table. Large parties demand several tables, hopefully arranged for easy mingling before, during and after the party. Informal parties might be on the deck or in the kitchen nook. Formal parties are usually in the dining room and/or living room.

INVITATION

Depending on the type of party, invitations can be delivered by phone, internet, or mail. The type of invitation sets the tone of the party to follow. As most people these days have quite busy schedules it is best to invite well in advance of the event, at least one to four weeks in advance, especially if it is the holiday season. The invitation should include the type of party, date including day of week, time of day, address (possibly with a map), if gifts are appropriate, any special instructions and RSVP details. Unfortunately, these days many people do not respond to RSVP requests so follow-up calls a few days before the event may be necessary, especially if reserving at a hotel or restaurant. I often ask for information on any food allergy, food discrimination or food dislike so that I can plan a party that all will enjoy. If any guests have nut allergies, no nuts should be present in the home at all, especially on the menu.

AMBIANCE

If the venue is in a home, naturally a thorough cleaning is in order in every room of the house. Lighting outside the home and in the home, are important considerations. Think about burning candles without scent so as not to interfere with the aroma of the food and because some are allergic to fragrance. Plan to have simple seasonal decorations, flowers and candles. Determine where guests' coats and belongings may be stored during the party. The ambiance sets the initial tone of the party and can put the guest at ease if well planned. Part of that ambiance is the demeanor of the host. Plan on having all party tasks done at least one half hour before guests are to arrive. This will allow time to relax, feet up with a large glass of water in hand, refreshed and ready to enjoy the guest(s).

TABLE

Set the table first with a crisp, clean tablecloth and napkins. All too often these days, hosts prefer to use disposable or no linens. Linens make the guest feel special. This is key to the host/guest relationship. Yes, it takes time to clean and iron tablecloths and napkins but consider the reward. Informal tablecloths such as oilcloths are appropriate in settings such as the kitchen nook or deck. Next, the formal table is set with china, silverware and crystal. The informal table is set with appropriate dinnerware. If decorations such as candles and flowers are to be on the table, they should be low so that all guest can easily see one another. Slender, tall candles placed between guests' views can, however, create a warm mood in the evening. The focus should be on conversational ease.

MUSIC

This advice is from my music sommelier friend, Paul:

Music is a perfect complement to entertaining and dining. It can create the perfect mood for almost any occasion. To be successful, the music should be matched to the meal in much the same way food is paired with wine. It should also reflect who you are and music you enjoy, especially with meals.

There are some basic guidelines for music pairing and an important one is to emphasize instrumental music and to avoid vocals. The music should provide an ambience for conversation and dining. Vocal music tends to compete with conversation and can be distracting.

That being said, there are plenty of exceptions. For a very romantic setting, crooned ballads in the background are appropriate. Mexican fiesta theme and music that cries out for some corridos makes for fun. A dressy Italian themed dinner simply must have opera. For cocktails, livelier up-tempo music can stimulate conversation and create a merry mood. Transition to mellower mood music for dinner to allow your guests to relax and savor their meal.

Music playback settings are also critical to successful ambience. The music volume should be set appropriately so that it doesn't drown out conversation. Make sure no one is sitting in front of a speaker. For an intimate dinner with only a few guests, the volume should be fairly low. If you have a larger group, especially if they are talkative, the volume will need to be raised accordingly.

If you don't have your own music collection, there are alternatives. Some radio stations have appropriate music, but avoid commercials and talkative DJs as they will kill the mood quickly. There are also music streaming services that allow you to choose a music genre or select some appropriate pieces of music that the program will attempt to match. This gives you less control over what is actually played, but these programs are becoming more sophisticated and can introduce you to wonderful music you might otherwise miss.

MENU

There are numerous ways to determine an hors d' oeuvre and dinner menu, especially if the party has a specific theme. Consider the formality or informality of the event when determining what is to be served. Another consideration is if alcoholic beverages are served. If serving hors d' oeuvres before a dinner, plan on serving two or three varieties of individual hors d' oeuvres. For a party without dinner, plan on serving six or more individual hors d' oeuvres. Either way, plan on having two servings of each hors d' oeuvre per person per hour, possibly more if alcohol is being served. Printing a copy of the menu for formal parties is informative and well-advised.

The hors d' oeuvre menu can include nuts, olives, dips, chips, crackers, cheeses, canapés (open-faced sandwiches), savory pastries, eggs, seafood, meats, poultry, vegetables and fruits. One should stay away from overly sweet foods as they will curb the appetite. Any entrée or side dish recipe may be down sized to become an hors d' oeuvre. The dinner menu should have a good variety of foods. Try not to duplicate a type of food in a meal such as having hazelnuts on the salad then hazelnuts in the dessert. If it is summer

a salad prior to or after the entrée would be refreshing. If it is winter a hot bowl of soup can be welcoming. Some type of protein such as eggs, seafood, meats and poultry should be considered. Vegetables and grains, potatoes, or pastas should round out the selections. Keep in mind that all selections should be visually appetizing as well as very flavorful. Each individual dish should be garnished, preferably with a flavor complimentary to the contents. Finishing the meal with a delightful dessert will leave favorable lasting memories of the meal. Type out a formal menu including the invited guests and keep a log. The next time you invite that guest you will not want to duplicate the menu.

BEVERAGES

Plan on serving three non-alcoholic beverages per person, which may include sodas, fruit based beverages and mineral or sparkling water. If serving wine, plan on half a bottle per person and include a variety of selections, white and red. Advice from the local sommelier is usually the best way to pair that special wine with the menu at hand. Hold and serve each wine at specified temperatures for optimum enjoyment. If beer is indicated for the certain menu, plan on serving two bottles per person or more depending on the length of the party. Glassware should be appropriately shaped (depending on the beverage) and sparkling clean.

SHOPPING

Shopping should be done several days in advance with consideration for retention of product quality as a guideline. Flowers, ice, fish and delicate produce may be purchased a few hours before the event. Shop at several outlets to get the most economical and best quality ingredients. Always make a shopping list and stick to it.

FOOD PREPARATION

Write down an extensive "prep list" detailing what to do, when to do it, how to store it and how to serve. Professional chefs do this for special menus on a regular basis. Make the quality of product the determination on when to prepare ingredients for each dish. Many preparations can be made the day before the party. Read each recipe thoroughly and decide what can be prepared in advance. I usually shop three or more days before the event. Clean the house two days before and prepare many components of each recipe the day before. Some recipes demand that the dish be made the day before. Crossing off each "to do" provides confidence and prevents last minute anxiety attacks.

SERVICE

Most hors d' oeuvres are foods to be eaten with the fingers. Tooth picks and wooden skewers are helpful in managing some hors d' oeuvres. Others may require a cocktail fork and small plates. Yet with others, certain types of food become a service medium such as chips with dip, crackers or bread with cheese, or crudités (various vegetables) with dip. Plan to have two napkins per person. It is also important to have a designated area, tray or tub for the guests to deposit soiled and used service ware. Tidy up the presentation area from time to time to keep it appealing. When serving dinner on food presented plates have the plates chilled or pre-warmed depending on the course. If serving family-style the bowls or platters should be cool but not cold and warm but not hot to pass comfortably.

DINNER CONVERSATION

The best dinner parties I have attended or given have included pre-thought out conversation topics. Naturally at Thanksgiving one can ask all at the table what they are most thankful for that year. But other thought-provoking topics can be a source of lively conversation that makes the event memorable. It is best to avoid political or controversial topics. Better yet is to recall happy personal memories that will inspire all. This consideration is often absent from dinner parties but can enhance the moments of the meal and the host-guest connection.

P.S. A camera is always helpful to record those special moments.

Hospitality dictates attention to details in advance which enables the host to freely give unconditional attention to the guest.

Enjoy and cherish sharing the table.

Starters

APPETIZERS, HORS D' OEUVRES, TAPAS, ANTIPASTO, MEZZE, MEZAQ

The kitchen island has become the place to be for starters and beverages before and during the gathering for the main event. Having become comfortable with this custom, I now have a variety of nibbles to serve with a glass of wine or favorite beverage at one end of the island, which allows me to effortlessly put the finishing touches on the remaining dishes at the other.

Appetizer means "to tease the appetite" so they must be very flavorful and bold. The French call it hors d' oeuvre meaning "outside the meal." The Spanish call it tapa which comes from the custom of taverns to put a "lid" of food on top of the Sherry glass to keep the flies out. The Italians call it antipasti meaning "before the pasta." In Turkey or Greece, it is called mezé or mezze which literally translates as "a pleasant taste." This is probably derived from the Arabic word mezaq which means "the taste, the savor of a thing." They are also known as "kemia" in North Africa.

The first step to having a successful party is to query the guests before the party as to their likes, dislikes and food allergies, then plan accordingly. Serving a variety of appetizers may consist of cheese with crackers or bread, some type of spiced nuts or seeds, dips with tortilla, pita or chips, a colorful crudité platter of vegetables with a tasty dip, then an array of specially prepared finger foods.

These few beginning moments of any party set the tone for the whole party. Plan this course wisely and much fun is to follow!

DUNGENESS CRAB, SNAP PEAS IN TARRAGON TOMATO NAGE

Dungeness Crab, Snap Peas in Tarragon Tomato Nage

For several summers, I would spend a week in a condo with my parents on Yaquina Bay in Newport, Oregon. My father would buy bait fish at the local mini-market on the dock to stock his crab pot. He would go out on the dock at the appropriate time and cast his baited pot. Often, I would join him to bring in the catch, carefully measuring each to assure the legal size of crab. Back in the condo I would cook and pick the crab meat. One time I had an excess of crab. Looking in the refrigerator I found V-8 juice, white wine, lemons, fresh tarragon and sugar snap peas I later altered ingredients to create this recipe. Every time I prepare this dish I can see Dad out there on the dock casting and retrieving the crab pot, which brings a smile to my face and a tear to my eyes, as I miss him.

8 appetizer servings

Nage

6 Roma tomatoes diced

½ cup Sauvignon Blanc wine

1 ½ cups clam juice or cracked crab shell stock

3 tablespoons fresh tarragon, chopped

¼ cup fresh lemon juice

1 teaspoon lemon zest

sea salt and black pepper to taste

Assembly

3 cups sugar snap peas, stem and string removed

pea vines if available (optional)

2 teaspoons fresh tarragon, chopped

1 ½ cup fresh Dungeness crab meat

fresh lemon juice as needed

optional hot sauce like Tabasco

1. Bring the tomatoes, wine, clam juice or crab shell stock, three tablespoons tarragon, lemon juice and zest to a boil. Reduce heat and simmer for 10 minutes or until the tomatoes are soft. Puree the nage through a food mill. Discard the solids. Bring the broth back to a simmer and season with salt and pepper. **Taste, Think, Transform** with salt, lemon juice and/or just a drop or two of Tabasco sauce. Keep warm.

2. Blanch the peas and pea vines in boiling salted water just until they turn a vibrant green. Strain. Keep warm.

3. Toss the crab with the fresh tarragon and lemon juice. Heat the crab in the microwave until just warmed through, about one to two minutes.

4. Pour the hot nage into eight bowls. Distribute the peas into the broth. Top with the crab. Garnish with pea vines or alternatively with sprigs of tarragon. Serve warm.

To make a *crab stock* simmer the cracked crab shells in two cups of filtered water for twenty minutes. Strain through a fine mesh sieve. A nage is a French preparation of a shellfish broth infused with fresh herbs.

MANCHEGO CRAB STUFFED PIQUILLO PEPPERS

Studying Spanish cuisine, I was wondering why salted cod is often used in recipes like this one. It seems that the Scandinavian sailors would salt their beloved cod to preserve and take with them when traveling. They most likely introduced salt cod to Spain. Salt cod must be soaked in fresh water over several days to make it palatable. Since I am from the Northwest I thought I would take this recipe and substitute the salted cod for ever-abundant Northwest crab. The Piquillo peppers are grown in Northern Spain. Roasting the peppers over open fires imparts a rich, spicy-sweet flavor which pairs but does not overpower the delicate crab flavor.

8 to 12 appetizer size servings

2 tablespoons mayonnaise

2 tablespoons sour cream

2 teaspoons Dijon mustard

1 teaspoon fresh lemon juice

½ pound Dungeness or lump crabmeat (8 ounces)

1 tablespoon flat-leaf (Italian) parsley, finely chopped

1 tablespoon chives or scallions (greens only) sliced or minced

½ cup Manchego cheese grated

2 tablespoons extra virgin olive oil

9.9-ounce jar Piquillo peppers, drained, washed and pat dry

1. Preheat oven to 375°F. Coat a round baking dish (cazuelas) with the olive oil.

2. Mix the mayonnaise, sour cream, mustard and lemon juice together.

3. Mix together with the crab, parsley, chives and cheese.

4. Stuff each Piquillo pepper with the crab filling. Place in the oiled baking dish. May be refrigerated at this point for a few hours. Remove from the refrigerator one-half hour before baking.

5. Bake until thoroughly warmed and the cheese is melted (about thirty minutes).

6. Serve hot.

This makes a lovely first course to any meal. Likewise, it is a tasty bite to add to a tapa or hors d' oeuvre party.

. . . .

BLACK BEAN SALSA

This dish was created to become a bed for Roasted Achiote Turkey Tenderloins but can also be used as a dip for your favorite chip or as a topping for shredded lettuce as a simple salad or in a tortilla wrap. It is best in late summer or early fall when the tomatoes tomatillos, corn and peppers are ripe and at the peak of flavor.

8 servings

1 (15 ounce) can black beans drained and rinsed (about 1 ½ cups)

½ cup red onions, small diced

½ cup sweet red pepper, small diced

1 cup Roma tomatoes, seeded, small diced

2 husked tomatillos, small diced (about 1 cup)

½ cup frozen or fresh corn, chopped (blanch 3 minutes if fresh corn on cob)

2 serrano peppers or 1 large jalapeño pepper minced (about 1 ½ teaspoon)

1 ½ teaspoon garlic, minced

¼ cup cilantro leaves chopped

¼ cup lime juice

zest of 1 lime

1 teaspoon dried Mexican oregano

½ teaspoon ground cumin

¼ teaspoon Pimentón Picante or smoked paprika with pinch of cayenne pepper

2 tablespoons extra virgin olive oil

kosher salt and fresh ground black pepper to taste

1. Mix all the ingredients together. **Taste, Think, Transform** with kosher salt, lime juice and/or peppers.

2. Allow to macerate for one to two hours at room temperature.

This makes a lovely first course to any meal. Likewise, it is a tasty bite to add to a tapa or hors d' oeuvre party.

. . . .

GOAT CHEESE STUFFED FIGS IN PANCETTA

After trying to grow Black Mission figs in the cool Northwest to no avail, I was about to give up on this delightful fruit. Then I heard about the Italian Honey fig. We now have a large Honey fig tree on the south side of our home and enjoy this otherwise expensive fruit during the summer months. I have found them to be delicious on their own but fun to stuff and wrap.

8 servings

16 Black Mission figs or Italian Honey fig
½ cup fresh goat cheese, at room temperature
1 tablespoon Italian parsley, chopped
1 tablespoon fresh mint, chopped
sea salt and fresh ground black pepper
16 thin slices pancetta
good quality balsamic vinegar to taste
honey to taste

Preheat the oven to 350°F.

1. Wash and dry the figs. Cut off the hard stem tips. Slice down the middle of each fig twice to quarter, **leaving the base connected**. Indent the center with a thumb.

2. Mix the goat cheese, parsley, mint, salt and black pepper together.

3. Place a scant teaspoon of the goat cheese mixture in the center of each fig.

4. Place the slices of pancetta on a silicone mat or parchment paper lined sheet pan. Bake for one to two minutes or until the fat begins to render but is not crispy yet. Remove from oven.

5. Wrap each fig in the rendered pancetta. Place back on the lined sheet pan. Bake for twelve to fifteen minutes until warmed throughout and the pancetta is crisp. Remove from the oven and place on platter. Let them rest for five minutes.

6. Drizzle lightly with balsamic vinegar and honey. Serve warm.

This hors d' oeuvre can also be enjoyed as an appetizer too. Serve them plated on a tangle of arugula dressed with balsamic vinegar and extra virgin olive oil.

. . . .

CILANTRO AND PECAN VEGETABLE DIP

The starter to any party is a good dip surrounded by fresh crisp vegetables. This dip will bring a zingy bright and nutty flavor to any array of vegetables. It also enhances tortilla chips and crackers. It is best made the day before the party so the flavors can meld and marry. One might need to remind guests of the "no double dipping" rule once they taste this flavorful creation.

2 cups

1 bunch cilantro leaves and stems washed, dried (about 2 ounces chopped)
2 tablespoons onion, chopped
1 cup pecans
2 cloves garlic, minced
¼ cup sour cream
½ cup soft cream cheese (4 ounces)
¼ cup mayonnaise
2 tablespoons fresh lime juice
¼ teaspoon Pimentón Picante
½ teaspoon sea salt
¼ teaspoon fresh ground black pepper

1. Finely grind the cilantro, onions, pecans and garlic in a food processor by pulsing.

2. Add the sour cream, cream cheese, mayonnaise, lime juice, Pimentón, salt and pepper. Pulse until well blended. **Taste, Think, Transform** with salt, lime juice, Pimentón and/or Tabasco sauce.

3. Serve with a colorful assortment of fresh vegetables, tortilla chips and/or crackers.

Substitute Mexican Crema Agria for the sour cream to make for a tangier dip. Also, can substitute ¼ teaspoon smoked paprika with a couple of pinches of cayenne for the Pimentón Picante.

. . . .

CUMIN SCENTED GARBANZO BEANS

Spiced nuts are a great appetizer to stave off hungry guests while putting the finishing touches on the meal. This is a bit of a departure from nuts, however so yummy and easy to make. It is particularly appropriate preceding a Mediterranean menu. Sometimes it is a great substitute for popcorn while watching a good movie!

6 to 8 servings

2 (15-ounce) cans garbanzo beans

¼ cup extra virgin olive oil

2 tablespoons garlic, minced

4 teaspoons ground cumin

kosher salt to taste

1. Drain the garbanzo beans and rinse thoroughly in a colander. Pat them very dry on paper towels.

2. Heat the olive oil to medium high in a large sauté pan. Add the garbanzo beans and toss for five to seven minutes or until they form a light crust.

3. Drain the garbanzo beans through a sieve, discard the oil. Return them to the pan with the garlic. Toss for another minute or two. Dust with the cumin and salt. Mix well. **Taste, Think, Transform** with cumin and/or salt. Serve warm in a serving bowl.

PIMENTÓN SEARED SHRIMP

Slightly smoky, laced with thin garlic slices and anointed with a dry Sherry, this Spanish style shrimp charms guests as an enchanting appetizer or tapa. Appetizer is a French term which means "to whet or tease the appetite." Tapas, which are thought to have come from a time when a stage-coach would stop at a Spanish tavern so that the hot and weary-worn voyager could refresh themselves for the remaining trudge onward. A glass of sherry would be offered with small pieces of bread placed on top to discourage flies and dust from landing in the sweet Sherry. Hence tapa, which in Spanish means "to cover," became a standard wine complement. In due course, it became known as a multitude of tasty small dishes to accompany wine. This tapa is sure to tease and enchant!

8 appetizer servings

2 tablespoons extra virgin olive oil

1 pound raw medium shrimp, peeled and deveined (16/20 or smaller count per pound)

1 teaspoon kosher salt

4 each garlic cloves, peeled, thinly sliced

¼ teaspoon Pimentón Picante

2 tablespoons Fino Sherry (very dry Sherry)

¼ teaspoon fine lemon zest

1 teaspoon lemon juice

1 tablespoon chives or scallion greens, thinly sliced

fresh lemon juice to taste

salt to taste

Pat the shrimp dry on paper towels.

1. Heat a large sauté pan* big enough to hold all the shrimp, over medium high heat with the olive oil. When the olive oil shimmers add the shrimp one side down.

2. Sprinkle the shrimp with the salt and sauté until pink on one side (about one minute). Toss or turn to the other side.

3. Sprinkle with the garlic and Pimentón. Sauté for about one minute longer until pink on both sides.

4. Deglaze with the Sherry to release the fond (bottom drippings) for about a minute longer. The shrimp should be just barely opaque in the middle. Do not overcook as they will then become rubbery.

5. Transfer from the heat and to a serving dish. Scatter the lemon juice, lemon zest and chives over the top. **Taste, Think, Transform** with the lemon juice and/or salt.

*This may be made in two batches if the sauté pan does not hold all the shrimp flat at once. In that case divide the ingredients in half and use the directions twice, washing and drying the pan between batches.

Pimentón Picante is a hot, smoky paprika from Spain. If you can only find smoked paprika then add to the one quarter teaspoon of smoked paprika, one eighth or less cayenne pepper. This recipe can also be used to top a bowl of angel hair pasta to be served as an entrée.

· ·

CUMIN CARROT TAPAS

On a guided tour of Jerez, Spain we had the great pleasure of seeing how Sherry is classically produced. After the winery tour, we were presented with six glasses of different Sherries and then told that we had fifteen minutes until the tour bus would leave for our lunch destination. We rapidly downed those six glasses, rushed to the estate store to purchase a couple of bottles and barely made the bus. By the time we reached our lunch restaurant we were a bit tipsy and famished. Luckily, they had these splendid carrot tapas awaiting us. When we gobbled them down they brought more, to our great pleasure as we watched flamenco dancers twirl in their splendor. Once home, I recreated this tapa, which tastes divine, tipsy or not!

6 servings

1 pound organic carrots

2 tablespoons extra virgin olive oil

½ teaspoon cumin seeds

2 large cloves garlic, minced

¼ teaspoon dried oregano

½ teaspoon Pimentón Dulce or smoky paprika

2 tablespoons Sherry vinegar

sea salt to taste

1. Trim and peel the carrots. Place whole carrots in a sauce pot with filtered water to just cover. Bring to a boil, reduce to a simmer, cover and cook. Check the carrots at four minutes to test that they are tender but still slightly crisp. If not continue to cook until proper doneness. Drain and cool in an ice water bath. Slice into half–inch coins.

2. Heat the oil in a sauté pan. Add the cumin seeds and garlic. Cook briefly until just smelling aromatic. Remove from the heat. Add the oregano, Pimentón and vinegar. Pour over the carrot coins. **Taste, Think, Transform** with sea salt and/or Sherry vinegar.

3. Allow to marinate for at least thirty minutes to several hours at room temperature. Serve at room temperature.

It is imperative to use organic carrots. Their flavor is far superior to their commercial counter-parts. Buy them with tops attached to insure freshness.

· ·

PROSCIUTTO WRAPPED CARAMELIZED PEARS

While teaching Northern Mediterranean cuisine in the fine dining room, I had the students prepare an antipasto/tapas cart. This antipasto was an all-time favorite. It could also be served as a salad on a tangle of arugula, balsamic vinegar and olive oil. Or it could be served alongside a sampling of cheese for a dessert course. The beauty of antipasto is in their simplicity and use of high quality ingredients.

8 servings

4 firm Bosc pears, peeled

¼ cup unsalted butter

1 ½ tablespoon granulated cane sugar

12 thin slices prosciutto, sliced in half lengthwise

1. Halve and core the pears. Slice each half lengthwise into three equal pieces (6 slices per pear.)

2. Heat the butter in a large cast iron pan. Add the pears, sprinkle with the sugar and brown on one side. Turn over and brown on the other side. (This may be done in two or more batches depending on the size of pan.) Remove from pan.

3. When cool enough to handle, wrap each pear in prosciutto. Serve at room temperature.

This dish could be made three to four hours before serving at room temperature

. . . .

SPICY PEPITAS

When I lay out an hors d' oeuvre spread at the end of my kitchen island to welcome guests, I always try to include tasty seeds or nuts. This has become my favorite, so much so that I make them on a regular basis to have on hand just for snacking.

2 cups

2 cups raw pumpkin seeds
1 tablespoon extra virgin olive oil
2 teaspoons kosher salt
1 teaspoon ground coriander
½ teaspoon dried dill weed
¼ teaspoon Pimentón Picante

1. Preheat oven to 350°F. Toss the pumpkin seeds with the olive oil on a baking sheet pan.

2. Roast in the oven for three minutes. With a spatula, turn them over and roast for another three minutes. Turn them once more and roast another three minutes. They should be lightly golden in color. They continue to cook and make a popping noise when removed from the oven.

3. Sprinkle the spices onto the hot pumpkin seeds and toss. ***Taste, Think, Transform*** with salt and/or spices. Serve warm or at room temperature.

If Pimentón Picante is unavailable use smoked paprika with a dash of cayenne pepper in its place.

. . . .

ROSEMARY MARCONA ALMONDS

Marcona almonds are a special nut from Spain. Unlike its relative, the California almond, it has a sweeter flavor and softer texture. They are usually found without the peel and are round rather than elongated. In some stores, they come roasted in olive oil and salt and can be quite expensive. I prefer raw or lightly toasted Marcona almonds found online by the pound. Often found in the bulk section of a grocer or large box-stores at the most reasonable price, lightly roasted with salt.

2 cups

2 cups Marcona almonds
1 tablespoon extra virgin olive oil
1 tablespoon fresh minced rosemary leaves
½ teaspoon garlic powder (optional)
sea salt to taste

1. Preheat oven to 350°F. Toss the almonds with the olive oil, rosemary and optional garlic powder on a baking sheet pan.

2. Roast in the oven for three minutes. With a spatula, turn them over and roast for another three minutes or until lightly golden in color. They continue to cook when removed from the oven.

3. ***Taste, Think, Transform*** with salt and/or rosemary if desired. Serve warm or at room temperature. They will keep up to a week in an air-tight container.

BREADS AND SPREADS

HOME ROLLS, CASSEROLE BREAD, LEMON BRIOCHE, MUFFINS, COFFEE CAKE, RICOTTA CHEESE, FRUIT JAMS

There is nothing like the smell of fresh-baked yeast bread to kick the appetite into high gear! Old English has bread meaning a piece or morsel, but the Old High German brõt means to brew, obviously related to the fermentation action of yeast. Take that morsel while still warm, spread with a homemade ricotta and spicy jam for a treat any time of day.

This chapter was inspired by the baskets of fresh-baked bread and assortment of fruit jams experienced in guest houses and hotels throughout Europe, but especially in Germany.

The breads, muffins and coffee cake in this section are for the most part quite simple to make and yet are so very rewarding to serve. Homemade ricotta cheese is listed here, as it not only can be used in lasagna but is charming as a bread spread. It is amazingly easy to make and tastes so much better than store-bought. The fruit jams are best made in the summer then fun to give as Christmas gifts.

Before your guests arrive, take a warm slice of bread, slather it with high quality cultured butter or ricotta, and revive your energy with this tasty morsel. No one will know except you!

Whole Ricotta Cheese Italian Dessert Plate

WHOLE RICOTTA CHEESE

At a hill-top villa just outside Rome my culinary tour group was treated to a wonderful four-course meal. The final course, dolce, was sugar topped with rum, beneath fresh dairy-sweet ricotta cheese that was topped with coco powder. Accompanied by crisp almond biscotti and ripe red strawberries to lovingly scoop up the cheese mixture. This was not the ricotta cheese found in grocery stores here in the states. I set about learning how to create a comparable ricotta from scratch and found it quite easy to make. I have learned that it also makes a better lasagna and enjoy it quite simply spread on morning toast. As for that Italian dessert, the picture must suffice until you make your first batch!

About 2 cups

½ gallon whole milk (preferably organic)

½ cup heavy whipping cream (preferably organic)

1 ⅛ teaspoon citric acid (dissolved in ½ cup filtered water)

½ teaspoon canning or kosher salt

1. Place all ingredients in a non-reactive six-quart pan. Mix well and place over medium-low heat. **Heat slowly, stirring constantly** to prevent scorching on the sides and bottom of pan.

2. At 170°F small bits of cheese should appear on the surface. **Stop stirring.**

3. Continue to cook just until 190°F temperature is achieved. Remove from the heat.

4. Let the curds and whey rest for thirty minutes undisturbed.

5. Lay clean high quality cheese cloth in a large mesh sieve hung over a large bowl or bain marie. Gently ladle the curds into the sieve. Gently scrape the bottom of the cheese cloth to allow all the whey to pass through. Discard the whey or supplement the garden soil with it. Let the curds rest at room temperature for thirty minutes to an hour.

6. Cover the sieve and bowl with plastic wrap and refrigerate twenty-four hours. Invert the sieve to unmold the cheese onto a plate. Use within ten days.

I buy my citric acid online. It may also be found at wine-making supply shops or stores that stock canning supplies. Bain maries' are very handy holding vessels that can be found at a very reasonable price at restaurant supply stores. The cheese cloth must have a very fine mesh and be of high quality. To reuse the cheese cloth, wash and boil it for a minimum of three minutes in rapidly boiling water. Then wring out and hang to dry. Place it in a sealable plastic bag until using again.

LEMON BRIOCHE

In 1996 on a culinary tour we traveled to the small village of Torgiano, in the Umbrian region of Italy. In the basement cooking school of Hotel Le Tre Vasselle, the Executive Chef taught us how to make Capodanno Bread or a form of Lemon Brioche along with other traditional Umbrian recipes. The lemon in this bread brought brioche to a whole new level. Once I converted it from metrics I have found it to be delicious as a base for French (Italian) Toast, with a Berry Topping, Lemon Berry Bread Pudding, a base for strawberry shortcake or eating it slathered with crème fraîche. As with most baked recipes it is best to weigh the ingredients rather than measure, however both are offered here. The texture is tantalizingly cake-like and delicately lemon flavored.

1 two-pound loaf of bread

4 ounces unsalted butter (1 stick of butter)

¾ cup milk (warmed to 90°F)

1 package active dry yeast (2 ¼ teaspoons) (do not use rapid-rise or quick-rising yeast)

1 pounds, 2 ounces all-purpose flour (about 3 ½ cups)

1 teaspoon kosher salt

3 ½ ounces granulated cane sugar (about ½ cup)

1 tablespoon fresh lemon zest (zest on a rasp microplane about 2 lemons)

⅛ teaspoon lemon oil *(optional but recommended)* *

2 large eggs

1 large egg plus 1 teaspoon water for an egg-wash

1. Remove the stick of butter from the refrigerator and cut into small pieces. The butter should not be soft when used, but malleable when added.

2. Heat the milk briefly in the microwave to 90°F. Sprinkle the yeast on top to dissolve. Let sit for five minutes.

3. Mix the flour, salt, sugar, lemon zest, optional lemon oil, yeast in warm milk and eggs in a standing mixer with a dough hook for three minutes slowly until ingredients are blended into crumbs. Increase to medium speed and mix for five minutes until slapping the sides of the bowl, it becomes smooth yet sticky.

4. Add the butter pieces a few at a time on medium speed. It will take several minutes to incorporate.

5. Knead on high speed for another ten minutes until it comes together in to a ball, which will happen in the last minute. It will be very smooth, elastic and sticky.

6. Put dough in an oiled bowl.

7. Place in a warm, draft-free spot covered by plastic wrap and let double in volume (about two to two and a half hours).

8. Deflate the dough by lifting it out of the bowl with your fingers underneath. Let it fall onto a large piece of plastic wrap. Tap the dough down to about nine by six inches. Wrap tightly with plastic wrap, place on a small sheet pan and refrigerate overnight.

9. Oil a nine by five by four-inch loaf pan.

10. Remove chilled dough from the refrigerator. Unwrap the dough and turn over on the plastic wrap. Tap the dough with a rolling pin to a twelve by six-inch shape with the long end facing you. Fold the short ends onto the top to meet each other. Then roll front to back into a tight log.

11. Place in the oiled loaf pan and cover with plastic wrap. Allow the dough to double in size (about two and a half hours).

12. Twenty minutes before baking, preheat oven to 425°F.

13. Mix the egg and water for the egg-wash thoroughly. Lightly and evenly brush the top and exposed sides of the bread with the egg-wash.

14. Turn the oven down to 350°F. Place the loaf in pan on the bottom rack in the center of the oven and bake for twenty-five minutes until browned on top. Turn the pan around and tent with foil that does not touch bread surface and continue to bake for about thirty-five or more minutes until internal temperature reaches 190°F. Depending on the oven the total baking time will be from fifty to sixty minutes. It will be deep brown on top and sides. Move from the oven to a baking rack and remove the foil.

15. Allow to cool for thirty minutes in the pan. Run a knife around the edges of the pan to loosen. Invert pan

onto a cooling rack. Do not slice until the loaf is **completely cooled** to room temperature.

*I use Simply Organic Lemon flavor found in the spice section of most grocers.

It takes two days to make this bread but it so worth the time! Once this bread is baked and cooled, it may be halved, wrapped in plastic wrap, then foil and placed in the freezer for up to a month. One half loaf can be used to make the Italian Lemon Toast found in the Brunch chapter. The other half of the loaf can be used to make the Blueberry Lemon Bread Pudding in the Sweets chapter.

Ingredients ready to mix.

After three minutes of mixing, crumb texture appears.

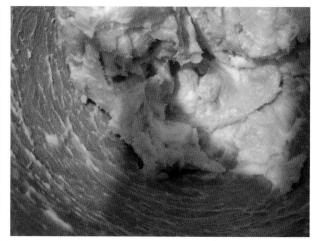

Butter incorporated and ready to beat on high speed for ten minutes.

Dough totally kneaded, away from sides of the mixing bowl in a ball.

Dough placed in an oiled bowl for first rising.

Fold the ends over to meet each other
Tightly roll the dough.

Place rolled dough in oiled loaf pan and let rise
until double in size.
Lightly brush the top and sides of the proofed dough.

Remove from the oven when internal temperature
reaches 190 F.

FLUFFY HOME ROLLS

A wonderful yeasty aroma would fill the whole house when Katie, my downstairs godmother would make these heavenly rolls. She would begin very early in the morning and by early afternoon we would be gently tearing them in half, buttering and spreading our favorite homemade jam on each warm half. They were light and fluffy as air. When I make them now I like to think that Katie must be looking down at me and smiling!

16 rolls

1 cup milk

½ cup soft unsalted butter

½ cup sugar

2 ¼ teaspoons dry yeast (¼ ounce)

¼ cup lukewarm water (90°F to 110°F)

2 large eggs

1 teaspoon salt

4 ½ cups all-purpose flour

1 tablespoon soft unsalted butter for pan

1. Heat the milk over low heat just until bubbles form on the side of the pan (scald). Add the butter and sugar and stir until butter is melted and sugar is dissolved. Remove from the heat and cool to 110°F.

2. Meanwhile sprinkle the yeast on the lukewarm water to soften.

3. Combine the milk mixture, yeast, eggs and salt in a crockery or heavy bowl. With a wooden spoon beat in half of the flour until well mixed. Slowly beat in the remaining flour.

4. Cover with a tea towel. Place in a warm, draft-free place and let rise until double in size (about one hour).

5. Beat down the dough with the spoon and let it rise for a second time.

6. Butter a nine by thirteen by two-inch baking pan Divide the dough in half and on a floured surface pat each into a disk shape. Cut each disk into eight equal pieces. Roll each into a round ball and place side by side, in three by five rows. The extra roll can

be placed on a small buttered custard dish. Preheat oven to 350°F. Cover and let rise until double (about thirty minutes).

7. Bake until golden brown (about twenty-five minutes). Remove from the oven. Cool in pan for five minutes then turn onto a baking rack. Serve warm or at room temperature.

The rolls may be made one day in advance and stored at room temperature, wrapped in foil. Or they may be wrapped in plastic wrap, then foil and frozen for up to one month. To reheat defrost the rolls at room temperature. Remove the plastic wrap if frozen and rewrap in the foil. Preheat the oven to 350°F. Place in the oven until heated through, about twenty minutes.

· ·

DILL CASSEROLE BREAD

At family gatherings, especially holidays, one food was always present at our table and that was what we called Dilly Casserole Bread. I think many families have a similar tradition as I have seen various renditions of this bread. It is very simple to make and can be made ahead of time which is a great convenience when cooking a holiday feast. It pairs especially well with ham. It is at its best when warm and slathered with butter. Unfortunately, there are rarely leftovers as it would make a great ham sandwich.

1 loaf

2 ¼ teaspoons dry yeast (¼ ounce)

¼ cup lukewarm water (90°F to 110°F)

1 cup small curd cottage cheese

2 tablespoons cane sugar

2 tablespoons mince onion

3 tablespoon unsalted butter (divided in 3 parts)

2 teaspoons dry dill weed

1 teaspoon salt

¼ teaspoon baking soda

1 large egg

2 ¼ to 2 ½ cups all-purpose flour

kosher salt for topping to taste

1. Sprinkle the yeast on the lukewarm water to soften.

2. Heat the cottage cheese, sugar, onion and 1 tablespoon butter until the butter is melted.

3. In a mixing baking bowl combine the warm cottage cheese mixture, softened yeast, dill weed, salt, baking soda and egg.

4. Add the flour and beat with a wooden spoon until well blended. Cover with a tea towel. Place in a warm, draft-free place and let rise until double in size (about one hour.)

5. Butter an eight-inch round casserole baking dish with 1 tablespoon butter. Stir the bread down and form a round shape. Place in the buttered baking dish. Cover with a tea towel and let rise for forty minutes until light.

6. Preheat the oven to 350°F.

7. Bake until dark golden brown (about one hour).

8. Remove from the baking dish by running a knife around the edges and inverting on a baker's rack. Rub the top of the warm bread with the remaining 1 tablespoon of butter. Sprinkle with the kosher salt. Let rest for ten minutes before slicing. It is best served warm.

The bread may be made one day in advance and stored at room temperature, wrapped in foil. Or it may be wrapped in plastic wrap, then foil and frozen for up to one month. To reheat, defrost the bread at room temperature. Remove the plastic wrap if frozen and rewrap in the foil. Preheat the oven to 350°F. Place in the oven until heated through, about twenty minutes.

ORANGE MUFFINS

Rather than reaching for the usual orange juice for breakfast try this spirited morning muffin. It has a moist, spongy and yet chewy texture that goes well with any morning egg dish. The cinnamon sugar topping complements the burst of orange zest essence. It has been a family favorite to enjoy with a steamy hot cup of coffee for many years now.

12 servings

1 ¾ cups all-purpose flour

1 teaspoon baking powder

½ teaspoon baking soda

½ teaspoon fine sea salt

2 tablespoons granulated cane sugar

1 large egg beaten

½ cup sour cream

½ cup fresh orange juice

¼ cup melted unsalted butter

zest of 1 orange (zest on a rasp microplane)

Topping

2 tablespoons butter

¼ cup granulated cane sugar

½ teaspoon ground cinnamon

1. Preheat the oven to 400°F.

2. Sift the flour, baking powder, baking soda, salt and sugar together in a mixing bowl.

3. In a separate bowl whip the egg, sour cream, orange juice, melted butter and orange zest together.

4. Immediately add the liquids to the dry ingredients. Mix with a large spoon for twenty seconds or until slightly blended. The mixture will be somewhat lumpy.

5. Distribute the batter to 12 paper-lined muffin tins with one-fourth cup scoop. Each should be filled about two-thirds full.

6. Bake for twenty to twenty-five minutes until golden brown on top, rotating pan after the first ten minutes.

7. For the ***topping*** melt the butter. Mix the cinnamon and sugar together in a separate dish.

8. Dip the warm muffin tops into the melted butter and then into the cinnamon sugar. Let muffins cool on a rack for at least ten minutes. Serve warm or at room temperature.

For a nice variation blueberries, raspberries, or rehydrated dried-cranberries can be lightly dusted in flour and added to the batter.

. . . .

SWEET POTATO PECAN COFFEE CAKE

My husband is a Texas transplant whose home town produces glorious pecans. I have found that this truly southern coffee cake embodies the goodness of southern flavors utilizing sweet potatoes, pecans and oranges. Served up with a steaming cup of coffee it is satisfying alone or as part of a breakfast or brunch.

12 servings

Coffee Cake

1 ¼ pounds sweet potatoes or yams (2 ½ cups cooked, mashed)

1 cup room temperature unsalted butter

2 cups granulated sugar

4 eggs

3 cups all-purpose flour

1 teaspoon baking soda

2 teaspoons baking powder

1 teaspoon ground cinnamon

½ teaspoon ground nutmeg

¼ teaspoon sea salt

1 teaspoon vanilla extract

1 ½ cups chopped pecans

1. Preheat oven to 375°F. Wash the sweet potatoes and pierce with a knife tip. Place on a foil lined baking dish. Bake until soft all the way through, about one hour depending on size and thickness of the potatoes. Cool, peel and mash. Measure exactly two and one-half cups to use.

2. Preheat the oven to 350°F.

3. Cream the butter and sugar well with a mixer. Add the eggs one at a time, mixing well before each addition. Add the sweet potatoes and mix well.

4. Sift the flour, baking soda, baking powder, cinnamon, nutmeg and sea salt together. Gradually add to the sweet potato mixture, blending well. Mix in the vanilla.

5. Remove from the mixer and fold in the pecans. Spray a ten-inch bunt pan with cooking oil spray. Spoon in the batter and place in the oven.

6. Bake for one hour and fifteen minutes or until a toothpick inserted come out clean. Cool in the pan on a rack for fifteen minutes. Turn the cake out onto a platter and let cool. This may be made a day before serving if covered with plastic wrap when cool and left at room temperature.

Orange Glaze

2 cups powdered sugar, sifted

2 tablespoons fresh orange juice

zest of 1 orange (use microplane)

1. Mix the powdered sugar gradually with the orange juice. Stop adding orange juice when thick and smooth. Add the zest.

2. Spoon the glaze over the top of the cooled coffee cake.

3. Slice and serve.

In the southern United States, sweet potatoes have an orange flesh. In the north, sweet potatoes are called yams. Orange flesh sweet potatoes are to be used in this recipe.

AMARETTO CHERRY JAM

Our first morning in my husband's ancestral home in the Black Forest we were delighted with the Gasthaus breakfast. The bread basket was filled with a variety of fresh baked rolls. Much to our enchantment they were accompanied by fresh churned butter and three house-made jams. Cherry jam was our favorite. So, when I returned home and the local cherries were in season I created this recipe to savour flavor memories with my own breads. It also makes nice hostess gifts.

4 to 5 eight-ounce jelly jars

3 cups pitted and finely chopped cherries (about 2 pounds sweet red cherries)

½ cup fresh lemon juice

¼ cup Amaretto liqueur

1 box natural fruit pectin (1.75-ounce net weight, MCP Premium Fruit Pectin)

½ teaspoon unsalted butter (to prevent excess foaming)

4 ½ cups granulated cane sugar

1. Wash six jelly jars, lids and screw bands in warm soapy water. Rinse thoroughly. Bring a boiling-canner two thirds full water to a simmer. Turn off the heat. Place the jars in the water. In a smaller pan heat the lids and rings in water. Place a clean salad plate in the freezer to be used to test the jell later.

2. Measure exactly three cups of finely chopped cherries. Measure all the other ingredients.

3. In a non-reactive sauce pot mix the chopped cherries and juice, lemon juice, Amaretto, pectin, and butter. Use a wooden spoon for stirring.

4. Bring the mixture to a full rolling boil. Stir in the sugar and bring back to a full rolling boil. Boil for exactly two minutes until jelled, which is determined by a drop of jam onto a cold salad plate. Let set for a moment and run your finger through. It should cause a clean swipe through the jell. If it does not continue to cook for another minute or two and test again.

5. Remove from heat and skim and discard foam, if any, off the top.

6. Remove the hot jars from the hot water. Quickly fill the jars with jam one eighth of an inch from the top. Wipe the rim with a clean wet cloth. Place the lids on top. Screw the bands on until slightly snug, then give another half turn. (Not too tight! Air must be allowed to escape for a good seal.)

7. Place in the boiling-canner on a rack. The water should be one to two inches above the jars. Cover with a lid. Bring to a gentle boil. Simmer for ten minutes (elevations above 1,000 feet simmer an additional five minutes). Remove the jars and place on a towel to cool. When cool, test the top of the jars by pressing in the middle of the lid with a finger. The lids should not spring back. If they do, place in the refrigerator and use within a month. Allow to sit for twenty-four hours. Wash with a wet cloth, label and date each jar. All other jars should be stored in a dark, cool place for up to one year. Refrigerate after opening.

• •

HONEY FIG JAM

My husband and I grow Italian Honey figs as Black Mission figs do not grow well in our area. I have found, however that we enjoy the taste of an Italian Honey fig much better. It has a green skin which needs to be peeled before preserving as opposed to the purple-black skin of a Black Mission fig. This year our crop was so large that we could not eat it all fresh so I made this jam. Now we thoroughly enjoy the flavor of this jam on toast or served with cheese as a first course.

6 eight-ounce jelly jars

6 cups peeled and chopped Italian Honey figs

6 tablespoons fresh lemon juice

1 tablespoon calcium water (as prepared in instructions from Pomona's Universal Pectin)

¼ teaspoon ground cinnamon

½ teaspoon unsalted butter (to prevent excess foaming)

1 tablespoon pectin powder from Pomona's Universal Pectin

1 cup local honey (I use a local blackberry honey)

1. Wash six jelly jars, lids and screw bands in warm soapy water. Rinse thoroughly. Bring a boiling-canner two thirds full water to a simmer. Turn off the heat. Place the jars in the water. In a smaller pan, heat the lids and rings in water. Place a clean salad plate in the freezer to be used to test the jell later.

2. In a non-reactive sauce pot add the chopped figs, lemon juice, calcium water, cinnamon, and butter

3. Mix the pectin powder thoroughly into the honey. Set aside.

4. Heat the chopped fig mixture on medium-high heat until simmering.

5. Add the honey and pectin mixture and increase the heat to high. Bring to a full rolling boil that cannot be stirred down. Boil and stir with a wooden spoon for one to two minutes until jelled, which is determined by a drop of jam onto a cold salad plate. Let set for a moment and run your finger through. It should cause a clean swipe in the jell.

6. Remove from heat and skim foam off the top if necessary.

7. Remove the hot jars from the hot water. Quickly fill the jars with jam one fourth of an inch from the top. Wipe the tops with a clean wet cloth. Place the lids on top. Screw the bands on until slightly snug, then give another slight back-turn. (Not too tight! Air must be allowed to escape for a good seal.)

8. Place in the boiling-canner on a rack. The water should be one to two inches above the jars. Cover with a lid. Bring to a gentle simmer. Simmer for ten minutes (elevations above 1,000 feet simmer an additional five minutes). Remove the jars and place on a towel to cool. When cool, test the top of the jars by pressing in the middle of the lid with a finger. The lids should not spring back. If they do, place in the refrigerator and use within a month. Allow to sit for twenty-four hours. Wash, label, and date each jar. All other jars should be stored in a dark, cool place for up to one year.

I use Pomona's Universal Pectin because it contains no sugar or preservatives and requires low amounts of sweetener. It can be found at co-ops and some grocers. The directions inside the box will direct you to mix the calcium powder with water to be stored in the refrigerator. The calcium water activates the jell, thereby reducing the amount of sweetener used. But of course, the figs must be fresh, no older than one day to capture their irresistible essence!

. . . .

SPICY HONEY BLUEBERRY JAM

For twenty-some years my husband and I would collect wild blue huckleberries at our Cascade Mountain cabin. They usually did not make it much past breakfast pancakes and syrup. While at our favorite Black Forest Gasthaus on our first morning in Germany, we were served an enchanting spicy blueberry jam with a spectacular basket of breads and rolls. When we returned, we planted our own blueberry bushes. Then I set about to recreate that wonderful spicy jam. It has taken several years but I finally found that honey was the final key to the puzzle.

6 eight-ounce jelly jars

6 cups mashed fresh blueberries (about 2 ½ pounds)

6 tablespoons fresh lemon juice

1 tablespoon calcium water (as prepared in instructions from Pomona's Universal Pectin)

¼ teaspoon ground cinnamon

½ teaspoon ground nutmeg

1/8 teaspoon ground white cardamom

½ teaspoon unsalted butter (to prevent excess foaming)

1 tablespoon pectin powder from Pomona's Universal Pectin

1 cup local honey (I use a local blackberry honey)

1. Wash six jelly jars, lids and screw bands in warm soapy water. Rinse thoroughly. Bring a boiling-canner two thirds full water to a simmer. Turn off the heat. Place the jars in the water. In a smaller pan heat the lids and rings in water. Place a clean salad plate in the freezer to test the jell later.

2. In a non-reactive sauce pot mix the mashed blueberries, lemon juice, calcium water, cinnamon, nutmeg, cardamom and butter

3. Mix the pectin powder thoroughly into the honey. Set aside.

4. Heat the mashed blueberry mixture on medium-high heat until simmering.

5. Add the honey and pectin mixture and increase the heat to high. Bring to a full rolling boil that cannot be stirred down. Boil and stir with a wooden spoon for one to two minutes until jelled, which is determined by a drop of jam onto the cold salad plate. Let set for a moment and run your finger through. It should cause a clean swipe through the jell.

6. Remove from heat and skim foam off the top.

7. Remove the hot jars from the hot water. Quickly fill the jars with jam one-eighth of an inch from the top. Wipe the rim with a clean wet cloth. Place the lids on top. Screw the bands on until slightly snug, then give another slight back-turn. (Not too tight! Air must be allowed to escape for a good seal.)

8. Place in the boiling-canner on a rack. The water should be one to two inches above the jars. Cover with a lid. Bring to a gentle simmer. Simmer for ten minutes (elevations above 1,000 feet simmer an additional five minutes). Remove the jars and place on a towel to cool. When cool, test the top of the jars by pressing in the middle of the lid with a finger. The lids should not spring back. If they do place in the refrigerator and use within a month. Allow to sit at room temperature for twenty-four hours. Wash with a wet cloth, label and date each jar. All other jars should be stored in a dark, cool place for up to one year. Refrigerate after opening.

I use Pomona's Universal Pectin because it contains no sugar or preservatives and requires low amounts of sweetener. It can be found at co-ops and some grocers.

The directions inside the box will direct you to mix the calcium powder with water to be stored in the refrigerator. The calcium water activates the gel, thereby reducing the amount of sweetener used. But of course, the blueberries must be fresh, no older than one day to capture their enchanting essence!

· ·

VANILLA SCENTED STRAWBERRY JAM

A surprise gift of the most magnificent Northwest strawberries from friends who own a major berry farm was the inspiration for this jam. The farm is in the rich fertile Skagit Valley and produces a wide variety of sumptuous berries. Strawberries at their peak are best served simply over vanilla ice cream and shortcake. This jam extends the shelf life of this dessert, so one can enjoy it all year long whether on short cake, ice cream or in morning yogurt.

4 to 5 eight-ounce jelly jars

4 cups fresh strawberries (about 2 pounds berries)

½ cup fresh lemon juice

2 teaspoons calcium water (as prepared in instructions from Pomona's Universal Pectin)

1 vanilla bean

½ teaspoon unsalted butter (to prevent excess foaming)

2 teaspoons pectin powder from Pomona's Universal Pectin

¾ cup honey (I use local blackberry honey)

1. Wash five jelly jars, lids and screw bands in warm soapy water. Rinse thoroughly. Bring a boiling-canner two thirds full water to a simmer. Turn off the heat. Place the jars in the water. In a smaller pan heat the lids and rings in water. Place a clean salad plate in the freezer to be used to test the jell later.

2. Wash and discard strawberry stems. Cut the large ones in half or quarters. Mash strawberries with lemon juice and calcium water using a potato masher in a non-reactive sauce pot.

3. Cut the vanilla beans in half lengthwise. Scrape the beans from the pods. Add beans and pods to the mashed strawberry mixture. Also, add the butter

4. Thoroughly mix the pectin powder in the honey.

5. Bring mashed strawberry mixture to a boil. Add the pectin and honey mixture. Stir constantly with a wooden spoon until it returns to a full boil, until at the set point, which is determined by a drop of jam onto a cold salad plate. Let set for a moment and run your finger through. It should cause a clean wipe in the jell.

6. Remove from heat and skim foam off the top. Remove and discard the vanilla pods.

7. Remove the hot jars from the hot water. Quickly fill the jars with jam one-fourth of an inch from the top. Wipe the tops with a clean wet cloth. Place the lids on top. Screw the bands on until slightly snug, then give another slight back-turn. (Not too tight! Air must be allowed to escape for a good seal.)

8. Place in the boiling-canner on a rack. The water should be one to two inches above the jars. Cover with a lid. Bring to a gentle simmer. Simmer for ten minutes (elevations above 1,000 feet simmer an additional five minutes). Remove the jars and place on a towel to cool. When cool, test the top of the jars by pressing in the middle of the lid with a finger. The lids should not spring back. If they do, place in the refrigerator and use within a month. Wash, label and date each jar. All other jars should be stored in a dark, cool place for up to one year.

I use Pomona's Universal Pectin because it contains no sugar or preservatives and requires low amounts of sweetener. It can be found at co-ops and some grocers. The directions inside the box will direct you to mix the calcium powder with water to be stored in the refrigerator. The calcium water activates the jell, thereby reducing the amount of sweetener used. But of course, the strawberries must be fresh, no older than one day to capture their enchanting essence!

SOUPS

Is there anything more alluring than enjoying oneself over a hot, steaming bowl of soup? Soup is basically a liquid food made with various ingredients. The word originated from the Latin word "suppa" which means to dip bread or other food into a liquid or soak in a broth. It may be a delightful start to a formal meal or a one-dish meal. It may be thin or thick, hot or cold, sweet or savory. Soups can be garnished with an inclusive ingredient, or a textural contrast, or with bread or crackers that can be dipped.

When I think "soup," I think "rustic and comforting." No matter what country it originated in, it was a peasant staple that soon made it, in whatever form, to the tables of aristocracy. It is just that desirable.

Thin soups or broths often have sides of noodles, vegetables, stuffed pastas, meats, poultry or seafood to nibble on between the sips. Thick soups or potages frequently have the main ingredient puréed. Cream soups are regularly puréed then enriched with a cream finish. Chowders are creamy and chunky, usually with the addition of potatoes added to the main theme. Bean soups or chilies are generally chunky and hearty.

Soup will warm the cold day or cool the hot day. With the first taste of this liquid respite, it refreshes the body and the soul.

Roasted Garlic Crab Bisque

ROASTED GARLIC CRAB BISQUE

Newport, Oregon is a commercial fishing town as well as a bayside resort that I have visited often through the years. At my favorite seafood restaurant, there is an adjacent deli case filled with fresh fish and shell fish labeled as to where and how the seafood is caught which demonstrates ethical and fresh options. In the restaurant, I am always tempted to order their fresh fish-of-the-day tacos and a bowl of their sumptuous roasted garlic crab bisque. This soup is where my love affair for seafood bisque hit a crescendo. Here is my take on that charming soup.

4 first course or 2 main course servings

1 whole cooked Dungeness crab, cleaned by fish monger (about 1 ½ to 2 pounds)

½ cup extra virgin olive oil, divided

2 large carrots, small diced

½ cup onion, peeled, small diced

3 stalks celery, small diced

1 large shallot, peeled, minced

¼ cup brandy

½ cup tomato paste

2 ½ cup filtered water

1 tablespoon fresh tarragon leaves, chopped

¼ teaspoon cayenne pepper

10 garlic cloves

2 tablespoons all-purpose flour

1 tablespoon lemon juice

½ cup heavy cream

½ cup finely grated Parmigiano Reggiano cheese

1 teaspoon sea salt or more

1 teaspoon fresh tarragon leaves, chopped

Preheat oven to 450°F.

1. Crack and separate the crab meat from the shell. Break the shells into small pieces. Reserve the crab meat in the refrigerator.

2. In a non-reactive Dutch oven, heat one fourth cup olive oil. Toss the crab shells, carrots, onion, celery, and shallot in the oil. Place in the 450°F oven. Roast for thirty minutes, tossing every five minutes so they do not burn.

3. Remove from the oven and place over a medium high heat. Deglaze with the brandy. Stir in the tomato paste, water, one tablespoon fresh tarragon and cayenne pepper. Bring to a gentle simmer. Simmer for twenty minutes. Strain through a sieve and reserve the hot liquid.

4. In an eight-inch cast iron skillet heat the remaining one fourth cup of olive oil and garlic cloves over medium to low heat. Simmer gently until the garlic is soft and golden, about fifteen to twenty minutes. Remove and mash the garlic. Reserve the garlic and the garlic oil separately.

5. Place the garlic oil in a non-reactive pan. Add the flour and stir for one minute. Blend in the mashed roasted garlic. Slowly whip in small amounts of crab broth, whipping smooth before adding more broth. Add the lemon juice and bring to a simmer.

6. Finish by adding the heavy cream, cheese and reserved crab meat. Heat thoroughly. ***Taste, Think, Transform*** with sea salt and/or lemon juice. Garnish with the remaining one teaspoon chopped tarragon. Serve hot.

ASPARAGUS GARBURE

Enjoying as much asparagus as I can in the spring, I often choose to peel the asparagus and usually snap off one end at the breaking point and cut all other spears to the same length. That leaves a lot of peel and stem waste. While in school, we learned that vegetable waste could make a profit by turning it into a French soup called garbure which is usually made with carrot scraps cooked with potatoes, garlic, cabbage, green beans and salt pork. And what a flavorful garbure this one is!

8 servings

2 cups peel and green end scrap (from about 1 pound thick stalk asparagus)

1 tablespoon extra virgin olive oil

2 strips thick smoky bacon

1 medium onion ½ inch diced

pinch of cayenne

3 garlic cloves smashed

1 large Yukon Gold potato peeled, ½ inch dice

3 to 4 cups vegetable broth (see Appareils chapter)

1 teaspoon kosher salt or more

Optional Garnishes: chopped chives, chervil, or Greek yogurt sprinkled with sumac or zatar blended spices. The remaining asparagus spears can also be blanched and used as a garnish in this pureed soup.

1. Lay the asparagus flat on its side and peel with a vegetable peeler. Reserve this peel. Snap off the stem end of one piece of asparagus. Use this spear to cut off the other stem ends. Save the asparagus spears for eating cooked as a garnish or whole in another dish. Cut the stem ends into ¼ inch pieces. Discard any that are white in color as they will be bitter. Measure two cups of peel and stem end waste pieces to use in this soup.

2. Heat the olive oil and bacon in a saucepan. Cook until the bacon starts to become brown.

3. Add the onions. Sauté until translucent.

4. Add the asparagus, cayenne, garlic, potatoes and broth. Bring to a boil and reduce to a simmer until the potatoes are thoroughly cooked; about twenty minutes.

5. Puree the soup in a blender. **Taste, Think, Transform** with salt and more stock if the soup is too thick. Serve hot with one of the suggested garnishes.

A combination of carrot peels, cabbage and green beans could be used in in place of the asparagus peel for a more authentic French garbure.

. . . .

PANZANELLA SOUP

Panzanella is a classic Italian bread salad. With the abundance of cherry tomatoes in the early fall when the evenings have a crisp chill, I like to turn this summer salad into an autumn soup. It has the all the charm of a rich French onion soup gratinée with the addition of sweet small tomatoes.

6 to 8 side servings

4 to 6 slices of whole grain bread or sour dough bread, extra virgin olive oil, as needed

⅓ cup garlic cloves, thinly sliced (⅛ inch on a mandoline)

2 tablespoons extra virgin olive oil

3 cups sweet onions (Walla, Walla) thinly sliced with the grain (root to stem)

3 cups cherry-sized tomatoes, sliced in half *

½ cup Parmigiano Reggiano cheese, grated

½ cup basil, chiffonade (thinly sliced)

kosher salt and fresh ground black pepper to taste

6 cups rich chicken broth or more seasoned with kosher salt to taste (see Appareils chapter)

1. Preheat oven to 350°F.

2. Brush the sliced bread with the olive oil on both sides. Hand-tear each into approximately 2-inch squares. Place on a sheet pan and toast in the oven for ten minutes. Turn the bread over and toast until both

sides are golden brown about twenty minutes' total time.

3. Heat a sauté pan over medium heat. Add the onions and slowly cook until barely caramelized. Add the garlic and sauté until tender.

4. Coat a baking pan with olive oil. Place half the bread on the bottom of the pan. Top with half the onion-garlic mixture, half the tomatoes, half the Parmigiano and half the basil. Season with salt and pepper. Top with the remaining bread, onion-garlic mixture, tomatoes, and basil.

5. Pour the six cups of chicken broth over all. Top with the remaining Parmigiano. Cover with foil and bake for forty-five minutes.

6. Heat the broiler to 400°F. Remove the foil from the top and broil until golden brown. **Taste, Think, Transform** with salt and/or more hot broth. Serve piping hot.

* I usually use red, orange and yellow cherry-size tomatoes, however, peeled, seeded and large diced Roma tomatoes could be used.

Soup comes from the Latin word *suppa*, which originally meant to dip or soak stale bread in a broth. Up until this century bread was a thickening agent used in soups rather than flour.

. . . .

TORTILLA SOUP

The colors and flavors of the Oaxacan market were bright and enticing that spring when I attended the Women Chefs and Restaurateurs culinary tour. The smell of roasting chilies and corn tortillas lingered in the air. The small Oaxacan chilies were particularly delicious, although not usually found outside that region. Having tried many variations of this soup, I decided on this one to serve in our school's restaurant. It was a big hit, especially with the other chef instructors.

8 side servings

3 unpeeled garlic cloves

½ white onion peeled, sliced into large chunks

3 Roma tomatoes

1 ½ quart rich chicken broth, divided (see Appareils chapter)

3 tablespoon safflower oil, divided, plus extra for the tortillas

1 ½ teaspoons sea salt or more and ¼ teaspoon fresh ground black pepper

1 large or 2 small dried chipotle chilies (Oaxacan chilies if available)

4 corn tortillas (organic if available)

1 cup grated Monterey Jack cheese

2 avocados, peeled, pitted, small diced

½ cup sour cream

¼ cup cilantro, chopped fine

2 limes cut into wedges

8 paper doilies

1. Heat a cast iron griddle or skillet until smoky-hot. Toast the garlic, onion and tomatoes until slightly blistered black on all sides. Peel the garlic and add with the onion, tomato and one-fourth cup of chicken broth in a blender. Purée all together.

2. Heat two tablespoons of oil in a large heavy-bottom sauce pot over high heat. Add the purée and sizzle for two minutes. Lower the heat and simmer another five minutes or until the purée changes to a darker color. Add the rest of the chicken broth and simmer for fifteen minutes. **Taste, Think, Transform** with salt and pepper and/or reserve hot broth.

3. Discard the seeds and ribs of the chipotle (s). Slice into a very fine julienne. Heat a small sauté pan with one tablespoon oil. Cook the chipotle strips for thirty seconds. Do not allow them to get too brown or they will become bitter. Remove with a slotted spoon onto paper towels. Reserve.

4. Preheat oven to 375°F. Brush the tortillas on both sides with oil. Slice tortillas in half and then slice the four pieces into one-fourth inch batons. Scatter on a silicone baking liner or parchment paper lined sheet pan. Place in the preheated oven and bake until the chips are golden brown and crisp. Reserve. Heat the serving bowls.

5. When ready to serve, distribute in each hot bowl, the avocados, chilies, cheese and tortillas. Ladle the hot soup over the top. Place a dollop of sour cream on top and sprinkle with the chopped cilantro.

6. Place hot bowls on small plates with a paper doily to keep them from moving. Place a lime wedge on the side. Warn the guest that the bowls are extremely hot!

Two classical Oaxacan techniques are used in this recipe. The first is to toast the aromatic vegetables on a very hot cast iron griddle or pan until slightly charred. This creates a truly unique flavor. The second technique is called sizzle-frying which quickly caramelizes an aromatic purée. These are both vital to the depth of flavor in this soup.

. . . .

WILD MUSHROOM BISQUE WITH BRANDY CREAM

One crisp autumn day with three other chefs and two expert mushroom foragers in tow, I organized a trip to our Cascade mountain cabin for a day of good food and mushroom gathering. My husband had gone earlier to have a roaring fire in the stone fireplace to take off the chill. Each chef brought a dish to be shared with all. After a delightful meal and much laughter, we set out to find and identify wild mushrooms. I learned that day that mushrooms are the forest's natural decomposer because when they get wet they rot themselves and all around them. Therefore, never wash mushrooms until just before using them. I also use a mushroom brush to remove any debris stuck in the mushrooms. This rich soup is a tribute to that glorious day.

8 side servings

Soup

1 tablespoon extra virgin olive oil

3 tablespoons tomato paste

½ cup brandy

6 ounces chanterelle mushrooms (with an extra few for the garnish)

6 ounces oyster mushrooms (with an extra few for the garnish)

6 tablespoons unsalted butter, divided

3 tablespoons minced shallot (about one large shallot)

4 medium garlic cloves, mashed

⅛ teaspoon freshly ground nutmeg

½ cup Fino (dry) Sherry

3 tablespoons all-purpose flour

¾ teaspoon paprika

1 quart rich chicken broth (see Appareils chapter)

½ cup heavy cream

1 teaspoon sea salt or to taste

1. In a small cast iron skillet, heat the olive oil over medium heat. Add the tomato paste and slowly cook and stir often. When the mixture becomes dry add some of the brandy until all incorporated. When it is a dark reddish-brown remove from the heat. This mixture is called a *tomato pincer*. Reserve.

2. Thoroughly wash the mushrooms and trim the bad spots. Blot dry in paper towels. Hand-tear each mushroom into very thin long strips.

3. Melt three tablespoons of the butter in a sauté pan. Add the shallots and garlic. Cook until soft. Add the mushrooms and nutmeg. Toss until soft. Deglaze the mushrooms with the Sherry and cook for a few more minutes. Reserve.

4. In a sauce pan melt 3 tablespoons of butter. Mix in the flour and cook until blond in color and nutty in smell. Add the paprika and cook for just a minute before whipping in the chicken stock in small batches until all incorporated and smooth. Whip in the tomato pincer.

5. Add most of the mushrooms to the soup base and simmer uncovered for twenty minutes, stirring often. Reserve a few mushrooms for a top garnish. Add the cream, heat and season with salt. **Taste, Think, Transform** with more salt and/or Sherry.

Brandy Cream Garnish

2 tablespoons brandy

1 teaspoon demi-glace*

¼ cup heavy cream

1. Heat the brandy in a small sauté pan. Tilt the pan away from yourself and towards the flame to catch the brandy on fire. (If you do not have a gas stove, carefully light the brandy with a propane barbeque torch). When it burns out add the Demi-Glace. Heat until melted together. Cool completely.

2. In a small chilled stainless-steel bowl whip the heavy cream until soft peaks form. Fold in the cold brandy mixture.

3. At service time, top the hot soup with the brandy cream and a few pieces of mushrooms.

*demi-glace can be found in specialty grocery stores.

I make a larger batch of tomato pincer and keep it frozen so that I can use it to enhance the flavor of soups, stews and braises. I also make my own demi-glace by simmering homemade beef stock down until syrupy and it coats the back of a wood spoon. I also freeze this for use in many dishes. Both last for up to a year in the freezer if well wrapped in plastic wrap and sealed in zip-lock bag with all the air removed.

· ·

APPLE TARRAGON SOUP

In the autumn of the year, apples begin to appear in the farmer's markets. This is when they are at their prime. Tarragon is also at its prime. This soup is a lovely way to begin an autumn meal that may include a pork entrée. Apples and tarragon make a lovely pair.

8 side servings

2 tablespoons unsalted butter

½ cup sweet onion, (Walla Walla) small diced

¼ cup celery root, peeled, small diced

2 Granny Smith apples, peeled, seeded, sliced

1 tablespoon all-purpose flour

1 quart rich chicken broth (see Appareils chapter)

1 bay leaf

1 bunch fresh tarragon (8-12 sprigs)

1 cup half and half

Pinch of cinnamon

1 teaspoon kosher salt or more and fresh ground black pepper to taste

lemon juice to taste

1 small Granny Smith apple peel only, julienned

1. In a sauce pan, melt the butter. Add the onions, celery root and apples. Sauté until soft.

2. Add the flour and incorporate for a few minutes.

3. Slowly stir in the broth. Add the bay leaf and tarragon. Simmer for fifteen minutes. Discard the bay leaf and tarragon. Purée in a blender. Return to the sauce pan. Heat with the half and half and cinnamon until hot. **Taste, Think, Transform** with salt, pepper and/or lemon juice.

4. Pour hot soup into bowls and garnish with julienned apple peel.

· ·

GARLIC SAGE BROTH WITH PASTA

This soup is the epitome of simple, quality ingredients making an extraordinary dish. The aroma of this soup is tantalizing and the taste superb. All Italian pastas have names denoted by their shape. Literally translated from Italian, vermicelli means "little worms." If your guests have a good sense of humor, mention this fact as they slurp away.

8 side servings

1 tablespoon garlic cloves, finely minced (about 8 small cloves)

6 small fresh sage leaves

2 fresh sprigs of thyme, leaves removed from stems

3 pints rich chicken broth (see Appareils chapter)

6 ounces dried vermicelli

1 teaspoon sea salt and fresh ground black pepper to taste

2 tablespoons extra virgin olive oil

½ cup Parmigiano Reggiano cheese, grated

1. In a sauce pan bring the garlic, sage, thyme and chicken broth to a boil. Reduce to a simmer and cook, uncovered for twenty minutes. Remove the sage leaves. **Taste, Think, Transform** with salt and/or black pepper.

2. In the meantime, cook the vermicelli until al dente (to the bite) and according to the package directions. Drain and cut into bite sized pieces.

3. Place the vermicelli in hot bowls. Portion the sage broth into each bowl. Drizzle olive oil on top and garnish with Parmigiano. Serve hot.

. . . .

MOM'S POTATO ONION SOUP

Friends and family regarded my mother as a good cook, although she did not really enjoy cooking. To my benefit, she would teach me to cook and enjoyed cleaning the kitchen after me. How lucky was I? My favorite soups that she would make from her youthful farm memories were potato soup and bean with ham soup. The bean with ham soup would gently simmer all day in a built-in deep pot in our electric stove, which was probably the prototype of the slow cooker. The potato soup however was simple and easy. Nonetheless, I still make it often as it warms my soul on a cool winter night.

4 entree servings or 8 appetizer servings

1 ½ pounds russet potatoes, peeled, ½ inch diced (about 3 baker size potatoes)

1 medium yellow onion, peeled, ¼ diced (about 12 ounces diced)

1 ½ teaspoon kosher salt

filtered water to cover (about 2+ cups)

2 ½ cups whole milk

½ teaspoon fresh ground black pepper

2 tablespoons unsalted butter

optional: chopped fresh dill weed or chives as a garnish

1. Cover the diced potatoes and onions with the water and add the kosher salt. Bring to a simmer on medium high heat. Cook until potatoes are fork tender.

2. Drain the mixture leaving about one half cup of the water in the bottom.

3. Add the milk, black pepper and butter. Heat until bubbles form on the side of the pan and the butter is melted.

4. **Taste, Think, Transform** with kosher salt and/or pepper.

5. Ladle into bowls and serve piping hot.

6. If desired garnish with fresh dill weed or chives.

Mom's Potato Onion Soup

SALADS

CRISP GARDEN GREENS,
FRUITFUL, VEGETABALE-CENTRIC,
SLAW, COOL PASTA, GRAINY,
DRESSING, VINAIGRETTE

Summer is a wonderful time to grab the gathering-basket and wander the garden for the daily salad, looking for cucumbers hiding away, tomatoes glowing red in the sun, welcoming red cabbage, and emerging breakfast radish. Come winter the hunt is in the larder for beets, pears, apples, lentils, grains and pasta. With a splash of vinegar and a wash of flavorful oil, watch the magic happen.

Salad may be comprised of one ingredient or several, usually tossed with a tasty dressing and sometimes garnished with a sprinkle of the colorful or crunchy. The word originated from Medieval Latin "salata" meaning salt. Yes, do not forget the salt!

The salad may be the appetizer, before the soup, the entrée, after the entrée or the dessert. Now that's versatility! Let your imagination and food preferences be the guide. Don't like blue cheese? Try feta. Don't like red wine vinegar? Try sherry vinegar. How about a refreshing spritz of orange flower water? And after the salt, how about a grind of black pepper?

Invigorate the palate with a cool burst of tangy garden and larder spender.

SALADS

MANGO, AVOCADO, LETTUCE SALAD, SOUR ORANGE VINAIGRETTE

Caribbean cuisine uses a sour orange in salad dressings and marinades that produces a unique flavor. Since this orange is rarely available here in the northwest, I found that combining naval orange and lime juices create a good substitute. When planning a Latino menu for our school dining room I created this recipe with Caribbean influences. It is a very good side salad but is also wonderful topped with grilled Jamaican jerk chicken breasts as an entrée salad. A recipe for Jamaican jerk chicken breasts will be posted on chefsharingthetable.com.

6 to 8 side-salad servings or 4 entrée-salad servings

Vinaigrette

6 tablespoons safflower oil

1 tablespoon orange juice

1 tablespoon lime juice

1 tablespoon Sherry vinegar

⅛ teaspoon pure orange oil (optional)

½ teaspoon orange zest

½ teaspoon lime zest

1 ½ teaspoon honey

¼ teaspoon kosher salt or to taste

1. Mix all the ingredients together in a jar with lid and refrigerate, preferably overnight.

2. **Taste, Think, Transform** with salt and/or vinegar.

Salad

1 head romaine lettuce

1 head red-leaf lettuce

2 ripe mangos, peeled, seeded, diced

2 avocados, peeled, pitted, diced

6 radishes, thinly sliced

4 corn tortillas

kosher salt as needed

safflower oil as needed

1. Preheat oven to 400°F. Place the salad plates in the refrigerator.

2. Slice or tear both lettuces into bite size pieces. Wash and spin dry the lettuce.

3. Brush both sides of the tortillas with the oil. Cut into thin strips. Place on a silicone mat or parchment paper lined baking sheet pan. Bake until crispy. Lightly salt. Reserve dry. (Hide until ready to use or they may disappear to rogue tasters)!

4. Shake the jar of vinaigrette. Pour onto the lettuce and toss. Place on chilled salad plates.

5. Top each salad with mangos, avocados, radishes and tortilla strips.

. . . .

MINTED SUGAR SNAP PEA SALAD

Sugar snap peas are one of the first vegetables to emerge in our gardens and an all-time favorite to eat in a variety of ways. This salad is very refreshing on a hot summer day and makes a great side dish for a summer barbeque. We especially enjoy this with Tangerine Chili Glazed Black Cod found in the Seafood chapter.

4 side-salad servings

1 pint sugar snap peas (about 10 ounces)

1 tablespoon Aji-Mirin sweet cooking rice seasoning

1 tablespoon rice vinegar

1 tablespoon soy sauce

1 tablespoon granulated sugar

1 teaspoon toasted sesame oil

2 tablespoons toasted walnut oil

1 teaspoon fine sea salt

2 tablespoons finely shredded fresh mint leaves

1 tablespoon finely shredded fresh mint leaves for garnish

1. Snap the stem end and draw across the top of each pea to remove string (if tough) and wash the peas. Bring a quart of water to a boil. Drop the peas into the water and blanch until they turn from a garden green to a vibrant green and still have a crisp texture, about one minute. Drain in a colander and run cold water over the peas until they are cooled. Dry the peas in paper towels and reserve cold.

2. Whip the Aji-Mirin, rice vinegar, soy sauce, sugar, sesame oil, toasted walnut oil and salt together until the sugar and salt are dissolved. Reserve cold.

3. About one-half an hour before serving toss the peas with the vinaigrette and the shredded mint leaves. **Taste Think, Transform** with salt and/or vinegar. Toss again before serving. Garnish with remaining mint and serve cold.

If the peas sit in the vinegar too long they will turn an unappealing drab brownish green but will taste fine.

. . . .

TARRAGON GREEN BEAN SALAD

Dear friends chose to spend their fiftieth wedding anniversary here at our home a few years ago. What menu to prepare? No pressure here! Okay so I do what I normally do, I find the freshest, finest ingredients and prepare them simply but elegantly. I created this salad for that occasion and have gone back to it at the end of the summer when green beans and tomatoes are in their glory. It is an annual celebration of vegetable color and flavor.

8 side-salad servings

1 pound fresh green beans, stem end removed

1 teaspoon Dijon mustard

1 tablespoon minced shallots

2 tablespoons tarragon wine vinegar

4 tablespoons extra virgin olive oil

¼ teaspoon kosher salt and black pepper to taste

1 head of Bibb or butter lettuce, washed, dried and torn in bite-size pieces

4 Roma tomatoes, peeled, seeded and diced

1 tablespoon fresh tarragon leaves, chopped

1. Place the salad plates in the refrigerator.

2. Bring a salted pot of water to a boil. Add the green beans and simmer until the green beans are a bright green and are tender yet slightly crisp. Drain and shock the green beans in an ice water bath. Drain and keep chilled.

3. Combine the mustard, shallots, vinegar and olive oil in a small jar with a lid to make the dressing. **Taste, Think, Transform** with the salt and/or black pepper.

4. On eight chilled salad plates, distribute the torn lettuce.

5. Shake the dressing in the jar and toss with the chilled green beans. Place on the lettuce.

6. Top with the diced tomatoes and chopped fresh tarragon.

. . . .

ORANGE BLOSSOM SCENTED FRESH FRUIT

What is breakfast or brunch without a platter or bowl of fresh in-season fruit? During winter months, some fresh fruits are generally in season in the south but are often harvested when slightly under ripe to ship unbruised. It is especially at this time of year that the fruit needs a bit of help by being lightly perfumed with orange blossom water. I keep a small spray bottle of orange blossom water at the ready in my pantry for just those special occasions when the fruit can benefit from a light spray. I even sometimes use this trick on ripe summer fruit to give it an exotic touch.

fresh fruit, sliced or cubed

orange flower water or orange blossom water

several sprigs of fresh mint (optional)

1. Choose ripe fresh fruit in varying colors and shapes. Wash, peel and seed, if necessary. Melons need to be washed thoroughly before peeling as they have been in contact with pathogens in the soil. Slice and/or cube the fruit.

2. Lay the fruit on a platter or in a bowl. Garnish with fresh mint, if desired.

3. Lightly spray with the orange flower water. Serve at room temperature.

Orange flower water usually comes from France and can be quite expensive. Orange blossom water comes from the Middle East and is more reasonably priced.

. . . .

FENNEL APPLE COLESLAW

For over twenty years we enjoyed a snowy white Thanksgiving at our Cascade mountain cabin. We would carry all the provisions for a large Thanksgiving meal by Siberian husky-drawn sled. One year I decided to put a twist on the traditional Waldorf salad by substituting fennel for the celery and pistachios for the walnuts. This sweet and refreshing rendition became a new favorite.

4 side-salad servings

Dressing

¼ cup sour cream

¼ cup mayonnaise

2 teaspoons granulated cane sugar

1 teaspoon fresh lemon juice

¼ teaspoon sea salt and fresh ground black pepper to taste

Whip together the sour cream, mayonnaise, sugar and lemon juice. Season with salt and black pepper.

Salad

1 large Red Delicious or Rome apple, preferably organic

1 tablespoon fresh lemon juice

1 fennel bulb

2 tablespoons pistachio nuts, chopped

2 tablespoons dried currants

1. Peel and core the apple. Finely julienne the apple peel and reserve in ice water for a garnish. Julienne the apple flesh and toss in the lemon juice.

2. Trim and core the fennel. Finely julienne the bulb and toss with the apples. Chop one tablespoon of the fennel fronds (leaves) and add to the salad.

3. Toss the pistachios currants and salad dressing with the apples and fennel. ***Taste, Think, Transform*** with lemon juice, sugar and/or salt. Place on chilled salad plates and garnish with the julienne of apple peel.

If the currants are a bit on the dry side, pour boiling water over them and soak five or more minutes. Drain thoroughly before using.

. . . .

PEAR, WALNUT AND GOAT CHEESE SALAD

My go-to fall and winter side salad has become this caramelized pear salad. The soft sweetness of the pears is balanced by the nutty flavor of the crunchy walnuts and creamy tang of goat cheese. I have found a pear infused white balsamic vinegar that I use to intensify the flavor of the pears. The pears can be sautéed ahead of time but if they sit too long they turn from slightly crispy to weepy and therefore not as desirable.

8 side-salad servings

Vinaigrette

3 tablespoons white balsamic vinegar

6 tablespoons roasted walnut oil

¼ teaspoon kosher salt and fresh ground black pepper to taste

Salad

2 large Bosc pears, peeled, cored, sliced into 12 equal slices

¼ cup cane sugar

4 tablespoons extra virgin olive oil, divided

6 cups mixed Bibb lettuce

sea salt and fresh ground black pepper as needed

1 cup walnut halves, lightly roasted in a 350°F oven (about 5 minutes)

¾ cup goat cheese crumbled

1. Place the salad plates in the refrigerator.

2. Place the vinegar, oil, salt and pepper in a small jar with lid and shake.

3. Dredge the pear slices into sugar just before sautéing.

4. Heat a large sauté pan with two tablespoons of oil. Lay half of the pear slices into the oil. Sauté until golden brown, flip them over with tongs and repeat on the other side. Remove from the pan and reserve at room temperature. Wash and dry the pan. Sauté the second batch, remove from the pan and reserve.

5. Shake the vinaigrette and toss with the salad greens. **Taste, Think, Transform** with salt and/or black pepper. Pile salad high on each chilled plate. Lay three pear slices around the salad. Sprinkle the walnuts and goat cheese around each salad. Serve immediately.

I use White Balsamic Pear Infused Vinegar by Alessl in place of the white balsamic vinegar but know this may be difficult to find. Extra virgin olive oil could replace the roasted walnut oil if desired.

· ·

ORANGE, AVOCADO, FETA SALAD WITH HONEY MUSTARD VINAIGRETTE

In the winter when oranges are plentiful I find this salad to be a stimulating course that could be served after the entrée to refresh the palate. Or served as the first course to get the taste buds activated. Either way, this is a tasty winter salad.

4 side-salad servings

Dressing

¼ teaspoon Dijon mustard

½ teaspoon honey

2 tablespoons grapeseed oil or avocado oil

1 tablespoons Sherry vinegar

2 tablespoons fresh orange juice

½ small shallot, minced

¼ teaspoon kosher salt

1. Whisk the mustard and honey together. Slowly whisk in the oil. Then slowly whisk in the vinegar, orange juice. Add the shallot and salt. Store in a jar refrigerated for at least two hours or overnight.

2. Chill the salad plates in the refrigerator.

Salad

3 cups red leaf lettuce or mixed soft greens

2 Cara, Cara or navel oranges, peeled, sliced ¼ inch rounds, halved

1 avocado, peeled, pitted, sliced

2 tablespoons fresh dill, chopped

½ cup feta cheese, crumbled

1. Shake the salad dressing in the jar.

2. Toss the lettuce with the salad dressing and place on the chilled salad plates.

3. Top each salad with the sliced oranges and avocados.

4. Garnish with a sprinkling of dill and feta cheese. Serve immediately.

Chilling salad plates for cold salads is that finishing touch that tells the guests that you have thought of every detail that would make the salad extraordinary.

WILTED GARDEN GREENS WITH FIGS AND PECANS

In my Northwest garden, three things grow profusely: cabbage, kale and chard. I have a variety of ways to prepare them. At the same time, figs from my Italian Honey fig bush become ripe. This recipe is one that utilizes all to the greater good. The salad is hearty enough to be served as an entrée but is equally good as an appetizer-salad course. It is especially appealing when the evenings turn cool.

8 side-salad servings or 4 entrée servings

Dressing

2 tablespoons balsamic vinegar

1 tablespoons Sherry vinegar

½ cup extra virgin olive oil

4 strips bacon, small diced

1 large clove garlic, mashed (about 1 teaspoon)

2 scallions, sliced thin

Salad Base

¼ head red cabbage, cored, shredded

1 bunch Swiss chard leaves, stems removed, sliced in 1 to 2 inch ribbons (about 13 leaves)

1 bunch green kale, stems removed, sliced in 1 to 2 inch ribbons (about 13 leaves)

sea salt and fresh ground black pepper to taste

½ cup blue cheese, crumbled

8 fresh figs, stems removed, quartered

(In the winter months use rehydrated dried figs, diced)

½ cup pecan halves, lightly toasted in the oven

1. Mix the vinegars and olive oil together.

2. In a large sauté pan or wok, cook the bacon until crisp. Remove bacon and drain on paper towels. Discard the excess bacon grease.

3. Add the garlic and toss for a minute or two. Add the green onions, vinegar and oil. Heat for a couple of minutes.

4. Add the shredded greens and toss with the dressing until slightly wilted. **Taste, Think, Transform** with salt, black pepper and/or vinegar.

5. Divide the greens on eight salad plates. Top each with the bacon, cheese, figs and pecans. Serve immediately.

This is especially good if using a high-quality farmstead blue cheese such as Point Reyes. When figs are not in season, whole dried Black Mission figs may be substituted by dicing them into one-fourth inch pieces and rehydrating in hot water for ten minutes then draining. They will add a sweet counter-point to the salty bacon.

· ·

BEET AND ARUGULA SALAD WITH ORANGE WALNUT VINAIGRETTE

Beets are an all-time favorite winter vegetable in our household. As I often do, one evening I looked in the refrigerator for ingredients that would serve as a nice side salad to accompany the hot pasta that I was preparing. I found beets and baby arugula. From there I added a sweet vinegar and nutty oil and toasted walnuts for a bit of crunch. It was a hit! Sprinkle a salty cheese like feta or a tangy cheese like goats' cheese or a pungent cheese like blue cheese on top for added panache.

4 side-salad servings

4 small beets

½ cup walnut halves

4 loosely packed cups baby arugula

¼ teaspoons sea salt or to taste

3 tablespoons toasted walnut oil

1 tablespoon Orange Muscat Champagne vinegar

fresh ground black pepper to taste

optional cheese: either feta, goat or blue cheese

1. Place the unpeeled beets in a saucepan and cover with water by one-inch. Bring to a boil and reduce to a simmer. Simmer for one or more hours until very tender. Add more water as needed to keep the beets submerged. Drain the beets and peel under cold running water by rubbing the skins off. Slice the beets into one-fourth inch rounds.

2. While the beets are, cooking preheat the oven to 375°F. Toast the walnut halves until golden brown, about 7 to 10 minutes. With the first smell of toasted walnut check for doneness. Remove from oven and cool.

3. Toss the arugula with sea salt and walnut oil. Add the orange vinegar and toss. **Taste, Think, Transform** with salt and/or vinegar. Pile high on four plates.

4. Place the sliced beets on the arugula. Top with toasted walnuts and small crumbles of cheese. Grind black pepper to taste over the top.

If Orange Muscat Champagne vinegar is unavailable, use 1 teaspoon orange juice, ½ teaspoon of fine orange zest and 2 teaspoons of Sherry vinegar in its place.

. . . .

BELGIUM ENDIVE AND FUJI APPLE SALAD

Through the years, I would throw a sit-down Christmas party for thirty to sixty-five people in our home. For most people this would be a challenging endeavor. But with detailed planning and the help of two employed students I enjoyed the event. This is one of the recipes I created one year. It was plated on chilled salad plates and served to the guests. It has a sweet, slightly spicy flavor with a bit of crunch.

8 side-salad servings

Vinaigrette

1 teaspoon honey

1 teaspoon Dijon mustard

½ teaspoon fresh tarragon, stems removed and finely chopped

2 tablespoons grapeseed or safflower oil

1 tablespoon balsamic vinegar

¼ teaspoon kosher salt and freshly ground black pepper to taste

1. Place honey, mustard and chopped tarragon in a non-reactive bowl.

2. Slowly whisk the oil into the mixture to form a slight emulsion. Whisk in the vinegar. **Taste, Think, Transform** with kosher salt and/or pepper.

3. Refrigerate for at least one hour. Best if made a day before using.

Salad

1 tablespoon fresh lemon juice

2 cups filtered water

2 medium Fuji apples, peeled, cored, cut into ⅛ inch julienne

2 heads each, white and red Belgium endive (4 heads total)

2 tablespoons fresh tarragon stems removed and coarsely chopped

1. Place salad plates in the refrigerator.

2. Mix the lemon juice and water together. Dip the julienne apples into this water to prevent browning, drain and place on a paper towel.

3. On eight chilled salad plates, place three to five Belgium endive leaves, tips facing outward.

4. Toss the apples in the vinaigrette and place on the endive leaves.

5. Sprinkle the fresh chopped tarragon over the apples.

6. Serve chilled immediately.

The endive leaves can be shredded, although the whole leaves make for a better presentation. Just be sure to have an extra dinner knife for the guest if left whole.

Belgium Endive and Fuji Apple Salad

8 large Bibb lettuce (sometimes called butter lettuce)

4 radicchio leaves, shredded (optional)

1. Chill the salad plates in the refrigerator.

2. Toss the carrots, dill and dressing together. Place two lettuce leaves on each of four plates. Top with the carrot mixture. If desired, sprinkle the shredded radicchio leaves around the base of the carrots for added color and a slightly bitter note.

Organic carrots tend to be very sweet which is best suited for this recipe, rather than the regular commercial variety. Agave syrup by volume is sweeter than honey but either one goes well in this dressing.

CARROT SALAD WITH MUSTARD WALNUT VINAIGRETTE

A few years ago, near Stuttgart, Germany a friend served a simple but delicious raw, garden carrot salad in her home. Previously I experienced carrot salads that were overpowered with mayonnaise-based dressings. This version is light and has a pure sweet carrot flavor which I much prefer. The delicate Bibb lettuce gives a nice texture and color contrast to the crunchy, bright orange salad.

4 side-salad servings

Dressing

¼ cup roasted walnut oil

2 tablespoons Champagne vinegar

1 tablespoon honey

1 teaspoon Dijon mustard

¼ teaspoon sea salt or to taste

1. Whip together the oil, vinegar, syrup and mustard. **Taste, Think, Transform** with salt and/or honey.

Salad

2 large carrots (about 2 cups), peeled, finely julienned (preferably organic)

1 tablespoon fresh dill leaves chopped

POMEGRANATE COLESLAW

This tasty coleslaw is a great accompaniment to many Mediterranean dishes, including paella. Pomegranates are native to Iran but are grown throughout the Middle East and Mediterranean and now California. It is considered a super fruit due to its high nutritional profile with anti-inflammatory properties, flavonoids, natural enzymes, vitamins and minerals. In this salad, the seeds add a pleasant sweet-tart crunch and ruby red color to the slightly smoky, wilted cabbage.

8 side-salad servings

3 tablespoons extra virgin olive oil

3 large garlic cloves, thinly sliced

1 ½ pounds green cabbage, shredded (about ½ head of cabbage)

½ teaspoon sea salt or to taste

½ teaspoon Pimentón Dulce or smoked paprika

¼ teaspoon cumin seeds

3 tablespoons pomegranate vinegar

½ cup pomegranate seeds

1. Heat olive oil in a sauté pan over medium heat. Add the garlic and sauté until garlic is slightly golden brown. While still hot mix with the cabbage in a bowl.

2. Toss the salt, Pimentón, cumin seeds, black pepper and vinegar with the cabbage and let stand at room temperature at least 30 minutes. **Taste, Think, Transform** with salt and/or vinegar.

3. Garnish with the pomegranate seeds and serve at room temperature.

If pomegranate vinegar is unavailable use two table-spoons of Sherry vinegar and one tablespoon of pomegranate juice or red wine vinegar. To peel whole pomegranates without staining your clothing, peel and seed them **under** cold water in a bowl. Cut them into four sections. Pop seeds from the membranes. Discard any dull colored seeds, white membranes and peel.

· ·

HERBED TORTELLINI SALAD

During the spring and summer months, when my herb garden is at its best, I like to make this tortellini salad. Often, I mix and use whatever herbs are available and will brighten the flavor of the tortellini and feta cheese. "Tortello" is derived from a Latin word that means "stuffed." When there is an "ini" at the end of an Italian pasta name it means "small." When "oni" is at the end it means "large." Therefore, tortellini is small stuffed pasta. This is a perfect salad for a pot luck, buffet or picnic as it tastes best a room temperature.

6 servings

Dressing

¼ cup extra virgin olive oil

2 tablespoons red wine vinegar

Salad

1 (12-ounce) package of fresh tri-colored tortellini

1 cup Roma tomatoes, seeded, small diced (about 2 tomatoes)

½ cup Kalamata olives, pitted, quartered

1 bunch scallions, trimmed, sliced thin (white and green parts)

1 tablespoon fresh basil and/or mint thinly sliced

1 tablespoon fresh Italian parsley and/or chervil, chopped

1 tablespoon mixed fresh marjoram, thyme, dill and/or tarragon chopped

¾ cup crumbled feta cheese (3 ½ ounces)

¾ cup walnuts, lightly toasted, coarsely chopped (divided)

1 teaspoon sea salt or to taste

5 sprigs of fresh herbs (garnish)

1. Mix the olive oil, vinegar and salt. Reserve.

2. Cook the tortellini per package directions. It should be fully cooked as it will become tough when cold if not. Drain and shock with cold running water to stop the cooking. Pat dry with paper towels and place in a large mixing bowl.

3. Add the tomatoes, olives, scallions, fresh herbs, cheese and one half of cup of walnuts.

4. Toss with the salad dressing. **Taste, Think, Transform** with salt and/or vinegar. Place in a serving bowl and garnish with the one fourth cup of walnuts and fresh herb sprigs. Serve at room temperature.

BRUNCH

CROSTATA, FRITTATA, STRATTA, OMELETTE, GRATIN, SHIRRED, SAVORY TART, BENEDICT, CROQUE MADAME, ITALIAN TOAST

I love those lazy, late morning brunches which are equally as charming as a light supper in the early evening. Interestingly the word "brunch" was formed in the nineteenth century in England by the combination of the first two letters from the word breakfast and the last four letters of the word lunch, making br-unch a combination of breakfast and lunch. These congers up thoughts of a breakfast entrée complimented by fresh fruit or salad and possibly a simple coffee cake.

Various egg dishes seem most appropriate for a brunch entrée. Luckily, eggs, bacon, ham or sausage are not only tasty but are used in a great variety of brunch dishes.

Eggs are a nutritionally complete food and the properties of the whites and yolks make them suitable for many different purposes within recipes. They may be used to bind ingredients together, gives lightness and rising qualities, encrust breads, or be encased in a variety of crusts. The options seem truly endless. Fragrant fresh fruits or light salads often accompany and enhance these entrees and a sweet muffin or coffee cake can finish the course.

Pour a bubbly Mimosa or a spicy Bloody Mary and kick back for a leisurely and scrumptious mid-day meal.

Ricotta, Bacon and Asparagus Crostata

RICOTTA, BACON AND ASPARAGUS CROSTATA

When entertaining overnight guests, I enjoy having a special breakfast dish such as this one. The ingredients can be prepared the day before and combined in the morning. Crostata is the Italian name for tart or pie and this is a savory one, lightly scented with tarragon. It is a lovely dish for brunch or supper served with garden greens salad or fresh fruit.

8 servings

4 slices bacon, small diced

1 large shallot, minced (about 1 ½ ounces)

8 large spears asparagus (about 6 ounces) cut into one-inch green only pieces

1 ½ cups whole milk ricotta (see Appareils chapter for a homemade version)

½ cup Parmigiano Reggiano, grated

2 eggs, beaten

1 tablespoon bread crumbs

1 teaspoon fresh tarragon, chopped

pinch of cayenne pepper

½ teaspoon kosher salt

¼ teaspoon fresh ground black pepper to taste

pastry dough for a nine-inch pie pan

1. Preheat oven to 375°F.

2. Place the diced bacon into a sauté pan over medium heat. Cook until crisp. Transfer the bacon to paper towels. Drain off all but one tablespoon of the fat.

3. Sauté the shallots in the pan fat for a minute or two. Add the asparagus spears and cook until they turn bright green and are still firm. Remove from heat.

4. In a bowl mix the ricotta, parmesan and eggs well. Add the bacon, shallots, asparagus, bread crumbs, tarragon, cayenne, salt and pepper. Mix well.

5. Line the pie dough in a nine-inch pie pan. Crimp the edges of the pie dough. Fill with the ricotta mixture.

6. Place on a sheet pan and put into the oven. Bake for forty to forty-five minutes, until the top is browned and puffed. Rest at room temperature for at least five minutes before slicing into six equal pieces. Serve hot or at room temperature

Fresh whole milk ricotta cheese is so easy to make and very flavorful (recipe in Breads and Spreads chapter) however, Bellwether Farms from California also makes a delicious Jersey cow hand-dipped whole milk ricotta that would work nicely in this recipe.

SLOW AND LOW CREAMY SCRAMBLED EGGS

On a cool autumn morning in the kitchen of The Spring House Inn in upstate New York, I learned one of the most valuable lessons that an apprentice cook could learn. Proper technique can transform the simplest of dishes: scrambled eggs. I watched as the Sous Chef broke a dozen eggs into a bowl, whipped them with a simple table fork until they were thoroughly combined and fluffy. Then slowly he cooked the eggs over very low heat in a pool of butter gently folding the curds until they were creamy and almost set. What an "ah ha" moment! Prior to this, I had thought that it was necessary to add milk and salt before cooking and that the higher the temperature the sooner one would be enjoying the eggs. But alas, that method only yields dry, tough eggs. Patience and low temperature will produce the creamiest scrambled eggs. Often overnight guests will ask how I made the breakfast eggs taste so wonderful. It delights me to share this modest recipe.

4 servings

8 large eggs

3 tablespoons unsalted butter

1 teaspoon sea salt and ⅛ teaspoon black pepper or to taste

snipped chives or finely shredded sorrel (optional)

1. Break eggs into a bowl and whip with a table fork until combined and fluffy. (My pantry chef instructor at the Culinary Institute of America would say that they should be whipped side to side forty to fifty times.)

2. Over very low heat melt the butter in a ceramic or non-stick sauté pan.

3. Add the beaten eggs and stir and fold constantly with a high-heat spatula over very low heat. In about three to five minutes the curds will form, but will still be creamy. Cook to the desired doneness, still creamy. *Do not* allow the eggs to become thoroughly set and dry. Season with salt and pepper. Serve immediately.

4. Place on a plate and garnish with chives or sliced sorrel, if desired.

SIMPLE EGG CURD SCIENCE

Eggs are high in protein. Raw egg protein is in the shape of coil strands. As the egg is heated the protein strands become straightened (denatured). The longer they cook and/or the higher the temperature at which they cook, the individual strands begin to lightly link together forming visible curds (coagulation). If overcooked, the linked strands become tighter and squeeze water out of the egg protein, leaving a dry mass of curds. Salt, water, milk and acids will also denature egg protein, thereby not desirable to a creamy scrambled outcome.

Slow and Low Creamy Scrambled Eggs

SPRING ONION TART

While visiting a friend in Germany, her mother prepared several local traditional spring dishes from her garden. My favorite was a spring onion tart that had a light and fluffy texture with a mild onion flavor that melted in my mouth. When I converted it from metrics and recreated it I was amazed that she had used pastry flour in the filling. This truly made a difference in the texture. Fresh spring onions and chives are some of the first produce that I enjoy from my garden in spring time. Now I have this delicacy in which to enjoy them.

6 servings

1 tablespoon unsalted butter

16 spring or green onions sliced ¼ inch across (about 8 ounces)

2 tablespoons pastry or cake flour (½ ounce)

2 large eggs

1 teaspoon sea salt

⅔ cup sour cream

1 cup heavy cream

3 tablespoons chives sliced fine

1 pastry crust (yours or see chefsharingthetable.com for my recipe)

1. Melt the butter in a sauté pan. Add sliced green onions. Cook over medium low heat until soft. Cool slightly.

2. Preheat the oven to 400°F.

3. In a mixing bowl combine the cooked onions and pastry flour. Whip in the eggs and salt. Fold in the sour cream, heavy cream and sliced chives until smooth.

4. Pour this filling into a pie or tart pan lined with an uncooked pastry crust.

5. Bake in the oven for twenty-five minutes or more, until the crust is browned and a paring knife inserted in the center comes out clean. The top of the filling will be slightly browned.

6. Let the tart rest for at least ten minutes at room temperature before slicing into six equal pieces.

This tart may be refrigerated overnight and eaten cold or reheated briefly in a microwave oven.

. . . .

CRAB AND ZUCCHINI GRATIN

What to do with all that garden zucchini? The neighbors are not answering their phones and if left in the garden it will become a monstrous pest. At the same time of year, crab is in abundance as are local sweet Walla Walla onions. This sumptuous gratin recipe may help. It may even become an annual favorite supper or brunch dish. This recipe can be easily doubled. Why not knock on their door and invite the neighbors?

4 entrée servings

4 cups tightly packed zucchini, grated (about 1 ½ pounds)

½ teaspoon kosher salt

1 tablespoon extra virgin olive oil

1 cup sweet onions, finely chopped (preferably Walla Walla sweet onions)

½ teaspoon garlic, minced

2 large eggs beaten

¼ cup full-fat sour cream

1 teaspoon Dijon mustard

¼ cup fresh Italian parsley leaves, chopped, lightly packed

1 cup crabmeat (preferably Dungeness crab or lump crab)

¼ cup + 3 tablespoons Parmigiano Reggiano cheese, grated (divided)

½ teaspoon kosher salt

⅛ teaspoon fresh ground black pepper

olive oil to coat the baking dish

1. Coarsely grate the zucchini into a colander. Toss with the one-half teaspoon kosher salt. Let it sit while preparing the other ingredients, about thirty minutes.

2. Heat the olive oil in a sauté pan until it shimmers. Add the onions and garlic. Sauté until translucent and soft.

3. In a large mixing bowl combine the eggs, sour cream and mustard.

4. Preheat the oven to 350°F.

5. In a tea towel squeeze the zucchini in small batches to release excess moisture. It should be very dry so that the gratin will not be watery.

6. Toss the zucchini, parsley, crab, one fourth cup of the cheese, one-half teaspoon of kosher salt and black pepper into the egg mixture.

7. Oil a one quart baking pan with oil. Distribute the zucchini and crab mixture evenly in the pan. Place in the preheated oven.

8. Bake for thirty minutes. Sprinkle the remaining three tablespoons of cheese over the top of the gratin. Bake for another fifteen minutes or until puffed, browned on top and a paring knife inserted in the middle comes out clean. Serve hot.

Puget Sound Dungeness crab and Walla Walla sweet onions are best used in this dish. However, blue crab and either Maui or Vidalia sweet onions are acceptable substitutes.

CROQUE MADAME WITH LEMON SABAYON

Recently, I had the best Croque Madame that I have ever eaten. Better yet, the chef of the restaurant was a former student. Since then I have been in search of other good brunch recipes. So, when I could not make up my mind one morning if I wanted to eat Croque Madame or Eggs Benedict I had an "ah ha" moment. I decided to put the best of both recipes together. The main problem here was that if I used Gruyère cheese on the sandwich then the Hollandaise sauce would make the recipe too rich. To lighten it up I decided to make a savory lemon sabayon sauce or wine custard sauce. What a marvelous inspiration!

4 servings

Sandwich

8 slices whole wheat bread, crust removed or not

4 teaspoons Dijon mustard

1 cup Gruyère cheese, grated (about 2 ounces)

4 ounces thin sliced Black Forest ham

¼ cup soft unsalted butter, divided for bread and frying eggs

4 large eggs

Sabayon

4 egg yolks

2 tablespoons fresh lemon juice

2 tablespoons Sauvignon Blanc wine

¼ cup heavy cream, whipped to soft peaks, reserved at room temperature

2 small drops hot sauce like Tabasco

½ teaspoon sea salt or to taste

zest of 1 lemon

1. Preheat a griddle to 350°F.

2. Spread half of the butter on one side of all eight slices of bread.

3. On the opposite side of four slices of bread spread the mustard and top with the ham.

4. On the remaining four slices of bread distribute the grated cheese on the unbuttered side.

5. Place all eight slices of bread, butter side down on the preheated griddle and cook until golden brown on the bottom and the cheese is melted. Put the cheese sides together with the ham sides to form four grilled cheese and ham sandwiches. Reserve hot.

Sabayon

1. Bring one-inch of water to boil in the bottom half of a double boiler. The water should not touch the top pan. In the top pan place the egg yolks, lemon juice, wine and hot sauce. Whip the egg mixture non-stop over the boiling water. If the eggs begin to stick to the sides of the pan remove the top pan from the hot water pan for a few minutes while continuing to beat the mixture. Return until the eggs form a thick custard. Remove from the heat and whip in the whipped cream. **Taste, Think, Transform** with sea salt. Wrap the pan in a large bath towel to keep warm.

2. Heat the remaining butter in a large non-stick pan. Break four eggs into the pan. Cover with a lid and cook to sunny-side-up doneness, with the yolks not set or firm if desired. (Alternately if you are able, cook each egg separately in a small amount of butter and flip to cook over-easy).

3. Plate each sandwich, top with the egg and a portion of the sabayon sauce. Sprinkle each with lemon zest. Serve hot.

This dish would be perfect for partners cooking together. One could make the sandwiches and the other make the sauce. I found that the challenge here is to keep all components warm. Often, I use the closed space of the microwave to keep hot foods hot, like the sandwiches in this recipe. But I do not microwave them as that would toughen the bread. I also use large bath towels to keep some items warm like the sauce here that would separate if allowed to cool and reheat. Hollandaise and Sabayon sauces however will separate above 160°F, so the oven will not work. And the eggs must be fried at the last moment and not held, so that when cut into, the yolks will run and make everything taste great!

APPLE, ARUGULA AND BACON STRATA

The beauty of strata is that it can be prepared the night before, refrigerated. Pop into the oven upon awakening to have a lovely breakfast or brunch dish piping hot, when overnight company following their noses, wander into the kitchen. Add coffee, tea, juice and fruit to quickly complete this meal.

6 servings

3 cups crusty French or whole wheat bread, ½-inch cubes (8 ounces)

3 thick slices uncured smoked bacon, small diced

½ cup yellow onion, small diced

1 cup Granny Smith apple, peeled, pared, small diced (about 1 large apple)

2 tightly packed cups baby arugula (about 2 ½ ounces)

1 ½ cup whole milk

5 large eggs, beaten

¼ teaspoon fresh grated nutmeg

½ teaspoon sea salt

½ teaspoon fresh ground black pepper

1 ½ cup Gruyère cheese, grated (4 ounces)

1. Preheat oven to 300°F. Toast the bread cubes until golden brown.

2. In a sauté pan over medium heat, cook the bacon until crisp and brown. Remove and reserve the bacon. Drain all but one tablespoon of the bacon fat. Add the onions and apples. Sauté until soft and translucent. Add the arugula and cook just until wilted.

3. Whisk the milk, eggs, nutmeg, salt and black pepper together.

4. Toss the bread, bacon, onions, apples, arugula and Gruyère cheese together. Place in a seven by ten by two-inch or eight by eight ceramic or glass baking pan. Pour the custard evenly over the strata. Refrigerate covered for at least eight hours or overnight.

5. Preheat oven to 350°F. Let the strata stand at room temperature for thirty minutes.

6. Bake the strata uncovered for forty to fifty-five minutes until puffed and golden brown.

7. Serve hot.

. . . .

FIRE ROASTED TOMATOES AND CHILIES WITH POACHED EGGS AND FETA

Want to begin the day with a spicy, tangy egg dish? This recipe is for you. This Tunisian inspired one pot dish called Shaksuta is quick and easy to prepare for a tasty brunch. Likewise, it can be served for a light supper enhanced with a tossed greens or fruit salad. Serve with some crusty bread for sopping up the succulent juices.

2 large servings or 4 medium servings

1 tablespoon extra virgin olive oil

¾ cup onions, small diced

1 small clove garlic, minced (½ teaspoon)

½ teaspoon ground cumin

1 teaspoon Pimentón Dulce or smoked paprika

1 (14-½ ounce) can diced fire roasted tomatoes in tomato juice

¼ cup filtered water

1 (4 ounce) can diced fire roasted chiles

1 tablespoon harissa sauce, optional, for added heat (see Appareils chapter for a homemade recipe)

1 teaspoon sea salt and ⅛ teaspoon fresh ground black pepper or to taste

4 large eggs

½ cup crumbled feta cheese (2 ⅓ ounces)

½ cup chopped, fresh basil or cilantro

1. Heat an eight-inch, non-reactive sauce pan over medium-high heat. Add the olive oil and when it shimmers add the onions. Sauté until soft. Add the garlic, cumin and Pimentón. Sauté for a minute until fragrant. Add the tomatoes, optional harissa sauce, water and chilies. **Taste, Think, Transform** with salt and/or pepper to taste.

2. Bring to a simmer. Crack the four eggs into a bowl and slide them onto the tomato mixture. Cover the pan and turn the heat down to a low simmer. Cook for three minutes. Sprinkle with the feta cheese. Cover and simmer a couple of minutes more or until the eggs yolks are set to desired doneness (about six to seven minutes) or more for firmness and that the cheese has melted.

3. Remove from heat and garnish with the fresh chopped basil or cilantro.

4. Serve hot.

Offer hot pepper or harissa sauce on the side for those who desire more heat.

. . . .

ITALIAN LEMON TOAST

Lemon and berries of all types are a match made in heaven! In this recipe use brioche, challah bread or Lemon Brioche (found in the Breads and Spreads chapter) if possible. Add a couple link sausage, maybe a few whole berries and syrup to complete this decadent for-company brunch. The toast may be held in the oven until the guests arrive at the table.

6 servings

4 large eggs

½ cup half and half

1 tablespoon lemon zest

½ teaspoon vanilla extract

1 tablespoon honey

½ teaspoon kosher salt

½ loaf of lemon brioche (on page 17), divided (about ½ pound)

2 tablespoons unsalted butter

1. Preheat oven to 200°F. Place a sheet pan on the middle rack of the oven.

2. Whip together the eggs, milk, cream, lemon zest, lemon oil, vanilla, honey and salt.

3. Slice the bread into six three-fourth-inch thick slices.

4. Heat a cast iron griddle or sauté pan over medium heat.

5. Lay the bread slices in a baking pan and pour the egg mixture over the top. Turn the bread over in a minute or two. Soak until all the egg mixture is absorbed on both sides.

6. Melt a thin layer of butter on the griddle.

7. Cook half the bread on each side until golden brown. Do not crowd the pan. Place on the sheet pan in the oven.

8. Repeat cooking the remaining bread slices in the same manner.

9. Serve hot with butter and raspberry or blueberry syrup or preserves.

. . . .

SHIRRED HERBED EGG AND ARTICHOKES

Dear friends first served a rendition of this dish to me at their beach house. I was instantly enamored with this creamy herbed egg bake. It makes for a very fulfilling brunch or light supper accompanied by crusty bread to sop up the creamy goodness and fresh fruit. To utilize what you have on hand, change the herbs, cheese or vegetable. The French refer to this baked dish as "en cocotte," meaning in casserole dish.

2 teaspoons soft unsalted butter

1 quart water

1 teaspoon fresh, minced marjoram

½ teaspoon fresh, minced chives

½ teaspoon fresh, minced oregano

16 frozen quartered artichoke hearts, thawed

2 teaspoons grated Parmigiano Reggiano cheese (divided)

4 eggs (preferably organic, free-range)

4 tablespoons heavy cream
⅛ teaspoon sea salt and a pinch of fresh black pepper per serving or to taste

1. Preheat the oven to 400°F. Butter the bottom and insides of four 1-cup ramekins or custard baking dishes. Heat water to the boiling point. Mix the marjoram, chives and oregano together.

2. Place four artichoke quarters in the bottom of each ramekin. Top with ¼ teaspoon cheese and ¼ teaspoon mixed herbs. Crack an egg into each dish. Pour the cream around the top of the eggs. Season with salt and black pepper. Finish topping with ¼ teaspoon cheese and ¼ teaspoon mixed herbs.

3. Place the ramekins in a baking pan in the oven and pour the hot water into the pan to one-half of an inch from the top of each dish. Bake for fifteen to twenty-four minutes or until the eggs are slightly runny **or** set and lightly golden on the top. Serve hot, wrapped in napkins for safe handling.

SMOKED SALMON AND GOAT CHEESE FRITTATA

This is a great spring frittata as garden leeks that have wintered over and sugar snap peas are at their best. I generally use Steelhead that a friend smokes for me because it has a more delicate texture and rich flavor. The snap peas, leeks and red peppers add a crunchy vegetable dimension. Topping it with fresh goat cheese and dill is like icing on the cake. This makes a great brunch or supper dish.

6 servings

2 tablespoon extra virgin olive oil

1 small leek, halved, rinsed, thinly sliced

½ red bell pepper diced

1 ½ cups sugar snap peas halved on the bias (5 ounces)

4 ounces skinned smoked salmon or steelhead skinned, flaked

1 tablespoon fresh dill, stemmed, minced

6 large eggs, whipped smooth with a fork

1 teaspoon kosher salt

½ cup fresh goat cheese crumbled (about 4 ounces)

Preheat the oven to 400°F.

1. Heat a sauté pan. Add one tablespoon of the oil and when it shimmers add the leek and peppers. Sauté until soft. Add the sugar snap peas and toss just until the green color sets to a vibrant green. They should still be crunchy.

2. Add the remaining olive oil. Distribute the salmon and dill uniformly over the top of the vegetables. Season the eggs with salt and pour evenly over the top. Sprinkle with the cheese.

3. When the eggs set on the bottom, transfer the pan to the oven. As soon as the frittata puffs and sets, about eighteen minutes, remove from the oven. It will still be a bit moist in the center. Loosen with a flat rubber spatula. Cut into six servings. Serve warm or at room temperature.

ENTRÉES

Entrée means "enter into the main course" of the meal, creating the focus of a menu with complimentary dishes served before, with and after. Envision the guest's preferences, the season and the formality or informality of the meal. Wild fish, seafood and vegetables have distinct seasons for which they are at their best. Turkey, lamb, beef and ham are holiday favorites. Grilled entrées are ideal for informal outdoors parties. Roasted, baked, sautéed, fried, simmered or braised foods may go either formal or informal.

Entrées are usually the center of the plate. Often sides such as vegetables, grains, rice and fruit become the base on which to place or lean the entrée. Top with a chunky compote or a crunchy accent, or add a drizzle of sauce or vinaigrette and the dish is complete.

I was once invited to an East coast Italian home for Thanksgiving. The beautifully roasted turkey sat on the center of the side buffet for all to see but was never touched. Instead we thankfully devoured an antipasto platter, lasagna, eggplant parmesan and pasta Bolognese!

Enter the heart of the meal, the center of the plate with gusto and abandon!

PASTAS

Penne Rigate with Pistachio Mint Pesto

PENNE RIGATE WITH PISTACHIO MINT PESTO

On an Italian culinary tour, I had the great fortune to visit the hill top hunting villa of Sra Jo Bettoja about one hour northeast of Rome. On this Pentecostal Sunday, we were to sample the regional specialty of ember roasted, wild fennel stuffed suckling pig. However, for me the primo course, a heavenly casseruola of penne rigate anointed with rustic pistachio mint pesto was outstanding in its varying shades of green, bursting with fresco flavor and multiple textures. When I returned home I recreated this dish by flavor memory to share this bit of heaven with friends and family.

8 servings

Pesto

12 large garlic cloves, peeled

¾ cup extra virgin olive oil

½ firmly packed cup mint leaves

¼ firmly packed cup basil leaves

½ cup pistachios, lightly toasted

1 cup Parmigiano Reggiano cheese, finely grated

Pasta

1 pound penne rigate pasta

1 ½ tablespoon kosher salt

sea salt to taste

freshly ground black pepper to taste

Garnish

1 cup loosely packed mint leaves, roughly hand torn

½ cup loosely packed basil leaves, roughly hand torn

½ cup pistachios, toasted, chopped

½ cup Parmigiano Reggiano, finely grated

1. In a small cast iron pan, roast the garlic in the extra virgin olive oil until golden brown. Remove from heat and cool.

2. In a small sauce pan of boiling water, blanch the mint and basil leaves for thirty seconds. Strain and immediately shock in cold water. Squeeze dry. (This step will retain the bright green color of the herbs.)

3. Pulse the blanched mint and basil leaves with the pistachios in a food processor until crumbly in texture. Add the garlic, half cup of pistachios, one cup of Parmigiano Reggiano and half of the olive oil. Pulse until it comes together but not too fine. Add more of the garlic oil if the pesto appears too dry.

4. Bring a gallon of water to a boil. Add the kosher salt and penne. Stir until the water returns to a boil. Cook the amount of time designated on the package directions or until the pasta is al dente (to the bite). Drain in a colander.

5. Toss the hot pasta with the pesto. Add the rest of the garlic oil. Season with the sea salt and black pepper. Pour into a large pasta bowl.

6. Top with the remaining hand torn mint and basil leaves, chopped pistachios and Parmigiano Reggiano. Serve warm or at room temperature.

Penne rigate is commercial penne pasta with ridges. The ridges help hold the pesto to the pasta.

LEMON THYME CRAB AND SWISS CHARD CANNELLONI

Cannelloni means "large reeds" in Italian. Here, fresh pasta is rolled in a tubular "reed" shape around a crab and Swiss chard stuffing. I use Dungeness crab from the Puget Sound, delicately scenting it with lemon thyme cream and accentuate with local Gouda cheese from the Golden Glen Creamery. Serve bubbling hot and golden on top with fresh fruit or a tossed salad for an enjoyable brunch or supper.

6 to 12 servings (24 each cannelloni)

Dungeness Crab Stuffing

8 large garlic cloves, root ends cut off

1 sprig lemon thyme

1 teaspoon extra virgin olive oil

1 large cooked Dungeness crab
(about 1 ½ cups or 8 ounces crabmeat)

1 to 2 large bunch Swiss chard, stemmed
(about 8 ounces)

1 cup whole milk ricotta cheese
(carton or mine on page 25)

½ teaspoon sea salt

2 tablespoon chopped lemon thyme leaves

1. Preheat oven to 375°F. Place the garlic and sprig of lemon thyme in a piece of foil. Drizzle the olive oil over the cloves and bring the four corners of the foil to the top and seal. Bake on a sheet pan for about twenty-five minutes or until the garlic is soft. Remove the soft flesh from their skins and mash the garlic. Discard the lemon thyme and skins.

2. Pick the flesh from the crab shells. Pick again for any rogue pieces of shell. Reserve the shells for the sauce.

3. Wash the Swiss chard three times and spin dry. Chop it coarsely. Bring a pot of filtered water to a boil. Add the Swiss chard and cook until soft but still bright green, about two to three minutes. Drain, wash with cold water to cool and squeeze very dry by hand or by squeezing in a potato ricer.

4. Mix the garlic, crab meat, Swiss chard, ricotta cheese, salt and chopped lemon thyme. **Taste, Think, Transform** with sea salt. Reserve cold.

Fresh Pasta

1 cup unbleached bread flour (about 5 ounces)

1 large eggs, at room temperature

¼ teaspoon fine sea salt

1 ½ teaspoon extra virgin olive oil

1 ¼ tablespoons filtered water or more

extra bread flour for dusting or rice flour if freezing
as needed

1. In a food processor pulse the flour, egg, salt and olive oil until it looks like cornmeal. Drizzle with the water. Pulse again. Squeeze it in your hand to see if it comes together. If not add a bit more water. Place on plastic wrap and squeeze together in a firm smooth ball. Remove from plastic wrap and cut into two equal size balls. Wrap each ball separately in plastic wrap. Let rest at room temperature for thirty minutes.

2. Remove one portion of the dough at a time from the plastic wrap.

3. Form that dough into a flat rectangle about four by three inches. Flour the pasta rollers and the dough with extra bread flour.

4. Feed the dough through the machine at the widest setting.

5. Brush the excess flour from the top side of the dough. Fold into thirds and flatten with fingertips pushing from bottom to top. Roll the dough through the same setting again, bottom end first so excess air is pressed out.

6. Flour the dough and put through the rollers at a reduced width.

7. Repeat step 4, 5 and 6 three times, reducing the width each time. Then cut the pasta sheet in half and roll straight through, reducing the width setting

each time until the dough is at the desired thickness for stuffed pasta shapes (about one-sixteenth inch thick).

8. Repeat with remaining piece of dough.

9. Cut into four by three inch pieces (about twenty-four pieces in all). Sprinkle with bread flour to stack. Use within two hours or freeze the pasta sheets dredged in rice flour and tightly wrapped plastic wrap.

Lemon Thyme Sauce

crab shells, washed and cracked into small pieces

2 cups Sauvignon Blanc wine

½ cup fresh lemon juice (about 2-3 lemons)

zest of lemons

1 bunch lemon thyme

1 pint heavy cream

sea salt to taste

1. In a stainless-steel sauté pan bring the crab shells, wine, lemon juice, lemon zest and lemon thyme to a boil. Boil until reduced by half.

2. Add the cream and simmer until reduced and thick. **Taste, Think, Transform** with sea salt and/or lemon juice to taste. Strain the sauce through a fine mesh sieve. Reserve hot.

Cannelloni Assembly

1 tablespoon softened unsalted butter

Dungeness crab stuffing

24 uncooked pasta sheets

hot lemon thyme sauce

¾ cup medium Gouda finely shredded (about 3 ounces)

1 tablespoon lemon thyme leaves

1. Preheat oven to 375°F. Liberally butter a nine by thirteen-inch baking pan.

2. Divide and spread the crab stuffing onto the top of each four-inch side of the pasta sheet. Roll each up to enclose the filling. Cut off any excess pasta. Place in the baking dish with the cut side down.

3. Pour the hot sauce evenly over the top of the cannelloni. Sprinkle the Gouda evenly over the top.

4. Bake for twenty to thirty minutes until bubbling hot and golden on top.

5. Sprinkle the top with chopped lemon thyme and serve hot.

May use pre-picked crab meat and eliminate the shells in making the sauce. However, if you have the time and patience to pick crab from the shells, the crab shells do add extra flavor to the sauce.

. . . .

BEEF TORTELLINI IN BROWN BUTTER SAGE BRODO

Pasta in "brodo" which is Italian for broth is a particularly satisfying first course somewhere between soup and pasta. Equally enchanting as a dinner entrée served with a nice crisp salad. It can be quickly made by substituting round Gyoza wrappers for the fresh pasta as is sometimes done in restaurants. The outcome is sure to warm a chilly fall or winter dinner. A friend described it this way: "In one word, "spectacular". With the smiles and delights that this dish created at my family table, I cannot wait to try it with some of our friends."

8 first course servings or 5 entrée servings

Beef and Beef Green Tortellini (for 40 tortellini)

2 ounces lean top round or eye of round beef steak, diced

¼ cup onion, peeled, diced

1 tablespoon extra virgin olive oil

1 large garlic cloves, minced (about 1 tablespoon)

½ bunch beet greens, stemmed, thinly sliced, chopped (about 6 stems)

¼ cup beef broth

2 tablespoons red wine (Barolo, Barbera or Merlot)

¼ teaspoon kosher salt and fresh ground black pepper to taste

¼ cup Parmigiano Reggiano cheese finely grated

⅛ teaspoon fresh ground nutmeg

1 large egg yolk (save white for sealing pasta)

1. Pulse the beef steak and onion in a food processor until fine but not puréed.

2. Heat the olive oil in a large sauté pan over medium heat until it lightly ripples. Add the beef, onions and garlic. Sauté until cooked through.

3. Add the beet greens, beef broth and red wine. Cook until all the liquid evaporates. **Taste, Think, Transform** with kosher salt and/or black pepper. Cool.

4. Add the cheese, nutmeg and egg yolk. Mix thoroughly.

Fresh Pasta and Tortellini Assembly

2 cups unbleached bread flour (about 10 ounces)

2 large eggs, at room temperature, lightly beaten

½ teaspoon sea salt

1 tablespoon extra virgin olive oil

2 ½ tablespoons filtered water

1 tablespoon kosher salt

1 large egg white, beaten

⅛ teaspoon fine sea salt

½ cup rice flour

1. In a food processor, pulse the flour, eggs, salt and olive oil until it looks like cornmeal. Drizzle with the water. Pulse again. Squeeze it in your hand. Place on plastic wrap and squeeze together in a firm smooth ball. Cut into four equal size balls. Wrap each in plastic wrap. Let rest at room temperature for thirty minutes.

2. Remove one portion of the dough at a time from the plastic wrap.

3. Form that dough into a flat rectangle about four by three inches. Flour the pasta roller and the dough with extra bread flour.

4. Feed the dough through the machine at the widest setting.

5. Brush the excess flour from the top side of the dough. Fold into thirds and flatten with fingertips. Roll the

dough through the same setting again, open end first.

6. Flour the dough and put through the rollers at a reduced width.

7. Repeat step 13, 14 and 15 three times, reducing the width each time. Then cut the pasta sheet in half and roll straight through until the dough is at the desired thickness for stuffed pasta shapes (about one-eighth inch thick or less).

8. Beat the egg with the sea salt to make an egg wash. Allow to sit for at least ten minutes.

9. Cut the rolled pasta into three-inch circles. Brush the edges with egg wash. Place a scant teaspoon of filling in the center of the circle and press the edges firmly to seal with no air pockets, making half-moon shapes. Bring each end together and pinch. Place on a sheet pan dusted with rice flour to assist in drying and to keep each separate from the others. Repeat with remaining three pieces of dough. At this point they may be frozen or cooked within an hour or placed covered in the refrigerator for a few hours.

Brown Butter Sage Brodo

6 tablespoons unsalted butter

1 bunch sage, stems removed, hand torn into small pieces

3 ½ cups beef broth

¾ cup red wine (Barolo, Barbera or Merlot)

½ teaspoon sea salt and fresh ground black pepper to taste

5 quarts filtered water

1 tablespoon kosher salt

1. Place the soup bowls into a 200°F oven to warm.

2. In a non-reactive sauté pan, over medium high heat, cook the butter and sage until it begins to brown. Add the beef stock and red wine. Reduce to about two cups. Reserve hot.

3. Cook the tortellini in the five quarts of boiling water with kosher salt until al dente (Italian for to the bite). Drain.

4. Distribute the tortellini in eight appetizer or five entrée warm soup bowls. Whisk the sage brown butter broth and pour a portion into each bowl. Serve hot.

. . . .

KÄSEPÄTZLE

On a recent journey to Germany to discover our family history, we stopped at a Bavarian country restaurant for a light supper. My husband chose a delightful dish which was described as spätzle (a German noodle), fried onions and sauerkraut. As we shared this enchanting dish we became aware that the Swiss Emmentaler cheese, (cheese is known as Käse in German,) was the poignant flavor bringing all the components together. Once home, I set out to recreate this memorable fare. The results are as follows. Guten Appetit!

8 servings

Spätzle

2 large eggs beaten

½ cup whole milk

½ teaspoon fine sea salt

¼ teaspoon fresh grated nutmeg

¼ teaspoon fresh ground white pepper

1 cup all-purpose flour (5 ⅓ ounces) *

1 teaspoon kosher salt

4 tablespoons unsalted butter

1. Whip the milk into the eggs. Add the salt, nutmeg and white pepper.

2. Slowly sift the flour through a fine mesh sieve directly into the egg mixture while whipping to incorporate. The batter should be thick and smooth.

3. Cover and let it sit for at least one hour.

4. Bring two quarts of water to a boil. Add the kosher salt. Place half of the batter in a metal colander. With a wide silicone spatula, quickly force the batter through the holes into the boiling water. Place the colander in a cool pan of water until ready to make the remaining spätzle.

5. When the spätzle float to the surface, cook for one to two minutes. Using a skimmer or slotted spoon transfer the spätzle into a ice-water bath to stop the cooking.

6. Repeat with the remaining half of the batter.

7. Drain the spätzle well and place on a sheet pan lined with a white kitchen towel or paper towels. Allow to drain, then replace the towel with a dry one and refrigerate until ready to sauté.

8. Before assembling with the other ingredients melt two tablespoons butter in a non-stick sauté pan over medium high heat. Add half the spätzle. Sauté until golden brown. It is done in two batches so not to overcrowd the pan, which would prevent browning. Repeat with the second batch in the extra two tablespoons of butter

Onions and Assembly

1 ½ pound yellow onions (about 3 medium onions)

2 tablespoons unsalted butter (more for buttering the pan)

all-purpose flour as needed

2 cup safflower or sunflower oil

12 ounces drained sauerkraut

2 cups Swiss Emmentaler cheese, grated (4 ounces)

sea salt to taste

1. Peel the onions. Cut in half from root to stem. Slice the onions across into one fourth inch rings.

2. Melt the two tablespoons of butter in a sauté pan over low heat. Add two thirds of the onions and slowly sauté and stir the onions until deep brown, about thirty to forty-five minutes.

3. Preheat the oven to 350°F.

4. While the onions are browning heat the oil in a deep fryer or deep pan to 375°F. Lightly dust the remaining onions with flour. Add the onion rings in batches to the hot oil and deep fry until crispy brown. Place the onion rings onto a sheet pan with paper towels to absorb the excess oil.

5. In a buttered 8x8 inch baking pan layer half the onions, half the sauerkraut, half the spätzle and half the cheese. **Taste, Think, Transform** with salt. Repeat the layers with cheese on top. Bake in the oven for about 30 minutes or until lightly browned on top. Top with the deep-fried onions and serve immediately.

This can be made in eight individual casserole dishes instead of one baking dish. May also substitute canned onion rings for deep-frying from scratch. *For a high protein, low starch noodle replace the all-purpose flour with one cup of garbanzo bean flour and reduce the milk to one-fourth cup.

Käsepätzle

. . . .

PASTITSIO GREEK BAKED PASTA AND LAMB CASSEROLE

Dancing happily in the mouth with creamy, chewy and meaty panache, this is the magic of purely Greek comfort food, much as Zorba doing the sirtaki dance on a sandy Crete beach. Pastitsio is an early rendition of macaroni and cheese on top of lamb, eggplant and tomatoes. Although it has flavors from the Near East, its name is derived from the Italian word that means "mess" and is layered like lasagna. Enjoy it as a brunch entrée or as a casserole to nourish a hungry crowd.

8 to 12 servings

Lamb and Eggplant Mixture

1 pound lean lamb, cubed or ground lamb

1 tablespoon extra virgin olive oil

2 cups onion, small dice

2 cloves garlic, minced

1 ½ teaspoon sea salt

1 teaspoon ground cinnamon

½ teaspoon fresh ground black pepper

¼ teaspoon granulated cane sugar

1 ½ teaspoon dry Greek oregano or marjoram

1 pound eggplant, peeled, ½ inch dice (about 5 cups)

1 (28-ounce) can dice tomatoes

Cheese Sauce

3 tablespoon unsalted butter

3 tablespoon all-purpose flour

3 cup whole milk

3 whole clove

¼ teaspoon fresh grated nutmeg

1 ⅔ cup feta cheese, crumbled (about 8 ounces)

1 teaspoon sea salt

½ teaspoon fresh ground black pepper

3 large eggs, beaten

Pasta and Assembly

3 cups dry penne pasta

1 ½ tablespoon kosher salt

Lamb and Eggplant Mixture

1. Use ground lamb or if using cubed lamb pulse the cubes in a food processor until coarsely ground.

2. Heat the olive oil in a four-quart heavy bottom non-reactive pot. Add the onion and cook until soft and translucent. Stir with the ground lamb over medium high heat until no longer pink.

3. Sprinkle with the garlic, salt, cinnamon, black pepper, sugar and oregano. Stir for about two minutes or until fragrant.

4. Stir in the eggplant and tomatoes. Simmer, barely bubbling and cover with a lid over low heat until the eggplant is tender, about forty minutes, stirring often.

Remove the lid and continue to cook uncovered until thick. **Taste, Think, Transform** with salt.

Cheese Sauce

1. Meanwhile, melt the butter in a one-and-half quart or larger sauce pan to prepare the cheese sauce. Stir in the flour and cook for two minutes, stirring constantly. (see Appareils chapter for review of Béchamel)

2. Gradually whisk in a small portion of milk, whipping it smooth before each subsequent addition of milk.

3. Drop in the clove and nutmeg.

4. Bring to a boil stirring constantly. Reduce to a gentle simmer and stir for about five minutes until it coats the back of a spoon (the French call this "nappe" which refers to a sauce with good body, not watery). Discard the cloves.

5. Whip in the cheese, salt and black pepper. Simmer for two minutes until smooth. **Taste, Think, Transform** with salt. Reserve hot.

Pasta and Assembly

1. Preheat the oven to 425°F.

2. Bring one-gallon of filtered water to a boil. Add the kosher salt. Add the pasta and boil until al dente (Italian for "firm to the bite"). Strain through a colander.

3. Just before assembling, gradually whip the cheese sauce into the beaten eggs.

4. Toss half of the pasta with the cheese sauce.

5. Toss the other half of the pasta with the lamb and eggplant mixture.

6. In a ten by fifteen-inch **or** four-quart (glass or ceramic) baking dish pour the lamb, eggplant and pasta mixture, evenly covering the bottom of the dish.

7. Top with the cheese sauce and pasta, spreading evenly.

8. Bake uncovered on a sheet pan until bubbling and browned on top, about twenty-five to thirty minutes.

Let it stand at room temperature for five minutes before serving.

. . . .

RAGÙ BOLOGNESE

Ragù which is derived from the French word 'ragoût' roughly means "to awaken the appetite." The French nobility were probably first to create ragout as a savory stew rich with generous chunks of meat. Marriage between French and Italian nobility began the exchange of cuisines. When Italian country folks of Bologna in the Emilia-Romagna region, known for its outstanding dairy and meat products, began to prepare a ragù, meat was scarce, therefore the meat was ground and became a sauce for pasta rather than a one-pot dish. Ragù Bolognese truly will awaken the palate of a hungry crowd.

6 to 8 servings

1 large onion, peeled, cut into small pieces (about 1 ¼ pounds)

2 stalks celery, trimmed, cut into small pieces (about 4 ounces)

2 carrots, peeled, cut into small pieces (about ½ pound)

1 pound round beef steak, cut into small pieces

8 ounces lean pork steak, cut into small pieces

8 tablespoons unsalted butter (1 stick) divided

2 tablespoons extra virgin olive oil

3 ounces pancetta, sliced thin and minced

½ cup   dry white wine

⅛ teaspoon freshly ground nutmeg

3 tablespoons tomato paste

2 cups   beef broth

1 or 2 pieces of Parmigiano Reggiano cheese rind (optional)

1 cup whole milk

to taste, sea salt and freshly ground black pepper

1. Pulsate the onions, celery and carrots in a food processor until finely chopped. Remove and pulsate the beef and pork until coarsely ground.

2. Heat four tablespoons (half) butter and the olive oil in a large sauce pot. Sauté the pancetta and chopped

vegetables until the vegetables are translucent and soft.

3. Add the beef and pork to the pan. Sauté, stirring for a few minutes over medium heat until it is lightly browned.

4. Deglaze the pan with the wine. Season with the nutmeg, tomato paste, beef stock and optional Parmigiano Reggiano rind.

5. Turn the heat down very low. A range top simmer plate would be helpful here. Partially cover.

6. Simmer slowly for two hours adding a few tablespoons of milk occasionally until all the milk is incorporated. Stir in the remaining four tablespoons of butter. Discard the Parmigiano-Reggiano rind before seasoning.

7. *Taste, Think, Transform* with salt and/or pepper.

Serve over fresh cooked tagliatelle or use to make lasagna. Top with freshly grated Parmigiano Reggiano cheese. My local co-op carries Bionaturae, organic tagliatelle made in Italy that is a great substitute for fresh.

VEGETABLE MAINS

Fennel, Lentil and Rice Bake

FENNEL, LENTIL AND BROWN RICE BAKE

Often in the winter months we enjoy this hearty vegetarian entrée. Enticing aromas slowly begin to fill and warm the kitchen as it gradually bakes. Along with being very nutritious it has a nutty, satisfying flavor. As with many casseroles it is even better reheated the next day. Serve with a fresh, light winter salad like the orange, avocado, feta salad with honey mustard vinaigrette.

6 entrée servings

Base

½ cup onion, peeled, small diced

1 cup fennel bulb, trimmed, small diced, reserve the fronds

¾ cup brown lentils, rinsed

½ cup long grain brown rice, rinsed

1 teaspoon fresh garlic, minced

1 teaspoon fennel seeds, finely chopped or ground in a mortar

½ teaspoon dried marjoram

½ teaspoon dried oregano

½ teaspoon dried thyme leaves

½ teaspoon fresh ground black pepper

1 teaspoon sea salt

¼ cup Sauvignon Blanc or alcohol-free apple cider

2 ¾ cups vegetable broth (see Appareils chapter)

1 cup Gruyère or Swiss cheese, grated

Finish

½ cup Gruyère or Swiss cheese, grated

optional: ½ teaspoon each fresh basil, marjoram and thyme minced

reserved fennel fronds

1. Preheat oven to 350°F.

2. In a seven by seven by two-inch baking dish or a one-and-a-half-quart casserole dish mix all the base ingredients together. Cover with a tight-fitting lid or foil and place in the preheated oven. Stir occasionally as it bakes. Bake for one and a half to two hours until all the liquid is absorbed and the rice is tender. In the last five minutes' top with the finishing cheese and let it melt uncovered.

3. Serve hot topped with the fresh herbs and garnish with the reserved fennel fronds.

If you are skeptical of lentils here are words from a friend: "I am not a huge lentil fan. But I loved this! My husband loved this and he doesn't like lentils at all! Amazing combination of ingredients." Try it you might be surprised.

· ·

PECORINO RISOTTO WITH FENNEL AND TANGERINE BRAISED IN OLIVE OIL

Do you ever wonder what to cook in those winter months when the farmer's markets are somewhat barren? This dish may be the solution. Here the fennel flavor is mellowed and heightened by being braised in extra virgin olive oil and with the addition of tangy tangerines. Served on the top of a Pecorino risotto it is a warming winter's dream.

4 servings

Braised Fennel and Tangerine

1 large fennel bulb, trimmed, sliced thin on a mandolin (Reserve fennel fronds for garnish)

2 small tangerines, sliced very thin (Use with a **thin skin** intact. Otherwise peel thick skin.)

6 garlic cloves, sliced thin

extra virgin olive oil, as needed

¼ teaspoon sea salt or to taste

1. Preheat oven to 350°F.

2. Oil a small baking dish. Layer half of the fennel, tangerines and garlic. Salt lightly.

3. Layer the remaining fennel, tangerines and garlic. Salt lightly. Compact by pressing down on the mixture.

4. Pour enough extra virgin olive oil to barely cover. Cover with a lid. Place in the oven.

5. Bake until soft and translucent (about forty-five minutes). Remove from the oven and reserve hot.

Risotto

2 cups vegetable broth (see Appareils chapter)

2 tablespoons the oil from the fennel

1 large shallot, minced (about ¼ cup)

2 garlic cloves, mashed

⅔ cup Vialone Nano rice (or Arborio rice)

⅓ cup Pinot Grigio wine

4 ounces Pecorino cheese, grated

2 tablespoons heavy cream

½ teaspoon sea salt and ⅛ teaspoon black pepper

1. Heat the vegetable broth and reserve hot.

2. In a wide-bottomed sauce pan, heat the oil until it shimmers. Add the shallot and sauté until soft or translucent. Add the garlic and sauté for another minute.

3. Add the rice and continue to cook without browning until the rice is coated with the oil and turns opaque, about two to three minutes.

4. Add enough hot broth to barely cover the rice. Stir the rice with the wooden spoon until the rice has

absorbed most of the broth and when the spoon is drawn through the rice it creates a wake.

5. Keep adding small amounts of the broth to the rice and stirring until the rice is creamy and has just a slight crunch. Add the wine and stir until absorbed.

6. Add the cheese and heavy cream. **Taste, Think, Transform** with salt, truffle salt and/or pepper.

7. Serve hot, topped with a portion of the braised fennel and tangerine. Garnish with fennel fronds

This dish is made even more amazing if Truffle Pecorino La Rustichella cheese is used in place of the Pecorino cheese but may only be found in specialty stores. Truffle salt is also a great enhancement.

. . . .

HARVEST VEGETABLE GRATIN

Having always loved vegetables from a young age, I find myself eating more and more vegetable entrées now. Concerned about environmental and health issues, this seems the wise thing to do. During late summer when our organic vegetable garden is heartily producing ripe vegetables; this dish is at its most flavorful moment.

8 entrée servings

Grains and Legumes

½ cup red quinoa

2 tablespoons extra virgin olive oil

½ cup Israeli couscous

½ cup red split lentils

3 cups vegetable broth (see Appareils chapter for a recipe) or filtered water

1 teaspoon kosher salt

1. Soak the quinoa in filtered water for one-half an hour or more. Drain well.

2. Heat a sauce pan over medium-high heat. Add the oil and when it shimmers add the couscous. Sauté the couscous until they turn light brown.

3. Add the lentils and quinoa. Toss until coated with the oil (about one minute).

4. Add the broth and salt. Bring to a boil, reduce heat, cover with a lid and simmer twelve to fifteen minutes until the liquid is absorbed. Remove from heat, uncover and reserve.

Gratin

1 large eggplant (about 1 ½ pounds), large diced

2 zucchini, large diced

1 red pepper, cored, seeded, large diced

1 yellow pepper, cored, seeded, large diced

1 large onion, peeled, cored, large diced

12 small garlic cloves, peeled, smashed but whole

1 tablespoon fresh rosemary leaves, minced

1 tablespoon fresh sage leaves, minced

¼ teaspoon black or Aleppo pepper or to taste

1 teaspoon kosher salt or to taste

½ cup extra virgin olive oil

4 small Roma tomatoes, large diced

reserved grains and legumes from above

1 cup Parmigiano Reggiano cheese, grated

1. Preheat the oven to 375°F.

2. In a fourteen-and-a-half by ten-inch baking dish, toss the eggplant, zucchini, peppers, onion, garlic, rosemary, sage, pepper, salt and olive oil. Place in the oven. Bake for fifteen minutes, stir and bake for fifteen more minutes.

3. Add the tomatoes and toss. Bake for ten more minutes.

4. Top the vegetables with the grains and legumes. Sprinkle the cheese over the entire top. Bake for an additional ten minutes until lightly browned on top. Remove from oven and serve hot.

ÉPIGRAMMES OF SPICY TOFU

Now don't be afraid of this tofu dish, it is tastier than you may think!

Just before graduation from the Culinary Institute of America, those of us who had volunteered to give weekly tours were given a dinner at the restaurant of our choice in New York City as a thank you. My group chose The Four Seasons Restaurant with chef Seppi Renggli at the helm. We could order dishes of our choosing from the menu. One of the dishes I chose was Épigrammes of Wild Boar as it sounded so exotic and it was. Originally épigrammes referred to slices of lambs' breast that are poached and pressed and then breaded and fried. This preparation of spicy tofu follows the pressing and breading but is also marinated and baked to render a crispy tofu cutlet. Definitely a meatless Monday must try!

4 servings

1 pound firm or extra firm organic tofu

1 tablespoon soy sauce

1 tablespoon roasted garlic rice vinegar

1 tablespoon sweet Sherry

1 tablespoon toasted sesame oil

2 tablespoons filtered water

1 teaspoon Asian chili paste or Sriracha (as you like)

2 teaspoons ginger, finely shredded on a microplane or ginger grater

2 tablespoons cornstarch or more (preferably organic)

1. Drain the tofu, wrap in cheesecloth and place on several layers of paper towel lined plate. Place another plate on top and weigh down with a kitchen brick or heavy canned tomatoes. Let it stand for at least thirty minutes or more.

2. Combine the soy sauce, rice vinegar, sherry, sesame oil, water, chili paste and ginger in a shallow baking pan just large enough to lay the tofu slices side by side. **Taste, Think, Transform** with soy sauce and/or vinegar if necessary.

3. Gently squeeze the tofu to release more water. Unwrap. (the cheese cloth may be boiled for three minutes, hung to dry and stored in a sealed plastic bag for future use)

4. Cut the tofu in half. Slice each half into four slices. Cut all eight slices in half diagonally to form triangle slices.

5. Place the tofu triangles into the marinade. Cover and refrigerate. Turn over occasionally to marinate equally. Marinate for a minimum of two hours or overnight.

6. Preheat the oven to 350°.

7. Drain the tofu and place on a sheet pan. Place the cornstarch in a fine mesh sieve and sprinkle each side of the tofu, coating equally.

8. Line a baking sheet pan with parchment paper. Place the coated tofu on the parchment paper not touching.

9. Place in the oven. After about twenty-five minutes turn the épigrammes over and bake another twenty-five minutes or until crispy brown on both sides. Best served hot alongside Sugar Snap Peas with Red Peppers in the Sides chapter.

ITALIAN BRAISED BUTTER BEANS

An Italian heirloom white pole bean known as corona beans are difficult to find in their dried variety but well worth the search. Dry gigante beans or large lima beans are good substitutes. They are sometimes found canned and called butterbeans. They are transformed slowly by this braising technique into an entrée that would please even the most discriminating carnivore. Plan for a total cooking time of three to three and a half hours.

6 entrée servings

1 pound dried corona beans (about 3 cups) soaked refrigerated overnight in filtered water

2 tablespoons extra virgin olive oil

2 large carrots, peeled, medium diced

1 medium onion, peeled, medium diced

4 tablespoons tomato paste

3 large garlic cloves minced

1 small fennel bulb, medium diced **or** 2 stalks celery, medium diced

1 quart vegetable broth (see Appareils chapter)

6 large fresh sage leaves, minced

1 tablespoon fresh rosemary, minced

2 springs fresh thyme tied together with butcher's twine

1 dried bay leaf

1 teaspoon sea salt and ¼ teaspoon black pepper

2 pieces Parmigiano Reggiano cheese rind (optional but highly suggested)

2 tablespoons gremolata (equal parts of lemon zest, coarse sea salt, minced garlic & chopped parsley)

6 tablespoons grated Parmigiano Reggiano cheese

1. Cover the dried beans with warm to hot filtered water two inches above the beans. When cooled, refrigerate overnight to rehydrate beans.

2. Preheat oven to 350°F.

3. Heat the olive oil in a heavy gauge braising pan. Add the carrots and onions and brown over medium high.

4. Add the tomato paste, garlic and fennel or celery. Stir until the tomato paste begins to brown.

5. Deglaze with two cups of vegetable stock, stirring with a wooden spoon to incorporate the caramelized bits stuck to the bottom of the pan called "fond".

6. Add the herbs, salt, black pepper, corona beans and Parmigiano Reggiano rind. Add more stock if necessary to completely cover the beans. Bring to a simmer, cover with a tight-fitting lid and place in the 350°F oven.

7. Stir every thirty minutes for two hours or more. Add more vegetable stock to keep the beans submerged in liquid as they braise. Continue braising until the beans turn from white to golden brown and are very soft. The stock will become thickened into a sauce. Add more stock if the beans become too dry. **Taste, Think, Transform** with salt if needed.

8. Discard the thyme springs, Parmigiano Reggiano rind and bay leaf. Divide into six servings and top each with the gremolata and grated Parmigiano Reggiano. Serve hot.

Using dried beans are key here to absorbing the flavors of the braise. The gremolata is a classic finishing touch that brightens the flavor of braises after the long-cooking time.

. . . .

CRISPY HAZELNUT AND BLACK RICE CROQUETTES

For several years while I was teaching at Seattle Culinary Academy we hosted an annual Harvest Dinner in conjunction with Seattle Central Community College Foundation to raise money for scholarships. We would invite a renowned Chef to create the menu and execute it with the instructors and students help. It became a well-respected annual event in Seattle. One year, early in the afternoon of the event, word came in that we were going to host five individuals who were vegetarians. Having no entrée suitable for them, I was asked, with the help of two students, to create and prepare an elegant entrée, worthy of the occasion. This is the dish that I created. It was warmly received by those individuals.

6 servings (12 croquettes)

Rice

½ cup black rice (or Thai black sticky rice)

1 pint filtered water

½ teaspoon kosher salt

1. Bring the rice water and salt to a boil in a sauce pan. Turn the heat down to a simmer. Cover with a lid and simmer until tender, about forty to sixty minutes, until all the water is absorbed. The rice will be shiny.

2. Uncover, spread on an oiled sheet pan and cool in refrigerator.

Mornay Sauce

1 ½ teaspoons unsalted butter

1 tablespoons all-purpose flour

¼ cup plus 2 tablespoons whole milk

⅛ teaspoon fresh grated nutmeg

¼ teaspoon kosher salt and ⅛ teaspoon black pepper

¼ cup Gruyère cheese grated (1 ounce)

2 tablespoons Parmigiano Reggiano cheese grated

1 egg yolk

1. Melt the butter in a small sauce pan. Add the flour and cook for three minutes, stirring with a whip constantly. Slowly whisk the milk, two tablespoons at a time, into the flour mixture, beating smooth after each addition. **Taste, Think, Transform** with nutmeg, salt and/or pepper. Simmer until thick and reaches a maximum temperature of 200°F. (see Appareils chapter for a review of Béchamel sauce)

2. Add the cheeses. Stir until melted. Remove the sauce from the heat and cool.

3. When cool slowly whip the egg yolk into the sauce. Chill.

(The recipe to this point may be made several hours to a day before.)

Croquettes

¾ cup hazelnuts peeled, toasted, (see Appareils chapter) coarsely chopped (divide into ¼ and ½ cups)

¼ cup Gruyère cheese grated (1 ounce)

½ cup Panko breadcrumbs

1 egg, beaten

1 teaspoon filtered water

1 teaspoon olive oil

¼ teaspoon kosher salt

¼ cup all-purpose flour

olive oil spray as needed

1. Preheat oven to 400°F.

2. Mix the cooled rice, Mornay sauce, one-fourth cup coarsely ground hazelnuts and one-fourth cup

Gruyère cheese together. Scoop up the mixture with a medium-sized oval scoop or roll into a long log and cut into twelve equal-size, compacted pieces. Use wet hands to shape each croquette.

3. Grind the remaining one-half cup of hazelnuts in a mini food processor until fine. Mix with the Panko breading.

4. Mix the egg, water, oil and salt together to make an egg wash.

5. Lightly dredge each piece of croquette in the flour. Shake off excess. Lay on a sheet pan.

6. Using one hand for wet and one hand for dry, dip in the egg wash. Next, coat with a mixture of finely chopped hazelnuts and Panko breading. Spray the bottom of the croquette and lay on a parchment paper or silicone mat lined sheet pan. Generously spray each with the olive oil spray.

7. Bake in the oven. After ten minutes turn each croquette over and continue to bake for about twenty to thirty minutes, until golden brown. Remove from oven.

Serve hot with sautéed chanterelle or shitake mushrooms sprinkled with chopped fresh fine herbs (parsley, chives, tarragon and chervil) on a bed of lightly wilted spinach with a splash of lemon juice if desired.

. . . .

DEEP DISH CHARD, FETA AND DILL PIE

Swiss chard is a lovely green vegetable in both my vegetable garden and flower beds. It is also a very delicious and nutritious vegetable, if prepared well. This dish is based on the savory Greek dish spanakopita, using chard in the place of the traditional spinach. Working with filo dough can be somewhat difficult but it is also very forgiving if following some very basic rules included in this recipe. This tart makes a charming vegetarian entrée. Cut into smaller pieces, it can be served as an appetizer or potluck offering.

6 to 8 servings

Filling

2 bunches Swiss chard, stem removed

1 bunch scallions, washed, roots removed, chopped fine

1 large leek, washed, white and 2 inches pale green, small diced

4 tablespoons extra virgin olive oil, divide

2 large eggs

1 large egg white

2 tablespoons extra virgin olive oil

1 ½ bunches dill weed, large stems removed, chopped

1 bunch Italian parsley, large stems removed, chopped

¾ teaspoon fresh ground nutmeg

½ teaspoon ground cumin

½ teaspoon sea salt

½ teaspoon fresh ground black pepper

2 tablespoons Parmigiano Reggiano cheese, finely grated

3 cups feta cheese, crumbled (12 ounces)

1. Chop the chard into one inch pieces. Wash and spin dry the chard three times to remove all soil.

2. In a wok or stir fry pan heat two tablespoons of olive oil. Sauté the scallions and leek until soft. Add the dry chard and toss the mixture with tongs until the chard is thoroughly wilted. Place in a colander to drain and let the mixture cool. Squeeze dry with hands or potato ricer.

3. In a large bowl mix the eggs, egg white, two tablespoons olive oil, dill, parsley, nutmeg, cumin, salt, black pepper, Parmigiano Reggiano, chard and feta cheese. Reserve.

Filo Assembly

½ box filo dough, defrosted overnight in the refrigerator

¼ to ½ cup extra virgin olive oil

1 large egg yolk

2 tablespoon milk

1 teaspoon sesame seeds (optional)

1. On a large countertop place two sheets of plastic wrap overlapping slightly with the filo dough rolled out on top. Completely cover the filo with plastic wrap, tucking the wrap under at the top of the filo. Place a wet and rung out dish towel over the top of the plastic wrap. Lightly oil a ten and one-half inch deep dish baking pan.

2. Working quickly, remove one sheet of filo, lay it flat and cover the rest up again. *Lightly* brush the sheet of filo with olive oil. Top with a second sheet of filo dough and lightly brush with olive oil. Continue this process until eight sheets have been brushed and placed on top of the others. Should a layer tear, just patch it with more filo dough.

3. Place the layers of filo in the oiled baking dish. With poultry shears trim the edges so they only come to the top of the baking dish rim. Evenly spread the chard filling in the filo pan.

4. Mix the egg yolk and milk together.

5. Preheat oven to 375°F.

6. Repeat step two, preparing a second set of eight layers of filo dough. **Do not** brush the top sheet with olive oil.

7. Place the eight layers over the filling. Trim excess filo with about one inch of excess dough to be tucked between the bottom dough and baking dish which will seal the tart. Quickly brush ***lightly and evenly*** the egg yolk and milk wash over the top.

8. Cut the tart all the way through into six equal pieces (or more if desired).

9. Sprinkle with optional sesame seeds.

10. Place on the middle shelf of the preheated oven. After fifteen to twenty minutes' check how brown it is on the top. Rotate the pan. If browned on top, lightly cover with foil to prevent further browning. Bake a total of forty-five minutes or until the filling is just set in the middle and crust is sufficiently brown.

11. Remove from the oven and let sit for ten minutes before serving. It may also be served at room temperature. Cover and refrigerate leftovers for up to two days.

It is possible to purchase a dry or old box of filo which can cause real problems. To ensure a better product, purchase the filo dough from a reputable store where it is restocked often. Refrigerate overnight before using. It is also possible to prep all the ingredients the day before, which is somewhat time consuming. Then cook the filling and bake the tart the next day.

Rather than a pie, it is possible to make this into a rectangular strudel form or individual triangles. Remember to score the strudel before baking so the crust won't crumble when cut into serving pieces.

SEAFOOD

Crispy Skin Salmon with Morel Cream Sauce

CRISPY SKIN SALMON WITH MOREL CREAM SAUCE

In the great Northwest, spring means fresh morel mushrooms from the mountains. Though it takes a bit of work to clean them, their alluring earthy flavor and texture pairs nicely with a tarragon, wine and cream sauce. Add crispy skin-side-up salmon fillets and spring asparagus for an enchanting dinner.

4 entrée servings

Morel Broth

8 ounces fresh morels, washed, halved lengthwise (about 2 cups)

1 cup room temperature filtered water

2 cups boiling filtered water

½ teaspoons sea salt

Salmon

1 ½ pounds wild sockeye or king salmon (divided into 4 fillets)

2 tablespoons safflower oil

Sauce

1 tablespoon unsalted butter

1 tablespoon extra virgin olive oil

½ cup shallots, peeled, minced

½ cup Sauvignon Blanc wine

2 tablespoons fresh lemon juice

2 cups mushroom broth (see directions below)

½ cup heavy cream

1 tablespoon fresh tarragon, chopped

½ teaspoon sea salt and fresh ground black pepper to taste

1. Place the morels in a heat-proof bowl with the room temperature water and salt. Pour the boiling water over the top. Cover with a lid or plastic wrap. Let sit for thirty minutes to an hour. Then lift the morels from the broth, leaving sediment on the bottom and reserve. Carefully ladle the broth from the bowl through a fine-mesh sieve over another bowl, leaving about one-half inch of broth and sediment. Reserve the strained broth. Discard the sediment broth.

2. Pat the four salmon fillets dry. Scrape the scales and dab moisture from the skin-side of the salmon with a paper towel.

3. Heat the safflower oil in a cast-iron pan over high heat. Add the salmon with the skin side down. Fry until the skin is crispy, about one minutes. Flip over and fry for another one to two minutes. The skin should be crispy and the flesh should be cooked medium-rare. Place on a plate skin-side up and in a closed area like a microwave to reserve (but do not cook).

4. To make the sauce, melt the butter and olive oil in a sauté pan over medium-high heat. Add the shallots and cook until softened. Raise the heat to high. Deglaze the pan with the wine, lemon juice, and reserved two cups of strained mushroom broth. Simmer until reduced to about three-fourths of a cup is left in the pan. Add the reserved mushrooms and cream. Simmer until the sauce is thickened to a nappe consistency (coats the back of a spoon).

5. Place the salmon, skin-side up on four plates. Pour the sauce and morels around or over the top of the salmon. Serve hot.

PAN ROASTED HALIBUT WITH FENNEL AND KALAMATA OLIVE COMPOTE

In the spring, pristine fresh halibut arrives locally from the waters around Orcas Island and the deep waters of Alaska. At the same time the winter leeks in my garden are at their prime and fresh fennel bulb is still available. This compote accentuates but does not overpower the mild flavor of the halibut. I use bronze fennel pollen that I collect and dry in the summer to highlight the fennel flavor, but if fennel pollen is not available finely ground fennel seeds will suffice.

4 servings

4 ounces leek, white part only (about 1 cup)

14 ounces fennel bulb with fronds (about 4 cups)

1 tablespoon unsalted butter

4 tablespoons extra virgin olive oil, divided

½ teaspoon sea salt or to taste

⅛ teaspoon fresh ground black pepper to taste

2 large Roma tomatoes, seeded and sliced lengthwise into ¼ inch batons

½ cup Kalamata olives, pitted and slice in half lengthwise

⅓ cup fresh squeezed lemon juice (about 1 large lemon)

⅔ cup Sauvignon Blanc wine (or a dry white wine without oak)

1 ½ pounds fresh halibut fillets cut into 4 equal portions (6 ounces each)

1 teaspoon fennel pollen or finely ground fennel seeds (in mortar and pestle)

½ teaspoon sea salt or to taste

1 tablespoon reserved fennel fronds roughly chopped

1. Preheat the oven to 375°F.

2. Cut the leek in half lengthwise, wash well between the layers. Slice one-fourth inch crosswise. Remove and trim the fennel fronds (stalks and leaves). Reserve

1 tablespoon of the fennel fronds leaves for garnish. Slice the bulb in half and wash. Cut into one-inch long by one-fourth inch wide batons.

3. Heat the butter and two tablespoons olive oil in a large oven proof sauté pan over moderate heat.

4. Add the leeks and fennel to the pan. Season with the salt and black pepper. Sauté until soft and slightly browned.

5. In the meantime, brush the halibut fillets with the remaining two tablespoons of olive oil. Sprinkle with sea salt and fennel pollen or ground fennel seed.

6. When the leeks and fennel are slightly browned add the tomato batons, olives, lemon juice and wine. Bring to a simmer and place the prepared halibut fillets on top. Place in the oven.

7. Roast the halibut until it turns from opaque to white and slightly flakes when a paring knife is inserted to the middle of the fillet, about ten to sixteen minutes depending on the thickness of the filets. Do not overcook. Remove the halibut filets to a warm place. Place the sauté pan over moderately high heat and reduce the juices until slightly syrupy. **Taste, Think, Transform** with salt and lemon juice.

8. Divide the fennel mixture onto four plates. Top with the halibut fillets and sprinkle with the fennel fronds. Serve hot.

. . . .

BAKED CHARMOULA AND ALMOND CRUSTED RED SNAPPER

Charmoula is a classic Moroccan fish marinade with a robust flavor that enhances most mild flavored types of white fish. In this preparation, the fish is first marinated and then rolled in ground almonds to form a crust when baked. The reserved marinade is then drizzled over the top, with the optional addition of finely minced preserved lemon and chopped parsley. Spicy, tangy moist and mellow fish bursts in the mouth upon the first bite of this Mediterranean delight!

4 entrée servings

¼ cup packed Italian parsley leaves, washed, dried

¼ cup packed cilantro leaves, washed, dried

3 cloves garlic, minced

1 ½ teaspoon sweet paprika

1 teaspoon ground cumin

⅛ teaspoon crushed saffron

¼ teaspoon cayenne pepper (or to taste)

½ teaspoon sea salt

¼ teaspoon fresh ground black pepper

3 tablespoons fresh lemon juice

¼ cup extra virgin olive oil

1 pound red snapper, cut into 4 fillets

½ cup ground almonds or almond meal

olive oil spray as needed

1 tablespoon doubled concentrated tomato paste

1 tablespoon preserved lemons, wash, pith removed, minced (optional)

1 tablespoon Italian parsley minced

1. To make the charmoula chop the parsley, cilantro and garlic, in a small food processor. Add paprika, cumin, saffron, cayenne, salt, pepper and lemon juice and blend thoroughly. Slowly add the olive oil into the mixture, blending well. Reserve one-fourth cup of the marinade for drizzling on the baked fish.

2. Wash and pat the fish fillets very dry. Remove any bones, if necessary. Rub both sides of the fish with the charmoula and place in a covered glass or ceramic dish and let sit for twenty to thirty minutes at room temperature.

3. Preheat oven to 400°F.

4. Dredge the fish in the ground almonds. Place on a sheet pan that has been sprayed with olive oil spray. Also, spray the tops of the fish and bake for eight to twelve minutes depending on the thickness or until the fish just flakes and crust is golden brown.

5. Mix the tomato paste and a bit of water into the reserved charmoula to make the sauce. **Taste, Think, Transform** with salt, cayenne, and/or lemon juice. Drizzle this over the plated fish and sprinkle with the optional preserved lemons and parsley.

. . . .

PAELLA MARINARA

On a cool but sunny spring day in Malaga, Spain my husband and I enjoyed a fresh and delicious seafood paella. I had been drawn towards this trip to Spain by my studies of the food and culture. Paella, among all Spanish dishes, represents not only the great flavors of Spain but the culture of the table as paella is a dish that is placed in the middle of the table or fire and all persons enjoy eating from the communal dish. The term "paella" is derived from the Latin word for pan "patella." It is the dimpled bottom seasoned steel pan that the rice, if prepared properly, will form a crust on the bottom of the pan called a socarrat.

8 servings (17 to 18-inch paella pan measured at widest point or two 12-inch cast iron pans)

36 fresh mussels washed, de-bearded

5 cup filtered water, divided

½ pound white fish bones (optional)

½ teaspoon saffron, finely crushed

8 garlic cloves finely minced

2 tablespoons minced flat leaf parsley

2 teaspoons Pimentón Dulce or sweet smoked paprika

1 tablespoon fresh thyme leaves

24 medium sized shrimp, peel, (save shells) devein

1 pound calamari, rings and tentacles cleaned

1 pound fresh white fish (halibut), boned and cut into 1 inch pieces

1 ½ teaspoons sea salt

½ cup extra virgin olive oil

1 large onion, peeled and small, diced

1 large green pepper, seeded and cut into small strips

3 large Roma tomatoes, seeded and cut into small dice

2 cups Bomba (or Arborio) rice

½ bunch flat leaf or Italian parsley, washed, dried and roughly chopped

1 large lemon cut into 8 wedges

1. Place eighteen mussels in a large sauce pan with one cup of water. Cover and bring to a boil. Remove the mussels once they are open (about ten minutes) and reserve cooled.

2. To the remaining mussel water add four more cups of water, fish bones if available, and the shrimp shells. Simmer for fifteen minutes. Strain the stock into another sauce pan. Add the crushed saffron and reserve hot.

3. In a mini-food processor grind the garlic, parsley, Pimentón and thyme leaves with a small amount of water to form a paste. Reserve.

4. Pat dry the shrimp, calamari, fish and remaining mussels. Sprinkle with a good quality sea salt and rest for ten minutes.

5. Heat a grill or barbeque to about 350°F

6. Heat a seventeen-inch paella pan on the grill. (May use two twelve-inch cast iron pans if no paella pan is available.) Add the olive oil. Add the onions, green peppers and tomatoes. Sauté until softened to create a sofrito, about ten to twelve minutes.

7. Stir in the rice and spice paste. Coat all with the oil. Spread out the rice until level and covering the bottom of the pan.

8. Pour in the hot broth carefully and bring to a boil. Reduce heat. Cover with a lid or another pan and simmer for twelve minutes, rotating if necessary to cook all the rice equally.

9. Arrange the shrimp, calamari, fish and mussels over the rice. Cover again and continue to cook for about six to ten minutes longer until the rice is *al punto* (al dente or to-the-bite) and the mussels are open and shrimp and fish are just cooked through.

10. Remove the pan to two large towels. Cover the pan with foil and then cover with the towel ends. Let rest at least five to ten minutes. (This will finish cooking the rice) Sprinkle with the remaining parsley and serve with lemon wedges.

Paella Marinara

2 teaspoons Chinese fermented black beans thoroughly rinsed and roughly chopped

½ teaspoon garlic, minced

½ teaspoon chili flakes

¼ cup sunflower seed oil or grape seed oil

1 ½ teaspoons toasted sesame seed oil

Black Cod and Sauce

1 ½ pound thick-end wild black cod filet cut into 4 portions

1 tablespoon Dijon mustard

1 tablespoon honey

1 tablespoon soy sauce

½ cup fresh tangerine juice

1 teaspoon Orange Muscat Champagne vinegar

1 tangerine sectioned (optional)

½ teaspoon sea salt or to taste

1. Several hours or one day before prepare the tangerine oil by combining all the tangerine oil ingredients. Bring to a simmer in a small sauce pan. Let gently bubble over very low heat for ten minutes. Remove from heat and cool completely. Refrigerate overnight if prepared the day before.

2. One hour before baking, scale the black cod skin by lightly scraping the skin against the direction of the scales under running water. Pat dry.

3. Place the black cod portions skin side down in an oven-proof baking pan lightly coated with tangerine chili oil. Top with three tablespoons of the tangerine chili oil. Reserve the remaining oil with fermented black beans and chilies. Let fish sit at room temperature for at least thirty minutes up to one hour.

4. Preheat the oven to 425°F.

5. Place the pan of black cod filets in the oven and bake for eight to twelve minutes or until the fish begins to flake when touched. Do not overcook.

6. While the fish is baking, combine the mustard, honey, soy sauce, tangerine juice, vinegar and remaining tangerine chili oil in a sauté pan over medium high heat. Simmer until it becomes a glaze that lightly

TANGERINE CHILI GLAZED BLACK COD

At an International Institute of Wine and Food conference held in Seattle, I had the great fortune to meet Barbara Tropp of San Francisco's China Moon Restaurant. She led a salt and soy sauce tasting class which I soon would recreate for my students. In her China Moon Cookbook, she has a recipe for a chili-orange oil on which this recipe is roughly based. I prefer the deeper flavor of a tangerine to that of an orange. I find it the perfect complement to enhance the flavor of black cod that is a delicate and luxuriously buttery fish, which is sometimes called sablefish. It is found in my local fish market in spring and again in the fall.

4 servings

Tangerine Chili Oil

1 tablespoon tangerine zest (from one large tangerine)

coats the back of a spoon. **Taste, Think, Transform** with sea salt and/or vinegar.

7. Plate the baked black cod filets and cover each with a portion of the glaze and optional tangerine sections. Serve hot.

Fermented black beans (Douchi) are found in Asian markets or from Amazon. They are black soy beans dried and fermented with salt. They come in bags and can be stored for months. You may find them in a jar, but the flavor is not the same. The Orange Muscat Champagne vinegar is a Trader Joe's staple.

. . . .

CRAB AND SPINACH CRÊPES GÂTEAU

I had the great fortune to meet Julia Child twice. Both times were at American Institute of Food and Wine events, the organization that she and Robert Mondavi founded. At the first meeting, I approached Julia with a well-worn original edition of Mastering the Art of French Cooking hoping for an autograph. She was most welcoming and was delighted that I was a chef instructor. She encouraged me in my teaching endeavors. It had been in the 1970's that I created this recipe for a fine dining nightly special, inspired by a recipe in that very book. At the second event, I also met Robert and Margrit Mondavi and was blessed with a kiss on each cheek! I think you will find this recipe delicious and worthwhile, though somewhat challenging and time consuming. This is my loving tribute to Julia.

8 to 10 entrée servings

Crêpes (15 nine-inch crêpes)

3 tablespoons unsalted butter

6 large eggs

2 cups whole milk

1 teaspoon salt

8 ounces sifted flour (about 1 ¾ cup plus 1 tablespoon sifted)

safflower oil as needed

1. Melt the butter in a small sauce pan. Simmer until it just begins to turn brown. Remove from heat and reserve warm but not hot.

2. Whisk the eggs and milk together.

3. Slowly whisk in the salt and flour. Stir in the melted browned butter. Let rest for at least one hour.

4. Heat a crêpe or sauté pan. Brush with the safflower oil. Whisk the batter again just before cooking. Pour in a slight one-quarter cup of batter and swirl to coat the bottom of the pan. The use of a small offset metal spatula is helpful to spread out the batter before it sets. Cook until lightly brown. Flip it over and cook for a few more seconds. Remove immediately and reserve slightly overlapping each crêpe on a sheet pan.

Mornay Sauce

4 tablespoons unsalted butter

5 tablespoons all-purpose flour

2 ¾ cups scalded milk (to scald milk, heat just until bubbles form on the sides of the pan)

½ teaspoon salt

⅛ teaspoon fresh ground black pepper

Pinch of nutmeg

¼ cup heavy cream

1 cup Gruyère cheese, grated (divided)

1. Melt the butter and add the flour. Cook until slightly grainy in texture but not browned. (review Béchamel technique in the Appareils chapter)

2. Whisk in the scalded milk and seasonings. Bring to a simmer. Stir in heavy cream.

3. Stir in all but two tablespoons of the cheese. Reserve hot.

Spinach Filling

1 tablespoon unsalted butter

1 tablespoon shallots, minced

1 cup chopped spinach, squeezed very dry (10-ounce bag of frozen spinach thawed)

½ teaspoon salt

1. Melt the butter. Add the shallots and cook until translucent.

2. Add the spinach and one cup of the Mornay sauce. Simmer for a few minutes while stirring. Season with salt and set aside.

Crab Filling

1 tablespoon unsalted butter

1 tablespoon shallots, minced

1 ½ cup picked Dungeness or blue crabmeat

(If picking your own crab use a whole crab weighing a minimum of 1 ¾ pounds).

1. Melt the butter. Add the shallots and cook until translucent.

2. Add the crab and one cup of the Mornay sauce. Set aside.

Assembly and Baking

About 2 tablespoons unsalted butter (divided)

1. Preheat oven to 400°F. Butter a round nine-inch bottom plate from a spring-form metal pan without the sides. The plate will make it easier to move to a decorative platter when baked. Place the plate on a larger sheet pan with rim.

2. Place a crêpe in the bottom and spread with a full one-fourth cup the spinach filling. Press another crêpe on top and spread with a full one-fourth cup of the crab filling.

3. Continue alternating layering crêpes and fillings with a total of fourteen crêpes.

4. Place the last crêpe on top. Pour the remaining Mornay sauce over the top and sides. Top with the remaining two tablespoons of cheese. Dot with four pea-sized bits of butter. At this point it may be reserved cold for a few hours before baking.

5. Bake for twenty-five to thirty minutes until heated thoroughly and browned. Cut into pie-shaped wedges to serve.

To ensure a smooth crêpe batter, sift the flour before measuring and again when adding to the egg and milk mixture. The batter will probably make up to twenty crêpes. Enjoy the excess crêpes with your favorite jam.

POULTRY

Wine Braised Duck Legs on Creamy Polenta

WINE BRAISED DUCK LEGS

The smell of duck slowly braising in an aromatic wine sauce will permeate the air of the entire home. Then nestle it into a bed of creamy polenta, adorned with sautéed mushrooms that will charm even the most reluctant guest. This is the dish to be served on a crisp autumn evening in the Northwest!

4 servings

Duck Legs

4 duck leg and thighs with skin attached

1 teaspoon sea salt and ⅛ teaspoon fresh ground black pepper

1 tablespoon extra virgin olive oil

½ small onion, small diced

1 large fennel bulb, small diced (about 12 ounces)

1 teaspoon fresh rosemary minced

2 tablespoons tomato paste

2 cups hearty red wine, plus more if necessary (Merlot, Zinfandel or Syrah)

2 tablespoons demi-glace (optional but delicious!)

2 tablespoons soft unsalted butter

Polenta

4 ½ cups rich chicken broth (a recipe in the Appareils chapter)

2 tablespoon unsalted butter

1 teaspoon sea salt

¾ cup polenta

½ cup heavy cream or more

¼ cup Parmigiano Reggiano cheese, finely grated (about 1 ounce)

Sautéed Mushrooms

2 tablespoons extra virgin olive oil

1 small shallots, minced

8 ounces chanterelle or cremini mushrooms, cleaned, sliced

1 teaspoon fresh rosemary, minced

1. Wash and dry the duck legs. Prick their skin all over with a fork. Season both sides with salt and pepper.

2. Preheat the oven to 325°F.

3. Heat an enamel lined Dutch oven or non-reactive braiser over medium high heat with the olive oil. Add the duck legs skin side down. Lightly brown both sides of the legs. Remove the legs from the pan.

4. Drain all but two tablespoons of the rendered fat from the pan. Add the onions, fennel and rosemary. Sauté until lightly browned. Add the tomato paste and stir until well blended. Deglaze with the red wine. Gently stir with a wooden spoon to dissolve any browned bits stuck to the pan.

5. Nestle the reserved duck legs into the mixture skin side down. Bring to a simmer, cover with a tight-fitting lid and place in the preheated oven. Braise for one hour.

6. Turn the legs over after the first hour of braising. If the sauce seems a bit dry add more wine. Braise covered for another hour.

7. In the meantime, prepare the polenta. Bring the stock or water, butter and salt to a boil. Whisk in the polenta. Bring back to a boil, cover with a lid and place in the oven for one hour. Remove from the oven. It will still be thin. Add the cream and cheese. Reserve in a warm place with lid on.

8. During the last few minutes that the duck legs are braising, heat a sauté pan with two tablespoons of the olive oil over high heat. Add the shallots, mushrooms and rosemary. Toss and sauté until golden brown. Reserve hot.

9. Remove the braised duck legs from the oven and pan, reserve hot. If the sauce is thin, place it over medium high heat and reduce until syrupy. Add the demi-glace, if using. Remove from the heat. **Taste, Think, Transform** with salt, black pepper and/or butter if desired.

10. On a platter or individual plates, place the creamy polenta. Top with the duck legs and wine-fennel mixture. Top with the sautéed mushrooms and garnish with a sprig of rosemary. Enjoy hot!

· ·

DUCK BREAST WITH RED CURRANT SAUCE

Years ago, when we owned a rustic cabin in the Cascade Mountains, we would forage for three kinds of wild huckleberries in late August. One was a sweet blue huckleberry, another was a tart purple huckleberry and the most floral scented was a tiny red huckleberry which would take hours to gather. I created this recipe to utilize these delicious berries. Since we no longer have access to these berries I began using fresh red currants in season which give a similar sweet tartness to the delicate gamy poultry.

4 servings

4 boneless duck breasts

1 teaspoon coriander seeds

½ teaspoon green cardamom seeds removed from pods (about 12 pods)

1 teaspoon dried juniper berries

½ teaspoon fresh ground black pepper

1 teaspoon kosher salt

1 tablespoon extra virgin olive oil

1 large shallot, peeled and minced (about 1 ½ ounce)

1 cup Sauvignon Blanc wine

2 tablespoons currant jelly

1 ½ cups fresh red currants, washed and stemmed (divided in half)

1 tablespoon superfine cane sugar

2 tablespoons Chambord liqueur

2 tablespoons room temperature unsalted butter

1. Wash the duck breasts and pat dry with paper towels. Trim any excess fat. Gently score the fat side making cross hatch marks with a knife, going almost but not into the flesh.

2. Lightly toast the coriander, cardamom and juniper seeds in a small sauté pan over moderate heat until the juniper skins turn shiny and give off a fragrant smell. Cool and grind in a spice grinder or mortar and pestle. Mix these with the black pepper and salt. Sprinkle this mixture on both sides of each duck breast and refrigerate overnight or for a minimum of four hours.

3. Heat a large sauté pan and add the olive oil. When the oil slightly ripples, add the shallots and sauté until they are slightly brown. Deglaze with the white wine, currant jelly and three-fourths cup of the currants. Simmer until the liquid in the sauté pan is reduced by half. Puree the sauce through a food mill and then strain through a fine mesh sieve back into the sauté pan. This sauce may be reserved cold for several hours at this point. Sprinkle the remaining ¾ cup of currants with the superfine sugar. Add to the Chambord liqueur and reserved sauce.

4. Heat a sauté pan over medium-high heat. (If working on a gas stove start with high heat. If working on an electric stove start with medium-high heat.) Pat dry the duck breasts and place fat side down in the hot pan. Cook for four minutes, basting the meat with hot rendered fat. Reduce the heat to low and cook for another ten to twelve minutes. Turn the breast over and cook for one more minute. Remove and keep warm while finishing the sauce. (The duck breasts must rest for at least five minutes before slicing.)

5. Drain and reserve the duck fat for another use. Heat the reserved sauce in this pan until simmering.

Remove from heat and swirl in the butter incorporating with a whip.

6. Slice each duck breast on an angle into one-quarter-inch slices with fat intact.

7. Pool the sauce on each plate and fan the duck breasts over the top. Serve immediately.

Rather than buy superfine cane sugar, which can be quite expensive, just pulse granulated cane sugar in a blender until superfine in texture. This superfine sugar also dissolves in hot and cold drinks much faster than granulated.

. . . .

ARROZ CON CHICKEN AND CHORIZO PAELLA

Do you consider rice a side dish? Well, this classic dish of paella from Valencia (Spain's eastern coast) is sometimes also called arroz con which means "rice with" for rice is the mainstay of this dish with other complimentary ingredients added to enhance. The Moors introduced rice and saffron to Spain, building elaborate irrigation systems making it possible to grow the rice in this arid country. Bomba rice from Valencia makes the best paella but Italian Arborio rice is an acceptable substitute although the texture will be creamier. Picada is the mixture of almonds, garlic, parsley, saffron and sometimes smoked paprika ground to a paste that gives a distinctive taste and yellow color to the dish.

8 servings (17 to 18-inch paella pan measured at widest point or two 12-inch cast iron pans)

8 boneless, skin-on chicken thighs (about 3 to 3 ½ pounds)

1 tablespoon kosher salt

2 tablespoons blanched Marcona almonds, chopped (about 20 almonds)

6 large garlic cloves, minced

¼ cup parsley, minced, divided in half

½ teaspoon Pimentón Dulce or sweet smoked paprika

¼ teaspoon saffron threads, crumbled

¼ cup extra virgin olive oil

5 cups rich chicken broth (a recipe in the Appareils chapter)

1 large onion, peeled and small diced (about 2 cups diced)

1 large green pepper, seeded and small diced (about 1 ¼ cups diced)

1 pound ground chorizo sausage

2 large Roma tomatoes, peeled, seeded and grated on a hand box grater

¼ cup dry Sherry

2 cups Bomba (or Arborio) rice

1 ½ teaspoons of kosher salt or to taste

1 (14-ounce) can of artichoke hearts, drained, washed and quartered

1 (10 ounce jar) roasted Piquillo peppers sliced ¼ inch lengthwise

1. Preheat a grill to medium.

2. Sprinkle the chicken thighs all over with the kosher salt. Place in a pan, cover and refrigerate for at least one hour or overnight. Rinse and pat dry with paper towels.

3. To make the picada, pulse the almonds to a fine crumble in a mini-food processor. Add and pulse the garlic, half of the parsley, Pimentón and saffron until very fine. Add two tablespoons of the broth and reserve.

4. Heat the remaining broth and keep hot.

5. Heat the oil in the paella pan on the grill. Place the chicken thighs skin side down and brown over medium heat being careful not to have skin stick to the pan. Turn over and brown the other side. Cook to internal temperature of 165°F.

6. Move the chicken to a dish in a warm place. Drain off all but ½ cup of the oil in the pan. Add the onions, green peppers and sausage to the pan. Cook until the vegetables are softened and sausage is browned.

7. Add the tomatoes and Sherry. Cook the Sherry until almost dry.

8. Add the rice and picada mixture. Coat the rice well with the pan mixture. Spread out the rice until level and covering the bottom of the pan.

9. Pour in all the hot broth. **Taste, Think, Transform** the broth with salt. Bring to a boil. Add the chicken back to the pan. Simmer uncovered for about twenty to thirty minutes until the rice is just tender, rotating the pan if necessary to cook all the rice equally.

10. Arrange the artichoke hearts and sliced Piquillos around the pan. Remove the pan to two large towels. Cover the pan with foil and then cover with the towel ends. Let rest at least five to ten minutes. (This will finish cooking the rice) Sprinkle with the remaining parsley.

I purchase the Marcona almonds at Costco, Bomba rice at the Spanish Table online and the Piquillo peppers at Trader Joes or our local Skagit Valley Co-op.

. . . .

ZUCCHINI AND TARRAGON STUFFED CHICKEN BREAST

At the hilltop Villa of Sra Lorenza de Medici near Coltibuono, Italy I attended a cooking class featuring a sumptuous boneless stuffed rabbit that was quite simply elegant. It was easy to prepare if one could find a rabbit and knew how to bone it out. Because that is a difficult task I went about recreating this lovely dish with chicken breast in place of rabbit. Interestingly, the stuffing is a zucchini frittata that would be great all on its own but even more delicious stuffed in a thinly pounded boneless, skinless chicken breast and served with a simple sauce of pan drippings, white wine and butter. Serve with sweet yellow peppers roasted with extra virgin olive oil, garlic and basil as a light but tasty accompaniment.

Serves 8

2 large zucchini (about 2 cups chopped)

4 tablespoons extra virgin olive oil, divided

1 tablespoon fresh tarragon, chopped

5 large eggs, whipped lightly

½ teaspoon sea salt and ⅛ teaspoon fresh ground black pepper

8 skinless, boneless halved chicken breasts

1 ½ tablespoons unsalted butter

1 ⅓ cup dry white wine (Pinot Grigio)

1. Wash and discard the ends of the zucchini. Cut into two inch rounds. Place in the food processor and pulse until chopped small.

2. Heat a sauté pan over medium heat. Add one tablespoon of the oil. Sauté the zucchini until most of the liquid is evaporated and the zucchini is cooked. Place in a fine mesh strainer or colander and allow to drain for a few minutes. Squeeze very dry with your hands or through a potato ricer.

3. Heat another sauté pan. Add one tablespoon of the oil. Add the zucchini, tarragon, salt, and pepper and mix well. Add the whipped eggs. Cook until the eggs are set on the bottom. Flip the mixture onto a flat plate or back of a sheet pan and then slide back into the sauté pan. Cook on the other side just until the eggs are barely set. Remove from the heat.

4. Preheat oven to 350°F.

5. Place the chicken breasts between two sheets of plastic wrap and pound gently until about one-quarter of an inch evenly thick. Try not to tear the meat. Discard the plastic wrap. On each chicken breast place a portion of the zucchini frittata down the center. Roll the chicken breast up and tuck in the ends. Use toothpicks to hold together, if necessary.

6. Spread the remaining two tablespoons of oil in a roasting pan. Lay the chicken rolls flap side down in the oil. Rub the top of the roulades (chicken rolls) with some of the oil. Season with salt and black pepper. Add the butter and half of the wine to the pan.

7. Place uncovered in the oven. Roast for about forty minutes, check temperature and continue to cook until the chicken is just cooked through to 165°F. Remove from the oven. Remove the chicken from the pan and keep in a warm place. Place the pan over a burner. Deglaze the pan with the remaining wine. Cook for a

few minutes. **Taste, Think, Transform** with salt and/or black pepper. Remove toothpicks. Slice the chicken breasts diagonally. Strain the pan juices over the top of the chicken slices. Serve hot.

. . . .

ROASTED ACHIOTE TURKEY TENDERLOIN

In the 1980's my husband and I took a trip to explore the wonderful restaurants of the San Francisco Bay area. We were amazed and awed at Chez Panisse and Stars. Then we headed north for wine sampling in the Napa Valley. On our way, we stopped at a wayside restaurant with a lot of cars in the parking lot. We were astonished to find the food at Mustards Grill to be so wonderful. Years later, when Cindy Pawlycyn wrote a cookbook, I cooked my way through that book. This recipe is my take on one of those dishes. Turkeys are abundant in Mexico and I have found the tenderloins to be a nice roast for a crowd.

8 servings

1 box achiote paste (3 ½ ounces), broken into small pieces

¼ cup Sherry vinegar

¼ cup dry white wine

½ cup fresh orange juice (about 1 large orange)

1 tablespoon orange zest (from 1 large orange)

1 tablespoon honey

1 tablespoon garlic, minced

1 tablespoon Mexican dried oregano

2 teaspoons ground cumin

½ teaspoon Pimentón Dulce or smoky paprika

½ teaspoon fresh ground black pepper

1 tablespoon kosher salt

⅓ cup extra virgin olive oil

2 pounds skinless, boneless turkey breast tenderloins (about 4 each)

1. In a blender thoroughly mix the achiote paste, vinegar, white wine, orange juice, zest, honey, garlic, oregano, cumin, Pimentón, black pepper and salt. Add the olive oil and pulse to blend.

2. Wash the turkey tenders and pat dry with paper towels. Place in a non-reactive pan and pour the achiote mixture over and under the turkey. Cover and refrigerate overnight.

3. Preheat the oven to 350°F. Remove the turkey from the refrigerator and let stand at room temperature for half an hour.

4. Place the turkey tenders on a rack in a roasting pan lined with foil. Roast on the middle shelf of the oven until the internal temperature of the turkey is 165°F in the thickest part, about thirty to forty-five minutes.

5. Place the turkey on a cutting board and tent with foil for twenty minutes or until juices are redistributed.

6. Slice thinly on the bias.

Serve the sliced turkey on a bed of Black Bean Salsa found in the Starters chapter. Drizzle with thin crème fraîche or sour cream thinned with milk.

. . . .

ROSEMARY LEMON CHICKEN

This Greek inspired roast chicken recipe has taken various turns through the years. It is a recipe that I make at least once a month. The vegetables on the bottom of the pan change according to the season. The marinade has changed very little. Begin marinating at least one day in advance. In the summer, I may grill the chicken, placing the vegetables on rosemary skewers but during cool weather it is roasted. The fragrance imparted is alluring.

4 servings

3 ½ to 4 pounds whole chicken

12 medium garlic cloves, peeled, finely chopped (about 1 ounce)

⅔ cup fresh lemon juice (about 4 medium lemons)

¼ cup extra virgin olive oil

2 tablespoons fresh rosemary, coarsely chopped (about 4 sprigs)

1 tablespoon kosher salt

½ teaspoon fresh ground black pepper

Additional salt and black pepper to taste

Extra virgin olive oil as needed

Optional vegetables:

(Use about 4 cups of mixed raw vegetables)

potatoes	Roma tomatoes
Picholine olives with pits	zucchini
baby artichoke hearts	red peppers
parsnips	yellow peppers
kohlrabi	fennel
cipollini	red onion slices with core attached
carrots	

1. Wash and pat dry the chicken. With poultry shears or knife remove the wing tips, excess fat, and tail. Freeze these parts to make stock at a future date. Discard any organ meats that may be inside the bird.

2. Mix the garlic, lemon juice, olive oil, rosemary, salt and black pepper.

3. Place the chicken in an oven plastic bag. Pour the marinade over the top. Tie the bag closed. Place in the refrigerator for one to three days, turning over every twelve hours.

4. Preheat oven to 400°F.

5. In a large baking pan place the desired vegetables cut into two-inch pieces. Place the chicken breast side up with the juices on the vegetables. Discard the oven plastic bag. Season with salt, pepper and drizzle with extra olive oil.

6. Roast for forty minutes. Turn the chicken breast side down and roast another twenty minutes or until 165°F measured between the thigh and breast.

7. Rest the bird for ten minutes tented under foil. Carve the chicken and serve with vegetables and pan juices.

8. **Taste, Think, Transform** with salt and/or black pepper.

CHICKEN AND PRESERVED LEMON TAGINE

Being paraded past a hot, steamy Moroccan kitchen lined with metal coucoussiers, a rounded pot with a round top steamer, I began to imagine the meal I was about to consume. I had read about the preparation of aromatic tagines in a bottom pot, while couscous steamed above but now I was to enjoy this fragrant preparation. After enjoying a lamb kefta and harira soup a bowl of couscous topped with chicken tagine was placed in front of me. The fragrant smell wafted upward and I enjoyed, much like one smells the bouquet of a fine wine before tasting the delightful flavors. What I then tasted was much more than I ever imagined. The meal was finished with honey cakes and traditional mint tea. Prior to leaving, a sprinkle of rose water was shaken on my hands from a quite decorative, round blue pottery vessel with a long tin neck. Ah, the fragrance of Morocco!

4 servings

Couscous

1 cups couscous

1 cinnamon stick

2 whole star anise pods

½ teaspoon cumin seeds

2 edible dried rosebuds (optional)

2 tablespoons cup extra-virgin olive oil

½ teaspoon sea salt

Tagine

1 cup Picholine olives with pits

2 tablespoons extra virgin olive oil

3 cups onion very finely chopped (about 1 large onion)

3 large garlic cloves mashed

½ teaspoon crushed saffron threads

½ teaspoon ground ginger

2 ½ cups rich chicken broth or more (found in the Appareils chapter)

8 chicken thighs with skin and bones **or** 1 whole chicken cut in 8 pieces

sea salt and fresh ground pepper to taste

¼ cup fresh lemon juice

2 tablespoons flat leaf parsley chopped

2 tablespoons cilantro chopped

1 preserved lemon, peel only finely julienned (optional but recommended)

Couscous (Prepare first and keep hot)

1. Fill a couscousière or pan with a steamer insert half way full of water. Place the spices in the water and bring to a simmer. Place the perforated steam basket on top to get hot. Cover with a lid.

2. Place the couscous in a bowl and toss using your fingers with a small amount of warm filtered water to just barely moisten.

3. Place the couscous in the top compartment of the couscousière over the simmering aromatic water. A few pieces may fall through the holes but most will stay in the top to cook. Steam uncovered for forty-five minutes.

4. Add more water to the steamer pan if running dry and bring to a simmer again.

5. Place the couscous in a bowl again and toss with the olive oil and salt.

6. Place the couscous in the top of the couscousière again and steam for another forty-five minutes.

Taste, Think, Transform with salt. Serve hot.

Tagine (Cook while the couscous is steaming)

1. Drain and wash the olives. Cover with water in a small sauce pan. Bring to a boil, turn down to a simmer. Simmer for ten minutes. Drain and cool. With the flat side of a chef's knife, gently flatten each olive to loosen and discard the pit. Reserve the meat.

2. In a heavy bottomed non-reactive pan heat the olive oil. Add the onions and sauté over low heat until soft.

3. Stir in the garlic, saffron and ginger. Cook for one minute. Add the chicken broth.

4. Place the chicken on top. Season with salt and black pepper. Cover the pan and simmer, turning the chicken occasionally. Add more broth if it begins to become dry. Simmer for forty minutes.

5. Stir in the lemon juice, parsley, cilantro, preserved lemon peel and olives. Simmer uncovered for another ten to fifteen minutes until the juices reduces slightly.

6. Serve the chicken on hot couscous with sauce poured over the top.

TRADITIONAL PRESERVED LEMONS

To make preserved lemons, wash and dry 4 whole lemons. Cut each lemon into eighths without detaching the pieces at the stem end. Pack tightly into a sanitized glass jar, squeezing as much of the juice from the lemons but keeping the peel intact. Pack 1 cinnamon stick and 1 bay leaf between the lemons. Pour in 1 cup of kosher salt and enough extra lemon juice to cover the lemons. Seal with a lid and shake the mixture. Refrigerate for a minimum of two weeks, shaking the jar occasionally. The lemons will keep in the refrigerator for up to six months. Preserved lemons can also be found in jars in specialty stores or online.

The recipe for couscous may be easily doubled. Cool unused couscous and make into a salad by adding garbanzo beans, diced red onions or scallions, diced, seeded roma tomatoes, diced red, yellow or green peppers, sliced Kalamata olives, chopped parsley or cilantro. Splash with fresh lemon juice and extra-virgin olive oil. **Taste, Think, Transform** with salt and/or lemon juice. Sprinkle with ras el hanout spice blend (found in the Appareils chapter).

PINOT NOIR BRAISED CHICKEN ON TRUFFLE SCENTED POLENTA

This dish is inspired by the wonderful Oregon Pinot wine and truffle products combined with the classic techniques of the French dish, coq au vin, and Italian polenta. On a trip to the France, I had the great pleasure of dining at Le Coq au Vin Country Inn in the small village of Julienas in the Beaujolais wine region. I purchased a Limoges plate there illustrated with a beautiful white rooster adorned by a bright red cockscomb stepping out of a cluster of grapes which now hangs in a place of honor in my kitchen. This entree is best enjoyed on a bright, crisp autumn day or for that matter to warm a cold winter's night.

6 servings

Chicken

1 whole chicken (2 ½ to 3 ½ pounds) preferably organic, free range

2 sweet Italian sausages, casings removed

4 tablespoons extra virgin olive oil (divided in half)

8 ounces cremini mushrooms, brushed, cleaned and quartered

1 bottle Oregon Pinot Noir wine

1 teaspoon minced garlic

all-purpose flour for dredging chicken

1 tablespoon fresh chopped rosemary

sea salt and fresh ground black pepper to taste

Polenta

4 ½ cups filtered water

2 tablespoons unsalted butter

½ teaspoon truffle salt

¾ cup polenta

½ heavy cream

1 truffle thinly sliced (optional)

truffle oil to taste (optional but yummy!)

1. With poultry shears or boning knife cut down one side of the chickens' back bone from neck to tail. Cut down the opposite side to remove the back bone.

Cut the skin between the leg/thigh and the breast to separate. Cut both legs and thighs apart at the joint. Remove the wings from the breast at the joint. Remove the last section of the wings. From the cavity side of the breast make a cut through the wish bone and cartilage. Remove the breast bone and cartilage and split the breasts apart. Cut each breast into two equal pieces. Wash and pat each piece dry.

2. Divide the sausage meat into one half inch pieces and brown in a sauté pan. Remove to paper towels to drain the excess fat. Reserve.

3. Heat a non-reactive sautoir (straight sided sauté pan). Add two tablespoons olive oil. When it ripples add the mushrooms and toss to coat with the olive oil. Sauté over high heat, tossing occasionally to brown all sides. Remove and reserve the mushrooms. Deglaze the pan with the Pinot Noir. Add the garlic and simmer for ten minutes to burn off the alcohol.

4. Preheat the oven to 325°F. Wash and dry the chicken pieces.

5. Meanwhile, heat the remaining two tablespoons of olive oil in a non-reactive pot or Dutch oven. Dredge each piece of chicken in the flour, shake to remove excess flour. Brown all sides of the chicken in the pan. This may need to be done in two batches.

6. Add wine, garlic, sausage, mushrooms, chopped rosemary, salt and pepper to the chicken in the Dutch oven. Bring to a gentle simmer. Cover with a tight-fitting lid and place in the oven.

7. After a half-hour, turn the chicken parts over and continue to bake for about another hour.

8. Begin to prepare the polenta. Bring the water, butter and truffle salt to a boil. Whisk in the polenta. Bring back to a boil, cover with a lid and place in the oven for one hour. Remove from the oven. It will still be thin. Add the cream. Reserve in a warm place with lid on.

9. Occasionally check the temperature of the chicken breasts. When they reach 180°F remove and reserve them in a warm place. When the other pieces reach

180°F remove the whole pan from the oven. Reserve the chicken parts warm with the breasts.

10. Over medium high heat, reduce the juices, with the sausage and mushrooms until slightly thick. **Taste, Think, Transform** with salt and/or pepper.

11. Divide the polenta onto six plates or one platter. Top with the warm chicken pieces.

12. Pour the pan juices with mushrooms and sausage on top. Drizzle each with truffle oil.

All removed bones can be frozen to make chicken broth later. Or buy a whole chicken that is already cut into eight pieces.

MEAT

Orange Scented Rack of Pork

ORANGE SCENTED RACK OF PORK

A few years back I created this recipe to serve at my husbands' Christmas staff dinner. I served it with a Chipotle Pear Compote. Both were a roaring success. At that time, I used a standing pork rib roast. I have since made it for smaller groups hence the use of a rack of pork. Either way the orange brine creates a succulent and tender pork roast that is sure to please even those leery of dry tasteless pork of yore.

8 servings

⅔ cup fresh orange juice (about 2 large oranges)

2 tablespoons orange zest (about 2 large oranges)

⅓ cup lime juice (about 2 to 3 medium limes)

⅓ cup honey

⅓ cup soy sauce

¼ cup toasted sesame oil

2 tablespoons garlic, minced

2 tablespoons fresh ginger, minced

1 tablespoon kosher salt

1 rack of pork (about 6 ½ pounds, 8 chops)

1 tablespoon extra virgin olive oil

¼ teaspoon fresh ground black pepper

1. Combine the orange juice, orange zest, lime juice, honey, soy sauce, sesame oil, garlic, ginger and kosher salt in a bowl.

2. Place the pork rack in a large oven bag. Pour the marinade over the top. Force all the air out of the bag and tie the top closed. Refrigerate overnight or up to three days.

3. Remove the pork from the refrigerator for an hour before roasting.

4. Preheat oven to 450°F.

5. Remove the pork from the marinade. Place the rack bones down, fat and meat side up in a roasting pan. Lightly oil the pork with the olive oil and generously sprinkle the black pepper. Cover the exposed bones with foil so they will not burn.

6. Roast at 450°F for fifteen minutes. Reduce the heat to 350°F and continue to roast until the internal temperature in the center of the rack reaches 160°F, about twenty minutes per pound.

7. Remove from the oven and rest for twenty minutes covered by foil to redistribute the juices. Slice into eight chops and serve with a generous serving of Chipotle Pear Compote (found in the Appareils chapter).

· ·

GRILLED BONELESS MARINATED LEG OF LAMB

Dare to dream of tender lamb slices without the presence of mint jelly! Imagine an exotic rendition of boneless leg of lamb with an intriguing blend of spices from North Africa. Add to that a refreshing yogurt, lemon juice and feta cheese sauce to tantalize. Lamb is a staple in Mediterranean and Middle Eastern cuisine with a variety of ways to prepare it. Most often it is grilled, staying tender by marinating the meat overnight. This version is based on the Tunisian blend of spices called ras el hanout that can be found at specialty spice stores or online. I prefer to make my own blend within a small coffee grinder that I reserve for spices only. (Recipe is in the Appareils chapter.) The yogurt, lemon juice and salt tenderizes the meat fibers. The outcome is perfectly tender, juicy and slightly spicy. This is a perfect dish for company as it is mostly prepared the day before entertaining. Accompanied by a couscous salad and grilled vegetables makes for an interesting summer meal.

6 servings

Yogurt Feta Sauce for the Table

½ cup whole milk Greek yogurt

1 ½ teaspoons ras el hanout spice blend (found in the Appareils chapter)

2 tablespoons fresh lemon juice

1 tablespoon extra virgin olive oil

½ cup finely crumbled feta cheese

½ teaspoon sea salt

⅛ teaspoon fresh ground pepper

Lamb Marinade

½ cup whole milk Greek yogurt

1 tablespoon ras el hanout spice blend

1 tablespoons garlic cloves, minced

1 tablespoons fresh lemon juice

2 tablespoons extra-virgin olive oil

Lamb

2 to 3 pounds boneless leg of lamb

1 ½ teaspoons kosher salt

½ teaspoon fresh ground black pepper

1 teaspoon sumac (optional)

1. Prepare the sauce for the table by processing the yogurt, ras el hanout, lemon juice, olive oil, feta cheese, salt and pepper in a small food processor. **Taste, Think, Transform** with lemon juice, salt and/ or black pepper. Can be made a day ahead and reserved in the refrigerator.

2. For the lamb marinade mix the yogurt, ras el hanout, garlic, lemon juice and olive oil together.

3. Wash and pat dry the lamb. Trim any excess fat or sinew. The lamb may be separated into several pieces depending on removing connective tissue and fat. The butcher can do this for you. It is okay to marinate and cook the lamb in several parts. Rub the lamb with salt and pepper. Then slather both sides of the lamb with the lamb marinade. Refrigerate

overnight. Remove the lamb and sauce from the refrigerator an hour before grilling.

4. Preheat the grill to medium high heat. Turn over after browning one side for four to ten minutes depending on the thickness of the cut and desired doneness. Grill on both sides to the desired doneness: rare 130°F, medium 145°F, well done 160°F.

5. Let the meat rest for twenty minutes tented with foil and then slice thinly against the fiber grain. Serve with the yogurt feta sauce. Sprinkle with sumac.

There are two basic cuts of meat based on muscles of locomotion and muscles of suspension. Muscles of locomotion can be tough and are best when cooked slowly at low temperatures whereas muscles of suspension are tender naturally and can be cooked quickly over high heat. Leg of lamb is an exception to that rule due to the young age of the animal. Even so, a leg of lamb should be sectioned, connective tissue and fat removed and marinated at which point it then can be grilled over high heat with tender results.

. . . .

RACK OF LAMB WITH OLIVE AND LEMON RELISH

While in Madrid, my husband and I enjoyed the smallest and most delectable lamb chops ever, served with olive oil deep fried potatoes. The next morning, we boarded a high-speed train to Malaga and the Costa del Sol. On the way, we passed grove after grove of olive and lemon trees and herds of sheep on rolling hills. This recipe is testament to that land of olives, lemons and lamb.

6 servings

Olive and Lemon Relish

1 jar Lucques or Picholine olives with pits (about 7 ounces)

2 tablespoons extra virgin olive oil

2 large Roma tomatoes, peeled, seeded, medium diced

1 tablespoon garlic, minced

2 teaspoon double-concentrated tomato paste

¼ cup filtered water

3 lemon slices, thinly sliced (about ⅛ inch thick)

½ teaspoon sweet paprika

¼ teaspoon Aleppo pepper **or** ⅛ teaspoon cayenne pepper

fresh lemon juice to taste

1. Drain the olives. Bring a medium pot of water to a boil. Add the olives, bring back to a boil and simmer for eight minutes. Drain. Smash each olive with the flat side of a Chef's knife and remove and discard the pit. Coarsely chop the olive meat.

2. Combine the oil, tomatoes, garlic and tomato paste in a heavy sauce pan. Bring to a simmer and reduce heat. Simmer for three minutes. Add the water, lemon slices, paprika, pepper and olives. Simmer until the liquid is reduced to a sauce consistency, stirring often (about five minutes). Remove the lemon slices and mince. Add 1 tablespoon of the minced lemon rind back into the mixture. **Taste, Think, Transform** with lemon juice and/or salt. Transfer to a bowl and reserve warm.

Rack of Lamb

1 teaspoon garlic, minced

1 tablespoon fresh rosemary, minced

1 ½ teaspoon sage leaves, minced

¼ cup extra virgin olive oil

1 teaspoon sea salt and fresh ground pepper to taste

3 rack of lamb Frenched (about 6 to 8 bones per rack)

2 tablespoons safflower oil, plus more as needed

1. Mix the garlic, rosemary, sage, quarter cup of olive oil, salt and black pepper together. Pat each lamb rack dry with paper towels. Rub the herb mixture on all sides of the racks. Refrigerate for at least two hours or more.

2. Preheat the oven to 450°F.

3. Heat a large cast iron pan. Add two tablespoons safflower oil. Add one rack at a time. Brown both sides

of the rack and place in a roasting pan. Add more safflower oil if necessary to brown the remaining two racks.

4. Place the pan with all three racks in the preheated oven for nine to ten minutes or longer. Roast to the desired doneness: rare 130°F, medium 145°F, well done 160°F.

5. Remove from the oven and let the racks rest for five minutes.

6. Cut into chops between each bone. Serve with the warm olive relish.

The Olive and Lemon Relish has a rich yet tangy flavor that offsets the fattiness of the lamb and which also makes it an excellent accompaniment to Crispy Skin Salmon in place of the morel sauce found in Seafood chapter.

· ·

STOUT AND CHERRY BRAISED PORK SHOULDER

A few years ago, my sister prepared a similar recipe for Christmas. The original recipe was a bit runny and bland. Seeing the possibility, I altered it to a tastier version. It is now a family keeper. The fork-tender meat drenched in a complex tart, tangy and sweet sauce melts in the mouth.

6 to 8 servings

1 pint Stout beer, preferably Oatmeal Stout beer (found at Trader Joe's)

½ cup balsamic vinegar

1 ½ cups dried cherries (about 6 ounces)

1 teaspoon whole allspice

3 bay leaves

4-inch square of double-layer cheese cloth and butcher's twine

5 ½ to 6-pound pork shoulder roast

2 tablespoons extra virgin olive oil

1 ½ teaspoons kosher salt and fresh ground black pepper to taste

3 large red onions, cut in half, ¼ inch slices from root to stem

6 large garlic cloves, minced

2 tablespoons tomato paste

¼ cup dark molasses

¼ cup dark brown cane sugar

1. Bring the stout, vinegar and cherries to a boil in a non-reactive pan. Remove from heat and cover tightly. Let rest for at least one hour.

2. Tie the allspice and bay leaves in a small cheese cloth bag secured with twine.

3. Preheat the oven to 325°F. Wash and pat dry the pork shoulder.

4. Heat the olive oil until it shimmers in a heavy bottom non-reactive sauce pan. Season the pork shoulder with salt and pepper and brown all sides in the olive oil. Remove the roast to a plate and reserve.

5. Remove all but two tablespoons of fat from the pan. Add the onions. Cook and stir until soft and translucent, about five minutes. Add the garlic along with the tomato paste and stir for a few minutes.

6. Deglaze the pan with the stout, vinegar and cherry mixture. Add the cheese cloth bag of spices with the molasses and brown sugar to the pan. Cook for a few minutes until the sugar is dissolved.

7. Place the pork roast in the pan. Bring to a boil, cover tightly and place in the oven. Turn the roast over after the first hour and a half. Braise the pork for a total of three hours.

8. Remove from the oven. Slice the pork roast. **Taste, Think, Transform** the sauce with kosher salt. (If the sauce is not thick enough, place over medium high heat and reduce to the desired consistency.)

9. Pour the sauce over the pork and serve warm. As with most braised roasts it will taste better reheated the day after.

WINE AND ONION BRAISED POT ROAST

My Mother would begin this sumptuous pot roast before we went to church on Sundays. When we came home, the air would be filled with a heavenly scent. I suspect that this recipe was an updated rendition of pot roast since I don't think we had decent red wine in the home before the sixties. It got me to wondering if Julia Child's Boeuf Bourguignon recipe had an influence on this process. Unfortunately, I will never know the answer but I sure do enjoy this simple yet elegant meal in a pot.

6 to 8 servings

2 large onions peeled

10 garlic cloves cut into ⅛ inch slivers lengthwise

2 ½ to 3 pounds beef chuck roast (preferably grass-fed)

½ cup all-purpose flour

1 teaspoon sea salt and é teaspoon black pepper

2 tablespoons safflower oil

1 bottle Merlot red wine

3 to 4 large carrots cut into 1 inch pieces

4 large russet potatoes peeled, cut into 1-inch pieces

1. Preheat the oven to 350°F. Slice the onions across the globe into four pieces. This will produce four sets of rings that should be kept in a solid piece.

2. Insert the tip of a paring knife into the chuck roast and insert a garlic sliver into the meat. Repeat this process all over both sides of the meat. Coat the roast with a dusting of flour. Season with salt and pepper.

3. Heat a large non-reactive Dutch oven. Add the oil. When the oil shimmers, add the meat. Brown the roast on both sides. Deglaze the pan with three-fourths of the red wine.

4. Secure onion ring sections to the top of the meat with toothpicks so that the meat is totally covered. Lay the other rings around the base of the roast. Bring the wine to a simmer, cover with a tight-fitting lid and place in the preheated oven.

5. Braise for two hours. Place onions that are around the base of the roast on the top of the roast and other onions. Randomly place the carrot and potatoes in the red wine. Add more wine to bring the depth of wine to one inch. Season the vegetables with salt and pepper.

6. In one-half hour turn the vegetables over to cover all sides with the wine. Continue to braise until the vegetables are soft, about another one-half hour.

7. Remove the vegetables and meat to a warm platter and cover with foil. Discard the toothpicks but leave half of the onions in the wine.

8. With an immersion blender purée the braised onions to create a wine-onion sauce. **Taste, Think, Transform** with salt and/or pepper. Serve the sauce in a gravy boat. The meat should be tender enough to pull apart with a fork. Serve with the carrots, potatoes and remaining onion rings, hot.

It is important to have a very large Dutch oven so that there is room for the vegetables to all be braised in the wine around the base of the meat. If you wish to have a Julia-style memorable dish, you might also add some diced bacon and/or mushrooms to the mix.

. . . .

RED CHILI PORK TAMALES

RED CHILI PORK FILLING

As a chef instructor in an ethnically diverse college, I often learned authentic recipes from my students. Rosie brought the most heavenly light and flavorful tamales to share on Cinco de Mayo. I asked her to teach me to make these tamales. This filling is one of two that she taught me and another student, Ana to prepare. Taking meticulous notes and a few liberties I came up with this rendition with the help of Ana. Rosie and Ana are now each chef instructors. My husband is originally from Texas so tamales are a Christmas Eve tradition in our home.

Filing for about 32 tamales

Pork and Broth

1 pound pork shoulder

¾ cup white onion, large dice (about 8 ounces)

3 large whole garlic cloves

1 bay leaf

1 quart filtered water or enough to cover the pork

Filling

2 cups dried chilies (Ancho Pasilla or a mixture of Ancho, Negro and Oaxacan chilies (about 3 ounces)

¼ white onion, peeled, roughly chopped

1 teaspoon garlic chopped

¾ cup pork broth

1 tablespoons safflower oil or grape seed oil

1 teaspoon Mexican dried oregano

¾ teaspoon ground cumin

1 ½ teaspoon kosher salt

granulated cane sugar, if necessary to counter bitterness in the chilies

1. Cut the pork shoulder into two pieces to fit into a sauce pot. Cover with cold water. Add the diced onions, whole garlic cloves and bay leaf. Slowly bring to a simmer over very low heat. Cook at about 160°F for four hours until the pork is thoroughly cooked. (This may also be done in a slow cooker on low setting.) Drain and reserve the broth for the tamal dough. Shred the pork with a fork while still hot. Chill the pork and broth separately in the refrigerator.

2. Wearing latex-free gloves discard stems, seeds and ribs of the dried chilies. Break into small pieces and pour boiling filtered water over the chilies in a non-re-active bowl. Cover tightly and let stand at room temperature for one-half hour or longer. Discard water, rinse the chilies in fresh water and drain.

3. In a blender purée the drained chilies, onions, garlic and pork broth until smooth. Press this purée through a fine mesh sieve to remove the skins. This should yield about one cup of chili purée.

4. Heat the oil in a large wok over high heat until it shimmers. Add the pork, oregano, cumin and kosher salt. Toss for a few minutes until heated thoroughly. Add the chili purée and sizzle-fry until the mixture turns from bright red to a deeper darker red.

5. **Taste, Think, Transform** with kosher salt. If it tastes too bitter add up to one teaspoon granulated cane sugar to moderate the bitterness.

The mixture can be chilled and kept to use as tamale, enchilada or quesadilla filling. It is also delicious used as a base to bake eggs and top with cheese for brunch. The broth will be used in the making of tamale dough.

TAMAL DOUGH

Rosie's tamales were the lightest tamales I have ever sampled. The texture was reminiscent of a savory corn soufflé. When asked, what made these tamales so blissfully light, she said that two elements to this recipe were vital to the outcome. First the lard, then the dough was beaten until a small dough ball would float in water. Secondly the pickled jalapeño juice reacts with the baking powder to give a nice leaven to the dough along with a clever flavor. Gather a group of friends to help roll the tamales and share good stories.

Dough for about 32 tamales

60 to 80 dried corn husks (2 cellophane bags)

4 cups masa harina (I use Bob's Red Mill)

4 teaspoon baking powder

1 scant tablespoon kosher salt

2 cups **cold** lard and fat reserved from the chili pork filling

2 tablespoons ice water

2 cup reserved pork broth

¼ cup pickled jalapeño juice (from a 7 ounce can)

more pork broth as needed

1. Separate the corn husks, discarding any with dark spots and pour boiling water over. Weight them down with a heavy plate and soak for at least one hour to soften.

2. In a bowl mix the masa harina, baking powder and salt together.

3. Place the lard and ice water in a standing mixer with a paddle attachment. Whip at least five minutes, until the lard is the consistency of a light frosting. Discard the water if not absorbed.

4. Add the masa mixture, jalapeño juice and a small amount of broth to the lard. Begin to whip, adding

more broth as needed. Whip for ten minutes, scraping the sides of the bowl occasionally. The dough is ready when a small ball of tamal floats in water. This may take quite a while, do not be discouraged.

5. Drain the corn husks and stack. Tear at least 32 strips of husk to use to tie the tamales together. Slather two heaping tablespoons of masa dough on each corn husk near the large end. Spread the dough about three inches wide by five inches long on the husk making an indentation in the center.

6. Place about one and a half tablespoons of filling in the center. Fold the right side of the husk to the left and then the left side to the right encompassing the filling in the dough. Fold the tail end of the husk over the tamale, tie with a husk strip and place tail side down.

7. In a steaming pan with water below a perforated rack stack the tamales upright with the large open ends facing upward. When completely full, place several corn husks over the top and a wet towel over all.

8. Cover and steam for sixty minutes. Check one tamale by removing and waiting for three minutes. Unfold and check that the tamale is thoroughly cooked. If necessary, continue to cook for fifteen minutes more. Tamales cannot be rushed! Serve steaming hot.

Store bought lard is okay, however I prefer to make my own lard. My local butcher saves several pounds of pork fat for me. I cut it into small pieces. Place them in a stock pot of cold filtered water. Slowly bring to a simmer. Simmer for several hours until most of the fat is rendered. Strain into another pot and chill in an ice water bath then overnight in the refrigerator. The next day the lard will be on top of the water. Discard the water. Excess lard may be stored for three months in the freezer.

SIDES

VEGETABLES, PASTAS, POTATOES, GRAINS, RICE, LEGUMES

Sides are dishes that accompany and hopefully complement a main or entrée dish. A side dish will at its best complete, fill up or make perfect that dish which it accompanies. Often a side will be a starchy complement to a protein main, such as potatoes, pastas, grains, rice and beans are to meats, poultry and seafood. Other times a multitude of vegetables will supplement an entrée. In this role of sidekick, attention must be made not only to enhance the flavor of the entrée but to also have a pleasing color, shape and texture.

Side may have a secondary role to the entrée but must never be overlooked as an important player. Much as a sidekick gives a counterpoint to a comedian, the side dish plays the straight part to bring attention to the entrée. At their best, they are codependent.

What would a hamburger be without French fries, ham without scalloped potatoes, steak without a baked potato or turkey without stuffing? Usually taking the lesser role, the sides really do complete the show.

Let the entrée reap the oohs and awes as the side dish casually elevates the entire plate.

Lemon Risotto

LEMON RISOTTO

It was on a culinary tour through northern Italy where I first encountered this tangy risotto.

At the hilltop estate, Villa of Sra Lorenza de Medici, the author and TV personality gave a cooking demonstration which included a lemon risotto as the first course. This is my take on that dish which is a refreshing first course or a base for seafood or fish. I like to sauté shrimp with garlic and deglaze with a Pinot Grigio wine to serve on this risotto for a refreshing light supper.

8 side-dish servings

5 cups vegetable or rich chicken broth (found in the Appareils chapter)

1 ½ tablespoons olive oil

5 tablespoons unsalted butter divided

⅔ cup onion, minced

2 ½ cups Vialone Nano rice (or Arborio rice)

1 ⅓ cups Parmigiano Reggiano cheese, grated

1 ½ large lemons, juiced

1 ½ large lemons zest

lemon oil to taste (optional)

¼ cup Italian parsley, chopped

2 teaspoons sea salt

¼ teaspoon fresh ground black pepper

1. Heat the chicken broth and reserve hot.

2. Melt half of the butter and olive oil in a wide-bottomed sauce pan. When the oil shimmers, add the onion and cook until the onion is soft or translucent. Stir with a wooden spoon.

3. Add the rice and continue to cook without browning until the rice is coated with the oil and turns opaque, about two to three minutes.

4. Add enough hot broth to barely cover the rice. Stir the rice with the wooden spoon until the rice has absorbed most of the broth and when the spoon is drawn through the rice it creates a wake.

5. Keep adding small amounts of the broth to the rice and stirring until the rice is creamy and has just a slight crunch (about twenty-five to thirty minutes)

6. Add the remaining butter cheese, lemon juice, lemon zest and parsley. **Taste, Think, Transform** with salt, pepper and/or lemon juice as needed.

There are three varieties of Italian Arborio rice. Superfino Arborio riso (rice) is widely used. In the Veneto region Vialone Nano rice is predominant. Carnaroli is another premium riso that is often used. In this recipe I prefer to use the Vialone Nano variety. If you cannot find this type, either of the other two will suffice.

. . . .

ROSEMARY ROAST FINGERLING POTATOES

French fried potatoes are just absolutely irresistible. However, they are difficult to make at home. So, roasting long thin potatoes in ample olive oil is a good substitute. Add some fresh rosemary and good quality salt and let the party begin!

6 servings

18 fingerling potatoes, washed, and halved lengthwise

¼ cup extra virgin olive oil

1 ½ tablespoon fresh rosemary, minced

1 teaspoon flaky sea salt or more

1. Preheat the oven to 400°F.

2. In a bowl, toss the potatoes with the oil and rosemary. Season with salt. Place on a sheet pan.

3. Place in the oven and roast for about thirty minutes, occasionally tossing to lightly brown all sides.

4. Remove from oven and serve warm.

This dish is even more interesting when using several kinds and colors of fingerling potatoes. It may also be made with small round potatoes too, however, cut them into fourths rather than half.

· ·

AMARETTO YAMS

My husband and I have epic tales of harnessing our Siberian huskies to a cargo sled in the middle of the night to pull our Thanksgiving supplies, including a sixteen-pound turkey and all the trimmings through one to three feet of snow to our cabin in the Cascade Mountains. Early on Thanksgiving morning we began to chop the wood which would fire "Big Bertha," our antique wood burning stove that would roast our bird to a lovely turn. The day usually consisted of stoking the fire, basting the bird, cross country skiing or sledding, and warming ourselves with hot chocolate or hot spiced wine around "Big Bertha." After several rounds of this, we would finally settle by candlelight to share our blessings and holiday feast. Being a chef, I usually tried new recipes each year for the turkey, stuffing, potatoes, gravy, vegetable, salad, and dessert. The amaretto yams, however, were a constant due to popular demand.

8 servings

Yams

2 pounds yams (about 2 large yams)

1 tablespoon unsalted butter

3 tablespoon brown cane sugar

1 ½ tablespoon Amaretto liqueur

1 ½ tablespoon orange marmalade

½ teaspoon ground ginger

1 teaspoon sea salt or to taste

Topping

12 each Amaretto cookies (about 1 ½ ounces)

4 tablespoon room temperature unsalted butter

1. Preheat oven to 350°F.

2. Pierce each yam with a fork and place on a foil lined baking pan. Bake for about one hour or until the interiors are soft.

3. While still hot, scrape the pulp from the skins into a food processor.

4. Add the one tablespoon butter, brown sugar, Amaretto, marmalade, and ginger. Purée. **Taste, Think, Transform** with salt. Place in a buttered baking dish. May be frozen or refrigerated at this point to finish later.

5. In a plastic bag place the cookies and four tablespoons of butter. Seal the bag and roll with a rolling pin to combine the two.

6. Top the yam mixture with the cookie topping and bake until warm and bubbly, about thirty minutes. Serve hot.

In the Northwest orange flesh sweet potatoes are called yam. This can be confusing because in the south they are called sweet potatoes. Although either could be used in this recipe the orange skin and flesh yams yield the tastiest dish.

ANGEL HAIR PASTA WITH GORGONZOLA CUSTARD TIMBALES

On special occasions, I enjoy making something out of the ordinary to entertain my guests. This timbale lends itself as a base in which slices of meat, poultry or vegetables can rest and enhance the plate's overall appearance and flavor. Delicate "Capelli d' Angelo" pasta is enriched with tangy Gorgonzola custard and crowned with a browned, crunchy topping. Let the festivities begin!

9 servings

2 quarts filtered water

1 ½ teaspoons kosher salt

5 ounces fresh angel hair pasta

olive oil spray as needed

1 cup heavy cream

8 ounces Gorgonzola cheese, crumbled (divided in half)

¼ teaspoon fresh grated nutmeg

1 teaspoon fresh ground black pepper

4 large eggs, beaten

¼ cup Panko breadcrumbs

¼ cup walnuts, coarsely chopped

1. Bring the water to a boil. Add the salt and pasta. Stir until it returns to a boil. Boil two minutes (longer if using dried commercial pasta). Drain and shock with cold running water to cool. Drain well.

2. Spray nine (one-half cup) timbale molds or baking custard cups with olive oil. Distribute the pasta evenly into the molds.

3. Preheat oven to 375°F.

4. Heat and stir the cream, four ounces of Gorgonzola, nutmeg and black pepper until the cheese is melted.

5. Combine a small amount of the hot cream mixture into the eggs to temper them. Mix all the eggs into the cream mixture. Remove from the heat. Distribute the custard into the nine molds.

6. Place the molds into a baking dish in the oven. Pour boiling water into the baking dish about half way up the sides of the molds. Bake until a knife tip inserted in the middle of the custard comes out clean, about twenty minutes. Remove the timbales from the oven and hot water bath onto a cooling rack.

7. Run a paring knife around the edge of the molds. Invert each to unmold. Place on a non-reactive pan. Preheat the broiler to 400°F.

8. Toss the remaining four ounces of cheese, bread crumbs and walnuts together. Top each timbale with this mixture. Place under the broiler until golden brown. Serve piping hot.

· ·

SEMOLINA GNOCCHI WITH OVEN DRIED TOMATOES

Most people are familiar with those fluffy little potato gnocchi. This style of gnocchi is ever much as traditional an Italian staple, but much less known. They are much easier to master also. However, one creamy bite and people will be in awe of the cook's skills. Adding a slowly roasted tomato and chiffonade of basil will transform this side dish into a façade upon which to gently rest any manner of sliced meat or poultry. These are so tasty that they can also be served as a first course appetizer.

6 side servings

2 ½ cups whole milk, divided

2 tablespoons unsalted butter

½ teaspoon kosher salt

⅛ teaspoon fresh ground black pepper

⅛ teaspoon nutmeg

¾ cup very fine semolina flour (4 ounces)

3 large egg yolks

¾ cup fresh grated Parmigiano Reggiano cheese divide

3 Roma tomatoes

virgin olive oil

sea salt and fresh ground black pepper to taste

4 fresh basil leaves, finely shredded

1. Reserve one tablespoon of milk; pour the rest into a sauce pan and heat the milk. The moment before it boils, add the butter and kosher salt, pepper and nutmeg.

2. Add the semolina, pouring in a continuous **slow** stream, at the same time mixing steadily with a heavy-duty whip. As soon as all the semolina is in the pan, quickly raise the heat so contents reach the boiling point almost immediately. Lower heat and allow mixture to simmer slowly for four to eight minutes, stirring with a flat wooden spoon continuously, until smooth, homogenous and very thick (spoon should stand-up-independently-thick).

3. Remove the pan from heat and let cool ten minutes.

4. Dilute the egg yolks with the one tablespoons milk, mixing well. Add the egg mixture to the semolina mixture with half of Parmigiano cheese. Stir until well incorporated.

5. Oil an eight-inch square baking pan. Spoon the mixture in the pan and spread with a wet flat spatula to make an even surface. Cover and refrigerate for at least one and a half hours or overnight.

6. Preheat the oven to 300°F.

7. On a sheet pan lined with parchment paper or silicone mat, place the tomato halves coated with the olive oil, cut side up. Sprinkle with salt and black pepper, then place in the oven for up to two hours. Cool for ten minutes.

8. Preheat oven to 400°F.

9. Cut semolina mixture into two and one-half inch round discs using a biscuit cutter or cutting rings.

Dredge the disks in the remaining parmesan cheese. Place the discs on top of each oven dried tomato.

10. Place in the preheated 400°F oven. When tops are golden brown, about 20 to 25 minutes) remove from oven. Sprinkle with the basil and serve hot.

. . . .

SUGAR SNAP PEAS WITH RED PEPPERS

Sugar snap peas are one of the first vegetables to be planted in our garden and one of the first to be harvested. My husband loves this vegetable and makes sure that there are several crops to harvest during the early summer. I am not sure how or why but one day I happened to have sugar snap peas and sweet red peppers on hand and I created this very simple but scrumptious and colorful side dish.

6 servings

1 pound fresh sugar snap peas

1 sweet red pepper

1 tablespoon safflower or grape seed oil

1 ½ tablespoons soy sauce

sea salt to taste

1. Wash and remove the stem end and attached string across the top of the sugar snap peas.

2. Wash, remove stem and ribs of red pepper. Slice into one inch by ¼ inch batons.

3. Heat a sauté pan over medium high heat. Add the oil and when it begins to shimmer add the sugar snap peas and red peppers.

4. Toss the pan occasionally (or stir if you dare not pan toss). After a few minutes add the soy sauce. Toss for a few minutes longer. The sugar snap peas and peppers should still be slightly crisp and lightly coated with the soy sauce. **Taste, Think, Transform** with salt if needed. Serve immediately.

SPAGHETTI SQUASH AND WALNUT GRATIN

What could be more comforting than a crunchy golden, walnut and crumb topped gratin of creamy, silken strand spaghetti squash accented by Parmigiano Reggiano cheese? Gratins are a favorite do-ahead party dish but why wait for guests? Once tried, it will quickly become a favorite fall and winter side dish.

6 servings

1 spaghetti squash (about 2 ½ to 3 pounds)

1 tablespoon fresh basil, finely chopped

1 ½ teaspoon sea salt

¼ teaspoon fresh ground black pepper

1 cup heavy cream

½ teaspoon minced garlic

¼ teaspoon fresh ground nutmeg

½ cup Parmigiano Reggiano cheese grated (divided in half)

½ cup walnuts, finely chopped

½ cup panko bread crumbs

2 tablespoon soft unsalted butter (divided in half)

1. Preheat the oven to 375°F. Butter a one and half quart round casserole baking dish with one tablespoon of the butter

2. Line a small sheet pan with foil. Cut the top off the squash and cut in half lengthwise. Discard the seeds. Place on the sheet pan cut sides up. Bake for about forty to sixty minutes or just until the flesh raked with a dinner fork flakes into separate strands.

3. Remove from the oven and rake the flesh with a table fork onto the sheet pan from the squash shell. Spread out into a single layer. Sprinkle with the basil, salt, pepper and half of the cheese. **Taste, Think, Transform** with salt and/or pepper.

4. Bring the cream, garlic and nutmeg to a simmer for a few minutes.

5. Toss the squash mixture into the buttered dish and pour the simmering cream equally over.

6. Mix the remaining cheese, walnuts and bread crumbs together. Spread equally over the squash. Dot with the remaining one tablespoon of butter

7. Bake, uncovered for about twenty to twenty-five minutes or until bubbly and golden brown on top. Serve hot.

. . . .

STEAMED ROMANESCO

Romanesco is a flower bud like broccoli or cauliflower that originates from Italy. It has a bright chartreuse color. Though looking like a head of cauliflower, it is fractal, with pointed spears or cones emerging from the head, making it a uniquely, attractive buffet dish when presented whole. It has a delicate, slightly nutty flavor and crunchy texture. Simply steam whole and serve hot, adorned with a butter sauce such as Herb and Almond Butter found in the Appareils chapter. With a squeeze of fresh lemon juice, it is especially impressive for a Christmas buffet.

Serves 4 to 8 side servings

1 head Romanesco, washed thoroughly

kosher salt to taste

½ small lemon

Herb and Almond Butter, optional but delicious (found in the Appareils chapter)

1. Gently remove the leaves and part of the core leaving the spears intact.

2. Bring two inches of water in a steam pot to a boil. Add the whole Romanesco to the perforated steam basket above the water. Steam until fork-tender, about eight to ten minutes.

3. Place on a round platter adorned with optional herb and almond butter. Sprinkle with salt and fresh lemon juice. Serve hot.

KOHLRABI SAUTÉ

The humble, homely kohlrabi, which means "cabbage-turnip" in German, is a much-misunderstood vegetable. Therefore, it is often overlooked as the truly delicious treat that it is. Though it is difficult to peel its sometimes-tough skin, it is well worth the effort. This dish was the hit of my Thanksgiving meal this year.

6 servings

6 small to medium sized kohlrabi (about 1 ½ pounds)

2 tablespoons extra virgin olive oil

¾ cup thinly sliced onion

½ teaspoon fennel pollen or finely crushed fennel seeds

2 tablespoons Dijon mustard

1 teaspoon finely chopped fresh dill weed

1 teaspoon kosher salt

1. Remove the leaves and stems from the kohlrabi bulb. Thoroughly peel the tough skin and any blemishes from the bulbs. Thinly julienne each into one-eight by one-eight by one inch long batons.

2. Heat the olive oil in straight sided sauté pan (called a sautoir) until it shimmers.

3. Add the kohlrabi and the onion. Toss and move them over medium high heat until they begin to soften. Add the fennel pollen or crushed fennel seeds and toss for a few more minutes.

4. Add the Dijon mustard and mix well. **Taste, Think, Transform** with salt to taste. When soft and well mixed toss in the dill weed. Serve hot.

Garden Kohlrabi

SMOKY BRAISED KALE

Kale is a good autumn, winter or spring side dish. In this recipe, it takes on a light smoky flavor from the bacon and sweet Pimentón. It brings back fond memories of cooking on our mountain cabin wood cook stove in the fall when it is cool enough outside to have a roaring fire inside. The smoky, tangy flavor is hearty enough to be served with grille steak, game birds or braised meats.

6 servings

2 bunches red or green kale, washed and dried

3 slices uncured smoked bacon, small diced

2 large cloves garlic, minced

⅓ cup filtered water

1 tablespoon Sherry vinegar

¼ teaspoon smoky paprika or Pimentón Picante

1 teaspoon kosher salt

¼ teaspoon fresh ground black pepper

1. Turn each kale stalk together exposing the stem, to remove the stem from the kale. Pile the leaves on top of each other and cut crosswise into one-inch slices.

2. In a large saucepan or wok over medium heat cook the bacon until brown, stirring often. Remove and reserve the bacon. Remove all but two tablespoons of the fat from the pan.

3. In the same pan, add the garlic to the rendered bacon fat. Cook for about one minute or until just fragrant. Add the kale and water. Cover and simmer until wilted, stirring occasionally (about five to ten minutes).

4. Toss with the Sherry vinegar, paprika, salt, black pepper and reserved bacon.

5. *Taste, Think, Transform* with Pimentón, salt and/or vinegar. Serve hot.

. . . .

BACON AND BRUSSELS SPROUT HASH

Mentioning Brussels sprouts to students, invariable brought numerous negative facial expressions. Memories of chomping down on a whole Brussels sprouts has ruined the reputation of this cruciferous vegetable, and rightly so. However, Brussels sprout petals or thinly sliced sprouts will neutralize the strong odor and taste and turn this scorned vegetable into an enjoyable side dish. They are best when the cool weather of fall or early winter arrives, usually in time for the holidays.

6 side servings

2 pounds Brussels sprouts (about 30 sprouts)

2 tablespoons extra virgin olive oil

2 thick slices smoked bacon, small diced

1 teaspoon caraway seeds

½ cup Sauvignon Blanc wine (or dry white wine)

2 tablespoons sour cream

1 ½ teaspoons Dijon mustard

1 teaspoon sea salt

¼ teaspoon fresh ground black pepper

1. Discard any bruised or wilted outer leaves of the Brussels sprouts. Cut out the core, freeing the bottom leaves with a paring knife. Carefully pull off the outer leaves one by one under cold running water until they no longer will come off in one piece. Reserve these leaves for steamed Brussels sprout petals. Slice the remaining hearts into very thin slices.

2. Heat the olive oil in a straight sided sauté pan (called a sautoir). Sauté the bacon until browned. Remove the bacon with a slotted spoon from the pan to a thick paper towel and reserve.

3. Add the sliced sprout hearts and caraway seeds to the pan and a small amount of sea salt. Sauté until wilted and slightly browned, stirring occasionally. Deglaze with the wine, gently loosening the browned fond in the bottom of the pan with a wooden spoon. Simmer until almost dry.

4. Stir the sour cream and Dijon mustard into the hash until thoroughly combined. Add the bacon bits. *Taste, Think, Transform* with the salt and/or black pepper. Serve warm.

. . . .

BRUSSELS SPROUT PETALS

The outer leaves of Brussels sprouts take on a completely different flavor than the core of the sprouts. When steamed, these delicate petals pair well with rich entrees. The first time I served these petals to company they asked what kind of charming new vegetable were they eating. Astonished, they replied that they did not like Brussels sprouts but loved this deliciously sweet dish, simply steamed. The petals may also be lightly sautéed in olive oil or browned butter.

6 to 10 side servings

2 pounds of Brussels sprouts

sea salt to taste

fresh lemon juice (optional)

1. Discard any bruised or wilted outer leaves of the Brussels sprouts. Cut out the core close to the bottom leaves with a paring knife. Carefully pull off the outer leaves one by one under cold running water until they no longer come off in one piece. Reserve the sprout hearts for other dishes like the Bacon and Brussels sprout hash.

2. Bring water to a boil in a pot with a steam basket above. Add the sprout petals. Steam a few minutes, just until they turn a bright green.

3. **Taste, Think, Transform** with sea salt and/or possibly lemon juice.

Lemon juice will turn the bright green petals to a drab green. So, sprinkle with the lemon juice just before serving.

. . . .

BUTTERED BEETS

During my culinary school days, I had the great fortune of learning from chefs whose opinions vastly differed on many recipes. One of the most memorable lessons was from an Italian chef who assigned me the simple task of preparing buttered beets. It was fashionable at the time to undercook or cook vegetables al dente (meaning "to the bite" in Italian). Therefore, when my simmering beets were still slightly crunchy I pulled them from the stove and began to peel them under cold running water. The chef immediately questioned whether they were done. "But chef, they are al dente!" He retorted something under his breath as I ran to the chef next door to ask his opinion. My Italian chef followed and I bowed out as the two chefs began a rather heated argument on the doneness of beets. Needless to say, I returned the beets to the stove and cooked the Dickens out of them. To my amazement, the flavor of the beets changed from a starchy to a sweet earthy flavor, which I found more desirable. Some lessons are hard learned.

4 to 6 side dish servings

2 bunches beets, purple and/or gold (about 1 ½ pounds)

2 tablespoon unsalted butter

1 teaspoon kosher salt

1. Trim the beet greens leaving the roots and one inch of the stems intact to prevent the color from leaching. Wash gently to remove all soil. Place in a sauce pan and cover with water well above the beets.

2. Bring to a boil and turn down to a simmer. Check the doneness after one hour and continue to gently simmer up to two hours depending on the size of the beets.

3. Remove from the heat, drain and under running water peel the beets while they are still hot. The skin should easily rub off the flesh. If not, put the beets back on the stove and continue cooking until they do!

4. Slice or dice the beets and toss with the butter and salt to taste.

. . . .

SAUTÉED BEET GREENS, ORANGE AND RED ONIONS

Eat your greens! Okay, so you may not relish the thought. However, consider the slightly wilted greens enhanced by the sweet flavor of orange and sweet onions. Now we are talking tasty! Besides, buying beets with their crisp greens attached ensures the freshness of the beets. It would be such a shame to throw away these delectable greens. Consider serving with the beets roasted or buttered.

2 to 4 side dish servings

2 bunches beet greens (about 8 to 10 ounces)

1 ½ tablespoon extra virgin olive oil

½ cup red onion, peeled, halved and sliced ¼-inch thick

1 teaspoon zest of 1 orange (zest using a microplane rasp)

1 ½ tablespoons Orange Muscat Champagne vinegar*

1 large orange peeled and diced

½ teaspoon kosher salt

¼ teaspoon fresh ground black pepper

1. Wash and spin or pat dry the beet greens. Slice into one inch ribbons.

2. Heat a large sauté or wok pan. Add the olive oil and when it begins to shimmer add the onions followed immediately by the beet greens and orange zest.

3. Over high heat toss the onions and greens constantly until slightly wilted.

4. Add the vinegar and diced oranges.

5. **Taste, Think, Transform** with salt, black pepper and/or possibly granulated cane sugar. Serve immediately.

Optional Roasted Beets:

3 large beets

1. Scrub clean three large beets. Lightly oil and place in foil sealed on a sheet pan in a 375°F oven for about an hour or until tender throughout. Peel while still warm. Dice and add to the cooked beet greens.

*Orange Muscat Champagne vinegar is available at Trader Joe's. If not available to you, mix 1 tablespoon orange juice with 1 tablespoon Sherry vinegar and add honey to taste.

. . . .

JALAPEÑO CORN FLAN

Spoonbread is a traditional southern comfort food. This recipe puts a Southwestern and Mexican spin on that old time favorite. Although it is at its best during fresh corn season, frozen corn can be used with decent results. Made in individual ramekins or flan molds allows for beautiful plate presentations. They are so comforting that they are even delicious reheated and served for breakfast!

8 (4 ounce) servings

2 each fresh corncobs (7 ounces) or defrosted frozen corn kernels

2 tablespoons corn pulp scraped from the corncobs after the kernels are cut off

1 tablespoon sunflower oil or grapeseed oil

1 teaspoon sea salt

vegetable oil spray as needed

1 to 2 large jalapeños, seeded, minced (1 ounce)

½ teaspoon garlic, minced

¼ cup shallots, minced

¾ cup whole milk

½ teaspoon sea salt

¼ cup cornmeal

1 cup Pepper Jack cheese, grated (3 ounces)

4 tablespoons softened unsalted butter

1 tablespoon maple syrup

2 large eggs separated

1 tablespoon tequila

jalapeño rings, thinly sliced (optional garnish)

1. Shuck and remove the silk from the corncobs. Slice the raw kernels from the cobs. Scrape the corn pulp left on the cobs with a spoon and reserve separately.

2. Heat a sauté pan over medium high heat. Add the oil and when it begins to shimmer add the corn kernels. Sauté and toss until the corn kernels are caramelized. Salt to taste. Set aside to cool.

3. Preheat the oven to 375°F. Spray eight half-cup ramekins or flan molds with vegetable oil spray.

4. In a saucepan over medium high heat bring the jalapeños, garlic, shallots, milk and one-half teaspoon salt to a boil. Immediately pour the cornmeal in a slow stream into the mixture whisking briskly until thoroughly incorporated. Lower heat and cook for one to two minutes or until thick. Remove from the heat and whip in the cheese, butter and syrup. **Taste, Think, Transform** with salt. Incorporate the tequila and half of the caramelized corn. Reserve the other half of the caramelized corn for the garnish. Set aside to cool slightly.

5. Boil one pint of water and reserve hot for the hot water bath.

6. In the meantime, whip the egg whites to a soft peak. Beat the egg yolks in a small bowl and stir into the

cooled cornmeal mixture. Fold the egg whites into this mixture.

7. Pour one-half cup of the mixture into each of the oiled molds. Place in a baking pan in the oven. Pour boiling water half of the way up the side of the molds. Bake in the oven until the tip of a knife inserted in the centers come our clean and the tops are browned and slightly cracked, about twenty to twenty-five minutes.

8. Run a knife around the edges of the molds. Invert each one onto a small plate, then invert again onto serving plate with brown side up. Top with the reserved caramelized corn and optional jalapeño rings. Serve hot. They may be reheated in a microwave, if necessary.

SWEETS

COOKIES, CAKES, CRISPS, CUSTARDS, FRUITS, PASTRIES, PIES, PUDDINGS, ICE CREAMS, TARTS, SORBETS

The first perceived taste of an infant is sweet and the last predominate taste of the elderly is sweet. All the moments between the two are enriched by a sweet bite here or there.

Like so many food courses, desserts are best when their main ingredients are in season. In the summer, it is difficult to resist a fully ripe fresh peach or that lovely farm stand ripe red raspberry. Come fall, Grandma's apple pie with a wedge of farmstead cheddar cheese is most appealing. Winter is warmed by pumpkin pie, chocolate cake or a peppermint torte. Spring brings forth rhubarb crisps. And what would the Fourth of July be without fresh berry shortcake?

"Dessert! It is for many of us the apogee of the meal, the best part reserved for the last, the reward for so many forkfuls of spinach shoveled down as little more than an exercise in carotene consumption. It is, in the end, the end for which we strive, gobbling our brisket while thoughts of sugarplums dance in our heads - unctuous cheesecakes, fudgy brownies, frozen creams that seduce the palate with their silky chill." –Elisabeth Rozin

Who is to say that dessert should be eaten after dinner? Why not have dessert before a meal or for that matter start the day with a sweet breakfast! Whenever you indulge the urge for sweets, be sure to savor each delightful moment, bite by bite.

Lemon Blueberry Bread Pudding with Blueberry Syrup

LEMON BLUEBERRY BREAD PUDDING

Once a year I would spend a week in Newport, Oregon with my parents who were avoiding the heat of their Arizona home. We had several favorite restaurants that we were certain to visit while there. One was down by the beach and had great clam chowder but what we really cherished was their warm raisin bread pudding. Here I have put a spin on that classic bread pudding by using Lemon Brioche in place of the bread and blueberries instead of the raisins. Having made this recipe for a crowd on Easter, it was convincingly a luscious way to end a marvelous feast. Truly, lemon and blueberries must be a match made in heaven!

12 servings

Bread Pudding

1 ½ tablespoons room temperature unsalted butter

½ loaf Lemon Brioche (found in the Breads and Spreads chapter) or 1 pound loaf plain brioche cut into 1-inch cubes (about 8 cups)

7 large eggs

½ teaspoons vanilla extract

⅛ teaspoon lemon oil (optional, I use Simply Organic Lemon flavor)

1 ½ cup heavy cream

2 ½ cups whole milk

1 tablespoon lemon zest

1 ¼ cup granulated cane sugar

⅛ teaspoon kosher salt

Blueberry syrup

3 cup fresh blueberries (divided)

½ cup granulated cane sugar

1 teaspoon fresh lemon juice

1. Preheat oven to 350°F. Lightly butter a thirteen by nine by two-inch baking pan or a two-quart oval baking pan two-inches high. Arrange the bread cubes in the pan.

2. In a large bowl, whip the eggs, cream, milk, lemon zest, one and one-fourth cup sugar, optional lemon oil and salt until smooth. If using plain Brioche or Lemon Brioche add one-eighth teaspoon lemon oil.

3. Pour the egg mixture over the bread. Sprinkle the one cup of the blueberries evenly around the bread cubes. Place a large plate or pan on top to weigh down the mixture and set aside for twenty minutes to let the bread absorb all the moisture. Remove the plate or pan.

4. Bake for about forty-five to fifty minutes in the oven until the center is set, it is browned on top and it puffs slightly.

5. While baking, make the blueberry syrup. Simmer one cup fresh blueberries and one-half cup filtered water for five to ten minutes until blueberries are broken down. Strain the blueberries, pushing with a high-temperature spatula through a fine-mesh sieve. Discard the pulp. While still hot mix with one-half cup of sugar and heat just until the sugar is dissolved. Cool, add fresh lemon juice and chill.

6. Cool on a baking rack for twenty minutes before serving. Top with the one cup of fresh blueberries and blueberry syrup.

CARAMEL FLAN

Is there anything more satisfying for dessert than a creamy flan with a splash of caramel coating? This dish, no matter whether considered French (crème caramel); Spanish, Portuguese or Mexican is based on the Latin word flado which means custard. Following a few basic techniques this is an easy and satisfying dessert and can be made up to one day ahead of serving.

8 servings

¾ cup granulated cane sugar

¼ cup filtered water

5 large eggs

¾ cup granulated cane sugar

1 pinch kosher salt

3 cups whole milk

1 cinnamon stick

1 strip of lemon peel without any white pith

1. Preheat oven to 325°F. Place eight six-ounce custard cups or metal molds in a baking pan with sides at least two-inches high.

2. Combine three-fourths cup sugar with the filtered water in a stainless-steel sauce pan. Place over medium-high heat and cook **without** stirring until the sugar melts and turns deep amber (280°F). **Quickly** pour a bit into each cup and tilt to cover the bottoms. **Do not touch the caramel!** Any remaining caramel clinging to the sides of the pan can be removed by boiling with water until dissolved and discarded.

3. Whisk the eggs, sugar and salt together in non-reactive bowl.

4. Heat the milk with the cinnamon stick and lemon strip until scalded (small bubbles will be clinging to the side of the pan but not browning) and steamy.

5. Gradually whisk the scalded milk into the egg mixture until the sugar is dissolved. Strain through a fine mesh sieve into a pitcher.

6. Pour the custard into the caramel lined cups or molds equally. Place the baking pan with filled molds in the oven. Carefully pour very hot tap water half way up

the sides of the molds. Close the oven door. Bake until the custards are firmly set in the center (about forty to sixty minutes). Remove from the oven.

7. Remove the molds from the pan. Cool slightly. Place in the refrigerator for at least four hours or overnight.

8. To unmold, dip each mold quickly in a dish with hot water. Run a knife around the edges to loosen and invert onto a serving plate.

Caramel Flan

RHUBARB OR APPLE CRISP

There are few desserts that I make just for my husband and me to eat alone. A fruit crisp is one that we deem worthy the sugar intake. First thing in the spring we enjoy rhubarb from the garden and in the fall, apples just seems to call our names. This is a foundation recipe that can be changed to accommodate the fruit of the season. Crisps lend themselves as a nice warm brunch side dish served with a pitcher of cream.

6 servings

Rhubarb Base

2 pounds rhubarb, washed, ends removed, ½-inch slices

¾ cup granulated cane sugar

3 tablespoons all-purpose flour

Apple Base

1 pound Granny Smith apples, peeled, cored, small diced

1 pound McIntosh apples, peeled, cored, small diced

1 tablespoon fresh lemon juice

¾ cup granulated cane sugar

3 tablespoons all-purpose flour

Topping

¾ cup brown cane sugar

dash of kosher salt

½ cup all-purpose flour

½ cup cold unsalted butter cut into ¼-inch dices

1 cup thick-rolled oats

1. Preheat the oven to 350°F.

2. In a large mixing bowl, toss the desired **fruit base** sugar and flour together. Mix in the chosen fruit. If apples, sprinkle with lemon juice. Place in a round or oval two-inch high baking dish.

3. Combine the **topping** brown sugar, salt and flour. With clean hands, rub the butter into the sugar-flour mixture until the size of small peas. Add the oats and mix well. Distribute over the fruit mixture evenly.

4. Place on a sheet pan and into the oven. After thirty minutes if the top is browning too fast lightly cover with aluminum foil and continue cooking for another thirty minutes or until golden brown and bubbly on sides and center.

5. This dessert is best served warm with vanilla bean ice cream melting over the top. It is also good with cream or milk poured over the top for breakfast!

The addition of one-half cup chopped walnuts or almonds to the topping adds a nutty crunch. One half a teaspoon of cinnamon and one fourth teaspoon nutmeg adds an apple pie dimension to the apple crisp. The brown sugar in the topping can be reduced if adding your favorite granola in place of the oats. Dark brown sugar can be used in the apple crisp and light brown sugar is best suited for the rhubarb crisp. Also, the addition of dried cranberries or blueberries in the topping adds a nice deviation. Orange ice cream is delicious on the rhubarb crisp! Mix and match to create your own rendition.

. . . .

ROASTED DOUGHNUT PEACHES WITH AMARETTO STUFFING

July and August brings the harvest of all varieties of peaches. My early love for peaches has become a lifelong quest for the ultimate peach. White doughnut peaches that are locally grown fulfill that criteria. The skin peels easily and the flesh sweetly melts in the mouth. Almonds and Amaretto cookies pair with this peach to make a delightful warm dessert. Serve with a scoop of vanilla bean ice cream to accentuate the almond peach flavors. Peaches and cream delights!

6 servings

6 large white doughnut peaches

3 tablespoons room temperature unsalted butter

6 tablespoons brown sugar

2 tablespoons almond paste

1 pinch sea salt

12 each Amaretto cookies (about 3 ounces)

3 tablespoons slice almonds, toasted

1. Preheat oven to 400°F.

2. Insert a paring knife into each peach around the pit and remove the pit. (The cook can suck on the pits for any clinging flesh while preparing the recipe!) Gently peel each peach. If the peel does not come off easily, blanch in boiling water for a few seconds until the skin does release easily. Place the peaches on a silicone mat or parchment paper.

3. Mix the butter brown sugar, almond paste and sea salt thoroughly.

4. Place the Amaretto cookies in a closed plastic bag and crush by gently smashing with a rolling pin. Toss

the cookie crumbs with the butter mixture. Stuff each peach where the pit had been overlapping on the top of the peaches.

5. Bake in the center of the oven for about fifteen to twenty minutes.

6. Serve the peaches while warm, topped with the toasted almonds.

Ginger snaps can be substituted for the Amaretto cookies changing the flavor dramatically.

. . . .

PEACH, PLUM AND ALMOND TART

Peaches and plums come in assorted varieties in July and August in the Skagit Valley. This is when an almond crust tart can highlight the robust flavors of these tasty stone fruits. The contrasting colors of the fruits add to the sensory appeal of this lovely tart.

8 servings

Crust
3 tablespoons almond paste
¼ cup granulated cane sugar
½ teaspoon sea salt
½ cup soft unsalted butter
2 cups all-purpose flour
1 large egg, beaten
⅓ cup whole milk

1. In a food processor blend the almond paste, sugar, sea salt and one half cup butter until well blended. Add two cups of flour and process until light crumbs form. Add one egg and the milk. Process just until it forms into a large ball. Flatten the dough with your hands in large circle (about ten-inches round) in plastic wrap. Refrigerate until very firm, about one hour or more. May be made a day ahead of time.

2. Remove from the refrigerator and roll the dough between sheets of plastic wrap fourteen inches in diameter. Place in a twelve-inch tart pan. Remove the top layer of plastic wrap and transfer the uncovered portion in the tart pan. Gently press dough into the bottom and sides of the pan. Remove the top sheet of plastic wrap. Place in the freezer for ten minutes.

3. Preheat oven to 350°F.

4. Line the tart shell with foil and place dried beans or pie weights to cover the bottom of the pan. Place in oven while still frozen. Bake for twenty minutes or until beginning to lightly brown on the edges. Remove the foil and weights and bake for ten more minutes or until lightly firm on the bottom. Cool on a baking rack.

Fruit
1 tablespoon soft unsalted butter
3 tablespoons brown cane sugar
⅓ cup Chambord liqueur
4 small Black Friar plums, stoned, quartered (about ½ pound)
2 large free-stone peaches, peeled, stoned, cut into eighths (about 1 pound)

1. Melt the butter and brown sugar in a sauté pan over medium high heat.

2. Add the Chambord and bring to a simmer.

3. Add the peaches flat side down. Cook for one minute. Remove the peaches to cool. Repeat cooking the plums in the same manner. Reserve the pan juices for the glaze.

Filling and Baking
¼ cup sliced almonds
¼ cup soft unsalted butter
¼ cup brown cane sugar
1 cup finely ground almond meal
3 tablespoons all-purpose flour
2 large eggs
2 teaspoons vanilla extract
½ teaspoon almond extract

1. While the oven is still at 350°F, place the almonds on a baking pan in one layer. Toast in the oven until lightly

toasted (about six minutes.) Cool on rack and reserve for the final garnish.

2. Preheat oven to 375°F.

3. In a bowl, thoroughly mix the butter and brown sugar with a hand mixer. Stir in the ground almond meal and flour. Add one egg at a time, beating after each until smooth then add the vanilla and almond extracts. Mix well.

4. Spread the filling evenly over the cooled crust. Arrange the fruit on top in a circular pattern.

5. Bake for thirty-five minutes or until the filling is just set in the center.

6. Remove to the baking rack and brush with the Chambord pan juices.

7. Top with the toasted almonds.

8. Cool at room temperature. Lightly cover or place a dome over the tart and let sit at room temperature overnight. Serve the following day.

This is best if made one day prior to serving. Choose firm but ripe fruit. Peel the peaches by dipping into boiling water for a few minutes until the skin loosens. Immediately stop the cooking by dipping into an ice water bath. Peel should come off easily but fruit should not be softened. Or use a serrated tomato/peach peeler to remove the skin.

QUINCE TART TATIN

In the town of Lyon, France I first encountered apple tart Tatin. It came to my table still warm from the oven with a dollop of crème fraîche. It was love at first bite! When I returned home, I made this tart every autumn in memory of that splendid moment. One year I decided to try using quince, an heirloom fruit that is quite tasty but only when cooked. It was a charming revelation enjoyed by all.

8 servings

½ cup unsalted butter

1 ¼ cups granulated cane sugar

¼ teaspoon kosher salt

5 medium quinces, peeled, halved, cored (about 2 ½ pounds)

1 sheet of frozen puff pastry (about 8 ½ ounces)

1 cup crème fraîche or sour cream (optional)

1. Preheat oven to 450°F. Roll out the puff pastry into a ten-inch circle on a lightly floured surface (the diameter of the cast iron pan). Dock (pierce) the pastry several times on both sides with a table fork and refrigerate on a sheet pan.

2. Melt the butter sugar and salt in a ten-inch cast iron pan over medium heat. Cook until just turning golden brown. Add the quinces, cut side down. Cook both sides of the quince until just soft and the syrup is caramelized. Arrange the quince round side down and place the puff pastry over the top.

3. Place in the oven for about twenty minutes, until the pastry is golden brown and puffed.

4. Remove the tart from the oven. Let it sit for two minutes. Using glove-style hot pads invert a serving platter over the top of the pan and flip over **very carefully** so as not to spill any syrup on yourself. Let sit a minute and remove the pan. Cool for at least ten minutes. Cut into eight equal pieces.

5. Cool a few minutes before serving with a dollop of crème fraîche.

Homemade crème fraîche is less expensive and much tastier than store-bought. Just plan to start it two days ahead. See my website for a recipe.

. . . .

COCONUT CREAM AND MACADAMIA NUT TART

Is there any dessert more luscious and creamy than a coconut cream pie? Well, this dessert just may raise that level of indulgence. When asked to create an island menu dessert for a fund-raising dinner party, I thought about a coconut cream pie and decided to add the macadamia nut crust. It was instantly a winner, a divine slice of island tart. Make room for this one, it's worth it!

one 11-inch tart or twelve 2-inch tartlets

Macadamia Nut Crust

¾ cup unsalted, raw macadamia nuts

¼ cup granulated cane sugar

½ teaspoon sea salt

1 ½ cups all-purpose flour

½ cup cold unsalted butter, cut into small pieces

1 large egg yolk

1. In a food processor pulse the nuts, sugar and salt until nuts are finely ground. Do not over process. Add the flour, pulse once. Add the cold butter and pulse fifteen seconds or until dough crumbles into pea size. Add the egg yolk and pulse just until the mixture begins to come together. Turn out and knead with fingertips until uniformly moist.

2. Place the mixture into one eleven-inch tart pan or into twelve tartlet pans. Gently press into pan(s). Cover with plastic wrap and refrigerate one hour or overnight.

3. Preheat oven to 375°F. Discard plastic wrap from tart(s). Dock (make small holes) the crust with a fork. Line with foil and fill with dried beans or pie weights.

4. Bake for fifteen to twenty minutes until the edges begin to brown. Remove foil and weights. Continue to bake until dry and golden brown. Cool on a wire rack. This crust may be made one day in advance.

Coconut Cream Filling

3 large eggs

1 cup granulated cane sugar

4 ½ tablespoons all-purpose flour

2 cups sweetened shredded coconut

3 cups whole milk

6 tablespoons unsalted butter cut into small pieces

1 tablespoon vanilla extract

1. Whisk the eggs, sugar and flour together in a mixing bowl.

2. In a sauce pan heat the milk and coconut until almost simmering over medium high-heat.

3. Temper the egg mixture by whisking small amounts of the hot coconut milk to the egg mixture, slowly bringing up the temperature of the eggs. Pour this mixture into the remaining coconut milk. Bring to a boil, whisking constantly. Reduce the heat and simmer for four to five minutes until thickened.

4. Remove from the heat and whip in the butter and vanilla extract. Chill in an ice water bath. Place in a bowl and cover tightly with plastic wrap. Refrigerate for several hours or overnight. This filling may be made two days in advance.

Cream Topping

2 cups heavy cream, chilled

2 tablespoons powdered cane sugar (optional)

1 tablespoon Dr. Oetker whipped cream stabilizer (optional)

1 teaspoon vanilla extract

½ cup sweetened shredded coconut, toasted

1. Just before serving, whip the cream with an electric mixer in a chilled bowl. Add the (optional) powdered cane sugar, (optional) whipping cream stabilizer and vanilla. Whip to firm peaks that hold their shape.

2. Fill the pre-baked macadamia crust with the coconut filling. Top with the whipped cream and toasted shredded coconut. Serve cold.

Dr. Oetker's *Whip It* is a whipping cream stabilizer that will keep the whipped cream stiff for hours without separating and can be found in the baking isle of most grocery stores or import marts.

. . . .

COCONUT WALNUT GLAZED OATMEAL CAKE

Is there a favorite family comfort dessert in your recipe box? Well this one is mine. It is easy to make and delicious to snack on. It is also great served at brunch. I am looking at a soiled and smeared recipe card that just says Oatmeal Cake. There is only one thing that I will be changing in this recipe which is substituting butter for shortening in the cake batter. This moist cake can become a favorite family recipe if you give it a try.

12 servings

Cake

1 tablespoon soft unsalted butter for lining baking dish

1 cup old-fashion oatmeal

1 ½ cups boiling water

1 ½ cups all-purpose flour

1 teaspoon baking soda

½ teaspoon cinnamon

1 teaspoon sea salt

1 cup brown cane sugar

1 cup white cane sugar

½ cup room temperature unsalted butter

2 large eggs

Topping

6 tablespoons soft unsalted butter

½ cup brown cane sugar

¼ cup heavy cream

1 teaspoon vanilla extract

1 cup sweetened shredded coconut

1 cup chopped walnuts

1. Preheat oven to 350°F. Butter a nine by thirteen-inch baking pan.

2. Mix the oatmeal and boiling water. Cook for a minute until slightly absorbed and then let stand for two minutes.

3. Sift the flour, baking soda, cinnamon and salt together on waxed paper or in a bowl.

4. Mix the brown sugar, white sugar, butter, and eggs well. Add the oatmeal mixture and blend. Add the flour mixture and blend until smooth.

5. Pour into the buttered baking pan. Place in the preheated oven and bake for thirty-five minutes or until a toothpick inserted in the center comes out dry. Cool for five minutes or longer. Preheat the oven broiler to 375°F.

6. Meanwhile mix the butter, sugar, cream and vanilla for the topping together. Then mix in the coconut and walnuts

7. Spread the coconut walnut topping evenly over the top of the cake. Place under the broiler and broil until the sugar dissolves and the coconut and walnuts brown slightly.

8. Remove from the oven and let the cake cool completely

LEMON COOKIES

Pucker power of the glorious lemon is probably what makes it the most versatile and widely used of all fruits. This sour member of the Rutacea family named citrus limon has a two thousand five-hundred-year history that has spread from Southeast Asia throughout the world. Paired with sugar, salt and butter it has a charming appeal as demonstrated in this cookie. Delightful during the holidays but well received year-round.

about 4 dozen cookies

Cookies

2 cups all-purpose flour

1 teaspoon baking powder

¼ teaspoon baking soda

¼ teaspoon kosher salt

⅔ cup room temperature unsalted butter

1 cup cane sugar

1 large egg

1 tablespoon lemon zest (about 2 medium lemons)

½ cup lemon juice (about 3 medium lemons)

1. Preheat oven to 400°F.

2. On a sheet of waxed paper sift the flour, baking powder, baking soda, and salt together. In the bowl of an electric mixer with a paddle attachment, cream the butter and sugar on medium high speed until light and fluffy. Scrape down the sides of the bowl. Add the egg and whip on high speed until combined. Add the lemon zest and lemon juice, blending on low speed.

3. Slowly add the flour mixture to the bowl and incorporate on low speed.

4. Drop two teaspoons full of dough one inch apart (preferably from a small scoop) onto an ungreased cookie sheet pan.

5. Bake for eight to ten minutes until just golden on the bottom. Rotate the pan half way through the baking time.

6. Remove from the oven. Let them sit for two minutes and then remove them to a wire rack to cool.

Frosting

2 cups powdered cane sugar

dash of kosher salt

2 tablespoons room temperature unsalted butter

1 tablespoon lemon juice (less than 1 medium lemon)

1 tablespoon lemon zest (2 medium lemons)

1. Blend the sugar, salt and butter. Add the lemon juice and zest. Mix until smooth. If necessary, add one or more teaspoons of hot water to bring together.

2. Frost the cooled cookies. Store in an air-tight container for up to one week.

SOFT MOLASSES COOKIES

Frequently after school, Katie would meet me at the door with cookies and milk. Most often, they were homemade chocolate chip or peanut butter. Occasionally Mabel, her sister-in-law, would have brought over these large, rich molasses cookies that would melt in my mouth. I made these for the young men at a fraternity where I cooked and could not keep enough at hand as they would come through the kitchen and grab one or two between classes. These are soft, not chewy cookies, best enjoyed by dipping in milk.

2 ½ dozen cookies

1 cup dark brown cane sugar

1 cup room temperature unsalted butter

¾ teaspoon kosher salt

2 well-beaten large eggs

¾ cup mild unsulfured molasses

¾ cup buttermilk

4 cups all-purpose flour (extra flour needed for rolling out the dough)

2 teaspoons baking soda

1 teaspoon ground cinnamon

1 teaspoon ground ginger

organic Turbinado raw cane sugar as needed

1. In a standing mixer with a paddle attachment thoroughly cream the brown sugar, butter and salt. Add the eggs and blend well. Add the molasses and buttermilk and whip until well incorporated.

2. Sift the flour, baking soda, cinnamon and ginger together. Add half of the flour mixture to the molasses mixture. Blend until smooth before adding the remaining flour mixture and blend smooth again.

3. Wrap the dough in wax paper and refrigerate for several hours.

4. Preheat oven to 400°F.

5. Lightly dust a clean surface with flour. Roll out the dough about ½ inch thick, using more flour as necessary but not too much. Cut into 3-inch rounds with a metal cutter dipped in flour.

6. Place on an ungreased cookie baking sheet pan. Bake for ten to twelve minutes. Cool on a baking rack.

Mabel's original recipe used vegetable shortening but I have substituted butter here due to unhealthy trans fats found in shortening. The organic Turbinado raw cane sugar is usually found at Trader Joe's. The flavor is predominately molasses enhanced with spices. For a more intense ginger flavor add one-half cup of minced candied ginger.

APPAREILS

BROTH, SAUCE, RELISH, CHUTNEY, CULTURED DAIRY, COMPOTE, PASTRY DOUGH, SPICE BLENDS, VINEGAR

An appareil, quite simply, is a recipe that is used within other recipes. One may call it a base or basics, while another may call it condiments. Appareil comes from the Latin word "apareiller" meaning to prepare or make ready. These dishes could quite possibly stand-alone but are often used to begin, compliment or finish another dish.

Take the white sauce named béchamel for example. It is used to make other small sauces such as Mornay sauce, thereby making it a base sauce. It is also used as a binder to hold together ingredients such as vegetable croquettes that are shaped, breaded and deep fried.

Early in my career at a large hotel, it was my job to prepare the base stock and sauces in large stock pots to be used by the different restaurants and banquets. I would prepare clarified butter from a seventy-five-pound block of butter, or I would make chicken, beef and vegetable stocks in very large quantities to be used in soups, sauces or specific dishes. All the different cooks would use these appareils to make their various dishes.

Begin with high quality basic recipes to help prepare, garnish, or season the final dish.

Red Wine Vinegar

RED WINE VINEGAR

After a charming lunch at FINI restaurant in Modena, Italy, my culinary tour group was treated to an educational excursion and tasting at the Acetaia Malpighi Balsamic Consorzio. The Malpighi family have been making traditional Balsamic vinegar since 1850. This was not your under-ten-dollar vinegar and neither was the slow topping-up traditional method that produced a vinegar so good that it was worthy of sipping like a fine aged Port. I began thinking when I got home that I might be able to produce a simple red wine vinegar. Then at Beringer's School for American Chefs we were each given a bottle of exotic tasting red wine vinegar, the results of a cask-gone-bad or good, depending on your perspective. I was hooked and began researching this very simple method of making a good red wine vinegar.

1 (750 ml) bottle of high quality red wine (or 3 cups left-over red wine)

1 (16-ounce) bottle of raw, unfiltered apple cider vinegar with the 'Mother'

1. Mix the red wine with the apple cider, making sure to include the dark gummy substance called 'Mother' at the bottom of the cider bottle.

2. Pour into a dark crock or bottle and secure cheese cloth on top with a rubber band.

3. Place in a dark spot, like a cupboard at room temperature and let age for three to six months.

4. ***Taste, Think, Transform*** asking "is this a good strong vinegar or does it need more time?"

5. When ready, strain through a fine mesh sieve. Reserve any sediment or 'Mother' for your next batch of vinegar. Each subsequent batch will improve the 'Mother' and flavor.

Egyptians were using vinegar as far back as 3000 AD. It is derived from the French word "vin aigre" or "sour wine." It is made by bacterial activity which converts fermented liquids such as wine, beer or cider into a weak solution of acetic acid. It is created by yeasts converting sugar to alcohol and then a thick, sticky skin bacterium known as 'Mother' converting the alcohol to acetic acid. Vinegars have varying percentages of acid which determines the amount of vinegar is needed in specific recipes. The stronger the percentage of acid, the less that should be used in a salad dressing or marinade. I often use a high-percentage vinegar like Sherry wine vinegar to balance out the final flavor of a dish when I ***Taste, Think, Transform***.

RICH
CHICKEN BROTH

What is it about homemade chicken broth? Is it that it has a soul-soothing flavor that seems to linger on the tongue? Or does it bring forth memories of warming up to chicken noodle soup on a cold winter day? Whatever the reason, I always have a batch in the freezer to quickly defrost and use in the recipe at hand. This recipe is enriched with wine and a whole chicken, giving it a distinctive sumptuous appeal.

1 gallon

1 large onion (about 8 ounces)

2 medium carrots (about 4 ounces)

2 large stalks celery with leaves if possible (about 4 ounces)

1 bay leaf

1 teaspoon dry thyme

12 whole black peppercorns

8 sprigs parsley

1 bunch fresh thyme (optional)

2 ½ to 3 pound whole chicken without giblets and liver

2 to 4 chicken feet (optional)

5 quarts **cold** filtered water

1 cup dry white wine like Sauvignon Blanc

1. Wash the onion. Discard the roots. Reserve dry peel if unblemished as this will give the broth a nice color. Wash but do not peel the carrots and celery. Discard any blemishes. Small dice the onions, carrots and celery to create what is called a mirepoix. Place in a large stock pot.

2. Place the bay leaf, thyme, peppercorns and parsley stems on top of the mirepoix. A bunch of fresh thyme can also be added if desired.

3. Place the whole chicken and chicken feet on top of mirepoix. Pour the water and wine over all. Place over medium low heat. Bring to a low simmer (185°F) and lower temperature to maintain bubbles barely breaking at the surface for four hours. Skim and discard the scum that rises to the surface.

4. Strain the broth into a metal pot. Reserve the chicken meat for use in salads or casseroles. Place in an ice water bath and stir until thoroughly cool (45°F). Refrigerate overnight or for several hours before discarding the fat that will solidify on the top. May be refrigerated up to three days or frozen for up to three months.

TECHNICALLY SPEAKING: The cold ingredients slowly brought to a simmer and held at a very low simmer will create a clearer broth than one that is boiled. Cold ingredients will also ensure that the maximum amount of amino acids or protein, especially collagen (the jelly-like consistency in homemade broths) will be extracted. If at all, possible find a source for the chicken feet as they will increase the collagen in the broth. The fat on top can be used to cook other poultry dishes and will last for a week in the refrigerator. Salt is not added to a broth as it may be used in other recipes which will be later seasoned with salt.

NUTRITION OF BONES: The adage of "chicken broth will cure the common cold" is not so far from the scientific truth. It seems that chicken contains a natural amino acid called cysteine, which can thin mucus in your lungs. Also, broth contains calcium, magnesium, phosphorus, sulfur, trace minerals, chondroitin sulfates and glucosamine that are helpful in joint pain and arthritis. And the list goes on. But science aside, there is nothing more soul-nourishing than a hot homemade chicken broth with vegetables and noodles.

Rich Chicken Broth

VEGETABLE BROTH

It is possible to buy vegetable broth, but the flavor difference shows and so does the love. The beauty of making a vegetable stock is the scrumptious fresh vegetable flavor it imparts in whatever recipe it may be used.

1 quart

6 black peppercorns, cracked

1 bay leaf

6 parsley stems, cut into small pieces

½ teaspoon dried thyme

1 teaspoon extra virgin olive oil

1 clove garlic, minced

1 teaspoon shallot, minced

1 small carrot, sliced (about 4 ounces)

1 small onion, sliced crosswise (about 8 ounces)

1 large stalk celery, sliced (about 4 ounces)

1 small leek (white and pale green) halved, rinsed, sliced (about 6 ounces)

1 medium Roma tomato, chopped (about 6 ounces)

1 quart filtered water

unblemished onion skins may be added for color

1. Prepare a sachet bag by placing the peppercorns, bay leaf, parsley stems and thyme in cheesecloth and tie together with butchers' twine. (A tea infuser could be used rather than cheesecloth).

2. Heat the olive oil in a sauce pot. Sweat the garlic and shallots over low heat until translucent. Turn the heat up to medium high.

3. Add the remaining ingredients and sachet bag. Bring to a boil and reduced to a simmer. Simmer for forty-five minutes to an hour. **Taste, Think, Transform** by considering if the flavor has been completely extracted. Cook longer if not.

4. Strain through a fine mesh sieve or chinois into a metal bain marie or stock pot.

5. Quickly chill in an ice water bath. Refrigerate. Remove any fat from the top of the stock before using.

Salt is never added to a broth because the broth may be reduced or added to a recipe that already calls for salt. May be refrigerated for a week or frozen up to three months.

· ·

BÉCHAMEL WHITE SAUCE

This basic white sauce was created in the eighteenth century by the French courtier, Louis de Béchamel. It is a foundation sauce to which other ingredients may be added to create a flavored sauce. Mornay sauce is made from béchamel to which Gruyère and Parmesan cheeses are added with the possible additions of egg yolk and cream and finished with salt and sometimes pepper. As an appareil, it sometimes is used to bind ingredients together as in croquettes, gratins, lasagna or macaroni and cheese.

1 cup

1 tablespoon unsalted butter

1 tablespoon all-purpose flour

1 cup whole milk

1 whole clove, *optional*

⅛ teaspoon fresh grated nutmeg, *optional*

1. Melt the butter in a small sauce pan. Stir in the flour and cook for 2 minutes, stirring constantly.

2. Gradually whisk in a small portion of milk, whipping it smooth before each subsequent addition of milk until all the milk is incorporated. Add the clove and nutmeg.

3. Bring to a boil stirring constantly. Reduce to a gentle simmer for about 5 minutes until it coats the back of a spoon (the French call this "nappe" which refers to a sauce with good body, not watery). It is done when it reaches 200°F. Discard the clove.

4. This sauce is now ready to be used in other recipes. It may be used hot or if it is to be refrigerated lay a piece of buttered parchment paper directly on the surface to prevent a skin from forming on the top of the sauce.

This recipe will produce a medium thick sauce. If the sauce is too thick it may be thinned with a small amount of milk. If it is too thin, continue cooking until it reaches the desired consistency. If the sauce is lumpy press it through a fine mesh sieve, reheat and adjust consistency. This sauce may be increased if needed without alterations.

CHERRY CHUTNEY

Is there any fruit that has such engaging depth of flavor as the fresh sweet cherry? Unfortunately, the cherry season is very short. This chutney will last in the refrigerator for up to a month. To conserve this lovely fruit longer it is necessary to preserve this chutney in jelly jars in a hot water-bath. This recipe can be multiplied or halved but the cooking time of the chutney will be longer or shorter accordingly. This is an excellent accompaniment to poultry, pork and mild cheeses such as Brie. It is an excellent alternative to cranberry sauce at Thanksgiving.

4 ½ cups

8 cups washed, stemmed, pitted fresh sweet cherries like Bing (about 3 pounds)

2 tablespoon grapeseed oil

1 ⅓ cups shallot peeled, minced (about 4 large shallots)

4 tablespoon fresh ginger peeled, minced

½ cup white granulated cane sugar

½ cup dark brown cane sugar

½ cup Kirshwasser (cherry brandy)

1 cup white balsamic vinegar

1 teaspoon kosher salt

¼ teaspoon fresh ground black pepper to taste

1. Cut the cherries in half.

2. Heat a two-quart non-reactive sauce pan over medium high heat. Add the oil and when it shimmers, sauté the shallot and ginger for two minutes. Add the cherries and sugar. Continue cooking for three to five minutes or until heated through.

3. Deglaze with the Kirsch and vinegar.

4. Lower the heat and simmer very slowly for one to two hours until a wooden spoon can be drawn through the mixture of chutney, to see the bottom of the pan for a moment.

5. Remove from heat and **Taste, Think, Transform** with kosher salt and/or pepper. At this point it may be refrigerated for up to one month.

6. Wash 4 one-cup jelly jars, lids and screw bands in warm soapy water. Rinse thoroughly.

7. Place the jars and lid in a water-bath canner with water and bring to a simmer. Turn off the heat.

8. Remove the hot jars from the hot water. Quickly fill the jars with chutney one half of an inch from the top. Wipe the tops with a clean wet cloth. Place the lids on top. Screw the bands gently just until it is snug, then a quarter turn back (not too tight).

9. Place jars in the boiling-canner on a rack. The water should be one to two inches above the jars. Cover with a lid. Bring to a gentle boil then down to a simmer. Simmer for twenty minutes (elevations above 1,000 feet simmer an additional five minutes). Turn off the heat and remove the canner lid. After five more minutes remove the jars and place on a towel to cool.

10. When cooled overnight, test the top of the jars by pressing in the middle of the lid with a finger. The lids should not spring back. Also, remove the bands and lift the lid between thumb and index finger. The lids should not come off the jars. If they do place in the refrigerator and use within one month or freeze up to three months. Replace the bands. Wash, label, and date each sealed jar. Jars should be stored in a dark, cool place for up to one year. Refrigerate after opening.

The dark brown and white sugars may be replaced with a light golden brown cane sugar. Add the kosher salt in small increments, tasting as you go. Because of the sugar and vinegar, it requires more salt to balance the flavor than you may think. This recipe will produce about one-half cup more chutney than is sealed in the jars. It is wise to have a room-temperature Brie cheese and crackers waiting to enjoy this fresh chutney.

CHIPOTLE PEAR COMPOTE

My dear friend made a compote much like this and served it with pork tenderloin in autumn at our cabin. The pairing of spicy pears and pork was a winning combination. So, for my Christmas crown pork roast I recreated this recipe. This spicy fruit compote has an Asian flair.

8 accompaniment servings

1 teaspoon ground dry chipotle pepper
(use ½ teaspoon for less heat)

¼ cup soy sauce

¼ cup dry Sherry

½ cup fresh orange juice (about 1 large orange)

2 tablespoons toasted sesame oil

¼ cup honey

2 tablespoons garlic, minced

1 teaspoon peeled ginger, finely grated

4 medium firm Bosc pears, peeled, cored, large diced
(about 1 ⅓ pounds)

½ teaspoon sea salt

1. Combine the chipotle, soy sauce, Sherry, orange juice, sesame oil, honey, garlic and ginger in a non-reactive sauce pan. Bring to boil, reduce to a simmer. Simmer over medium high heat until slightly syrupy, about fifteen minutes.

2. Add the diced pears and continue to cook until they are golden brown, about eight to ten minutes. **Taste, Think, Transform** with salt and/or chipotle pepper if needed.

3. Cool to room temperature or serve warm. Alternatively, cool and place in a jar with a tight lid for up to a week in the refrigerator.

This compote is a great accompaniment to grilled and roasted meats and poultry, especially pork. For an Asian touch throw a couple of star anise pods into the marinade, removing them before serving. It would make an excellent holiday gift-in-a-jar.

HARISSA SAUCE

Harissa sauce is a North African condiment used much as we use salsa, ketchup or hot sauce. It can be purchased but this homemade version is much tastier. Other chilies can be substituted, like chipotle if looking for a smoky flavor. Smoked paprika, Aleppo pepper or hot sauce can also be added. Once mastered, play with the flavors to your desired tastes. It can be used in soups, meats, vegetables and all varieties of dishes to add a bit of panache!

1 cup

8 dried ancho chilies (2 ounces)

4 dried guajillo chilies (1 ounce)

2 tablespoons reserved chili soaking broth

3 large garlic cloves, peeled, mashed

1 ½ teaspoon kosher salt

1 teaspoon ground coriander

1 teaspoon ground cumin

1 teaspoon ground caraway

1 tablespoon fresh mint, minced

1 ½ tablespoons fresh lemon juice

¼ cup extra virgin olive oil

1. While wearing latex-free disposable gloves, seed, stem and tear chilies into pieces. Carefully discard the glove after using. Pour boiling filtered water over the chili pieces and soak covered until soft, about one hour.

2. Drain the chilies thru a fine mesh sieve, reserving the 2 tablespoons of chili broth.

3. In a blender purée the chilies, 2 tablespoons of chili broth, garlic, salt, coriander, cumin, caraway and mint.

4. Slowly add the lemon juice and then the oil until paste is smooth.

5. Pass the paste through a fine mesh sieve to remove the chili skin, as it is bitter.

6. Place in a tight jar and refrigerate at least eight hours before using. The sauce will taste very different after the flavors have been allowed to marry and mellow.

Before using **Taste, Think, Transform** with salt, lemon juice and/or a pinch of granulated cane sugar (if too bitter).

HERB AND ALMOND BUTTER

Compound butters are used as sauces or toppings for a variety of dishes. This compound butter first is made into a pesto which is a combination of herbs, nuts and oil and then mixed into the soft butter. It can very easily be transformed with different combination of herbs, nuts, oils and even spices for a personal touch. Use it to flavor vegetables, grilled fish, meat or poultry.

½ cup

1 tablespoon lightly toasted almonds, chopped

½ teaspoon lemon zest

¼ cup Italian parsley, chopped

1 teaspoon fresh thyme leaves, chopped

1 teaspoon fresh marjoram leaves, chopped

1 ½ tablespoons extra virgin olive oil

¼ teaspoon sea salt

¼ teaspoon Aleppo pepper or fresh ground black pepper

4 tablespoons soft unsalted butter (2 ounces)

1. Process the almonds, lemon zest, parsley, thyme, marjoram, olive oil, salt and pepper in a mini food processor or grind with a mortar and pestle into a slightly chunky pesto.

2. Blend the pesto into the soft butter **Taste, Think, Transform** with salt and/or pepper.

3. Shape into a log, placed on plastic wrap. Roll and shape using the back side of a chef's knife. Squeeze and twist both ends of the plastic wrap until in a uniform roll. Refrigerate, freeze for later use or use immediately.

Herb and Almond Butter

RAS EL HANOUT SPICE BLEND

In a short visit to Tangiers, Morocco I was most impressed with huge colorful piles of aromatic spices in the marketplace. I was even more awed by the flavorful spicy cuisine. Later, I had the great privilege of spending a day in the kitchen with Paula Wolfert, cook book author and Chef Abderrazak Haouari of Tunisia at the Culinary Institute of America, Napa. Asking many questions, I learned of the use of various spice blends in North Africa. Ras el hanout, which means "top of the shop" in Arabic, is a blend of spices that has many variations depending upon the country and spice shop. Most often it is used as a complement to couscous, rice, chicken and lamb dishes.

3 tablespoons

½ teaspoon green cardamom seed, smashed and removed from the pod

1 ½ teaspoons coriander seed

1 teaspoon cumin seed

4 cloves

6 allspice berries

2 small dried rose buds (optional)

1 ½ teaspoons cinnamon

1 teaspoon grated nutmeg

1 teaspoon ground white peppercorn

¼ teaspoon cayenne pepper

1 teaspoon turmeric

1. Grind the cardamom, coriander, cumin, cloves, allspice berries and optional rose buds in a spice grinder or mortar and pestle until very fine.

2. Add the cinnamon, nutmeg, white pepper, cayenne pepper and turmeric. Blend well and place in a tightly closed jar for up to several months.

Use only freshly-bought spices from bulk containers in stores like Co-ops to make this mixture. Dried rose buds are available at Middle Eastern or specialty stores and are a special interesting addition to this spice mixture.

TOASTED HAZELNUTS

Most nuts are best when lightly toasted. The skins of the nuts, however can be quite bitter. So before toasting it is best to remove the skin. Originally, I was taught to remove the skin of hazelnuts (also called filberts) by roasting in the oven then rubbing them while still hot in a tea towel. This only partially removed the skins. The following method works much better.

1 cup hazelnuts

2 cups boiling filtered water

3 tablespoons baking soda

1 cup hazelnuts

1. Preheat the oven to 275°F.

2. Add the baking soda to the boiling water in a deep sauce pan.

3. Add the nuts and blanch for three to four minutes. Adjust the heat if it begins to boil over the top of the pan.

4. Drain and rinse the nuts. Discard the skins.

5. Place the skinned nuts on a baking pan in a single layer. Place in the oven and lightly toast, about fifteen to twenty minutes. The nuts will continue to toast for several minutes after removing from the oven.

If stored in an airtight container they may be frozen up to a year and defrosted just before using.

MAY YOU FIND JOY IN SHARING
YOUR TABLE

Index